FRANK ROBINSON: The Making of a Manager

Courtesy of the Cleveland Indians

Frank Robinson:
The Making of a Manager

Russell J. Schneider

Coward, McCann & Geoghegan, Inc. New York

The story by Ed Fowler from the *Chicago Daily News* of May 16, 1975 is quoted from with permission of author and publisher.

SBN: 698-10731-4

Library of Congress Cataloging in Publication Data

Schneider, Russell J
   Frank Robinson: the making of a manager.

   1. Robinson, Frank, 1935–   2. Baseball.
3. Baseball managing.
GV865.R59S36 1976   796.357'092'4 [B]   75-43864

PRINTED IN THE UNITED STATES OF AMERICA

76=08160

To those who mean the most to me . . .
    my wife,
    our children,
    and my parents . . .
who have shared the ambitions and the frustrations,
and who will share whatever achievements are yet to come

Acknowledgments

The most difficult task in completing this book, *Frank Robinson: The Making of a Manager,* comes after the final chapter, the final paragraph, the final word has been written: how to express my gratitude to those whose contributions and encouragement have meant so much.

To my wife, Kay, who always has been my severest critic, staunchest supporter, major source of inspiration, and best friend, and our children, Eileen, Rusty, and Bryan, who have all experienced (and suffered) the labor pains of this work, I can think of nothing more appropriate than, simply, thank you for your patience through the years and events that came before.

I regret that my parents, Mabel and Robert Schneider, did not live long enough to see the completion of this book and to share my satisfaction, because without their indulgence and encouragement, my interest in sports and sportswriting might never have developed. I shall always be thankful for having them.

I am also particularly grateful to Cynthia Williams of Albany, New York, a "super" editor in the truest sense of the word. Her tangible contributions were exceeded only by her encouragement and, yes, criticism.

There are others, too, whose assistance and interest are hereby gratefully acknowledged: my boss and my friend, Hal Lebovitz, sports editor of *The Cleveland Plain Dealer*; Barbara Krepop, who typed the manuscript (and never complained despite my impatience), and her husband John; Ted Bonda, president, and Phil Seghi, general manager, of the Indians, both my friends—most of the time; Randy Adamack, public-relations director of the Indians, and his assistants, Rosemary O'Connor and Carl Hoerig; the players and coaches of the 1975 Indians; and especially Frank Robinson, manager, without whose unflagging cooperation this book could not have been written.

I have tried to be as factual as possible. But, I suspect, the respect and admiration I now have for Frank Robinson may disqualify me as an entirely objective chronicler of his first season as major league baseball's first black manager.

Contents

FRANK ROBINSON: The Making of a Manager

Introduction

This book had its inception in October 1974, shortly after
Frank Robinson became major league baseball's first black
manager. It was conceived in the hope that the Cleveland Indians, under Robinson, would accomplish a miracle and win the
American League pennant in 1975.

Long before I began covering baseball for *The Plain Dealer*
in 1964—indeed, for as long as I can remember—the Indians
have been *my* team, especially in 1949 when I was a catcher
(good field, no hit) in their farm system, at Stroudsburg, Penn-
sylvania, of the now-defunct North Atlantic League.

My loyalty to the Indians was fortified in 1973 when one of
their minor league pitchers, a young man of considerable talent
named Eric Raich, married my daughter Eileen. Eric made it
to the major leagues in 1975 and won seven games, each of
them a very special occasion for me and my family.

However, aside from my personal interest, this book was to
be—and is, I believe—a factual account of Robinson's pioneer
effort, a day-by-day chronicle of the ecstasy and agony he ex-

perienced in a venture that black men previously were not given the opportunity to attempt.

It is intentionally unauthorized so as to portray more objectively all aspects of this breakthrough, coming as it did 28 years after another pioneer, Jackie Robinson, broke baseball's original color line as a player in 1947.

The Indians did not accomplish a miracle in 1975, but *Frank Robinson: The Making of a Manager* is a success story nonetheless.

It is a story of personal achievement: a man's determination to prove that the color of his skin is neither a liability nor an asset. It also is the account of a man who learned to cope with and overcome discouragement, disillusionment, frustration, and other negative emotions to establish that he is, indeed, capable of managing in the major leagues.

In the months from February to October it took me to write about the peaks and valleys experienced by the Indians in 1975, I spent more time with Frank Robinson than I did with my family. I shared with him elation, chagrin, laughter, despair, and hope for success in the future—as I do now.

Most certainly it was a baseball season that Frank Robinson will never forget.

Nor will I, even if it means I must wait another year for that miracle, a pennant.

Cleveland, Ohio   RUSSELL J. SCHNEIDER
November 10, 1975

1. *"We Don't Serve Niggers"*

—If I had one wish I was sure would be granted, it would be that Jackie Robinson could be here, seated alongside me, today.

—Frank Robinson, October 3, 1974

CLEVELAND, OHIO—Only the sweat on his brow betrayed the emotion within Frank Robinson. It was October 3, 1974, the day he broke the final barrier against black men in baseball.

Phil Seghi, the sophisticated but now nervous general manager of the long unsuccessful Cleveland Indians, made it official at 10:03 A.M.

"Gentlemen," said Seghi as he faced more than 100 newsmen, "we're very pleased to make this formal announcement of the selection of Frank Robinson as manager of the Indians."

Baseball commissioner Bowie Kuhn and American League president Lee MacPhail were present, underscoring the significance of the event. Neither had ever attended the announcement of the hiring of a manager before.

"The impact of Frank Robinson being named manager of the Indians, the first black manager in major league history, is second in importance only to Jackie Robinson's entry into baseball in 1947," solemnly announced MacPhail.

Kuhn was more subdued, though equally pleased.

"Now that it has happened," Kuhn spoke of the appointment of the 39-year-old Robinson, "I'm not going to get up and shout that this is something for baseball to be exceptionally proud of, because it is so long overdue."

Though accompanied by the steady hum of television cameras, the sporadic clicks of still cameras, and even an angry, muffled argument between a sportswriter and a photographer, Robinson conducted himself at the press conference as though he'd had 10 years to figure out how to answer the barrage of questions.

Robinson had dreamed of becoming a manager—not just the first black manager—for at least a decade. "I'm the first black manager only because I was born black," he said with simple logic.

Seghi, Nick Mileti, president of the Indians, and Alva T. (Ted) Bonda, executive vice-president, sat proudly at the head table, accepting what credit was due for their part in being the first to break the managerial color line.

Later Seghi would bristle at the suggestion that he was motivated by selfish reasons, that he would like to be remembered as a latter-day Branch Rickey.

Now Seghi smoked his pipe contentedly and said, "I wanted Frank Robinson because I wanted the very best man available. I had no reservations whatsoever about hiring him." His statements often seemed defensive. "I am not, and never was, interested in making history *that* way. I am not, and never was, looking for a monument. I only want to win a pennant."

It had been *his* decision, Seghi insisted, not Mileti's and Bonda's, but of course they endorsed it. "When I told them what I had in mind, they became as enthusiastic about Frank as I was," said the general manager. "But it was *my* idea to hire Robinson," he emphasized.

Were economics involved in the selection? The economics of attracting fans and generating publicity because of Robinson's color? "Never," Seghi replied. "The only economics involved were from the standpoint of drawing fans because Robby could make us a winner, and winning teams draw fans and make money."

Although vigorously denied by all concerned, the rumor had been circulating since the day he was purchased from the California Angels that Robinson would be the next manager of the Indians. "Frank has been obtained strictly as a player," Seghi maintained at the time.

However, the manner in which the news of the acquisition of Robinson was broken to then-manager Ken Aspromonte was a clue as to what was to follow.

Ordinarily a general manager and his field manager decide together to deal for a player. Seghi made his decision to purchase Robinson unilaterally.

Seghi informed Aspromonte at 1:55 P.M., September 12, that he had claimed Robinson from the waiver list.

"Hey slugger, I've got the right-handed hitter you've felt you needed to win this thing," Seghi blithely told Aspromonte.

"Who'd you get?" asked Aspromonte.

"Robinson," replied Seghi. "Frank Robinson."

Five minutes later the announcement was released to the media, and speculation immediately began that Robinson would become the new manager, and that Aspromonte would soon be out.

Just as the hiring of Robinson wasn't really unexpected, neither was the anticipated firing of Aspromonte a universally popular decision.

After three years as manager of the Indians, Aspromonte had become something of a martyr in Cleveland, winning over many admirers, including most of the players. He also had gained some advocates among the cynical Cleveland press corps, not a minor achievement considering the parade of losing teams and unsuccessful managers the writers had been covering since the mid-1950s.

Aspromonte had come to Cleveland in 1972, the choice of Seghi's predecessor, Gabe Paul. His imperfections outweighed his strengths the first two seasons, but in 1974, having learned the error of his ways, Aspromonte's relationship with press and players alike had vastly improved, except with a few.

Among the latter was George Hendrick, a sometimes moody,

sometimes excellent center fielder who could not or *would* not permit himself to coexist with or perform at his best for Aspromonte. Their relationship deteriorated as the 1974 season progressed and was reported accordingly in Cleveland's newspapers.

When Robinson joined the Indians to help spark the club's fading chances to win the American League's Eastern Division championship, Hendrick often was as outspoken in his praise for the future manager as he was in his defiance of Aspromonte. Hendrick had played for Robinson in the Puerto Rican Winter League. Robinson managed there for six years, gaining needed experience, but also determining in his own mind that he could and *wanted* to manage in the big leagues.

Later, Seghi would concede he decided to fire Aspromonte on September 15, just three days after acquiring Robinson, and that initially seven men were considered for the managerial job.

"We went into Baltimore for a four-game series," related Seghi. "At the time we were only 3½ games out of first place, behind Boston, and still had an excellent chance to win, I thought."

Methodically, the Orioles destroyed that chance by sweeping a doubleheader, 3–2 and 8–6, on September 13, and then beating the Indians, 7–1, on September 14.

Seghi didn't sleep well that night, and when September 15 dawned, with the Indians now 7½ games behind Boston, the general manager resolved to fire Aspromonte.

"I still wasn't sure who I wanted to replace him, but I knew Aspromonte had to go," said Seghi. "With all due respect for Kenny's industriousness, his Achilles' heel was a lack of communication with the players. He always meant well, but those good intentions never seemed to come off."

Of the other six candidates considered by Seghi, three were white, Dave Bristol and Frank Lucchesi, both of whom had previously worked for Seghi, and Bob Lemon, a former star member of the Indians, and three were black, Larry Doby, another ex-Indian great, Jim Gilliam, and Maury Wills.

"All were qualified, although with each passing day I developed more and more respect for Robinson," said Seghi.

The decision to tap Robinson was finalized, in Seghi's mind, on September 27. "Kenny came to my office that day," said Seghi, "to ask me what I was going to do, whether he was going to be back or not next season. I told him no, that I felt a change had to be made.

"I also told him no announcement would be made until the end of the season, and I thought he agreed that would be best for all concerned. I was surprised when he broke our agreement." Seghi also was angry, calling it "a matter of principle."

On that September 27, after the conference with Seghi, Aspromonte, very upset, returned to his office. Just after he did so, his contemplation was interrupted by shouts from the main clubhouse from Robinson and Gaylord Perry, one of the Cleveland fan favorites and the Indians' star pitcher.

An argument had developed between the two men because Robinson reacted angrily to a story in the papers quoting Perry as planning to demand in his 1975 contract "the same salary, plus a dollar more," as the $173,500 Robinson was being paid as a part-time player.

Perry and Robinson were separated by Aspromonte. It was ironic because Aspromonte had planned to use the delay to deliver his *coup de grâce*: to tell his players that he would not return as their manager, that speculation was in fact true Seghi had already decided to hire another manager.

The account of the Robinson–Perry quarrel might not have come to light except that the game that night was first delayed and then postponed by rain. If the game had gone on as scheduled, the writers would not have been in the clubhouse to learn of the dispute.

Of his quarrel with Perry, Robinson said, "I did what I thought was right. That's the way I am. If something bothers me, I like to get it off my chest. You've got to remember, at the time, I was only a player, same as Gaylord. Now, if I had been the manager, or *knew* I was going to be the manager, I probably would have handled it differently, more privately.

"As soon as we finished, it was over, done with. The important thing is that we got the problem cleared up." However, as it turned out, they didn't. It proved to be only a temporary truce.

After the Perry–Robinson argument, Aspromonte, an impetuous man whose emotions often overruled his better judgment, held his meeting with his players. Breaking his agreement with Seghi because he was anxious to make clear his availability to other organizations, Aspromonte confirmed his impending dismissal to the players and then to the media. Afterward he sighed and said, "Most of all I feel relieved, very relieved." Nobody doubted him.

Commenting on Aspromonte's speech, Robinson said, "I was surprised at the amount of effort he put into telling us. I guess he wanted the right words to come across. I never got to really know the man, but he treated me well the short time I was in Cleveland. So, yes, I felt sorry for him. It's always sad when someone isn't wanted anymore. I hope I never have to go through that kind of thing myself."

Both the Robinson–Perry argument and Aspromonte's announcement of his firing were the top stories on the sports pages of *The Plain Dealer* and *The Press* the next day, September 28.

That afternoon, during the opener of a doubleheader which was televised as NBC's backup game of the week, a bed sheet banner was unfurled in the Cleveland Stadium. It read: "Sickle cell anemia: the great white hope."

"Sure, I knew it was directed at me because of what happened the night before," acknowledged Robinson. "There was a time when something much less would have gotten through to me, but not this time, because I wouldn't let it. You can feel all kinds of anger inside you, but you have to think about what kind of a person would do something like that. It had to be a very sick person, and I kept telling myself that."

It also was during that doubleheader with the Yankees that Seghi, now sure he wanted Robinson as manager, contacted Robinson's agent, Ed Keating, then of Mark McCormack's International Management, Inc. Seghi asked Keating to meet with him the next day to discuss Robinson's future. It wasn't necessary to caution Keating about keeping the meeting confidential—even from Robinson. Keating knew. The game plan had been formulated much earlier.

Thus, Keating became the middleman in the unfolding drama. He met with Seghi, September 29, as the Indians were concluding their home season. Seghi formally offered Keating's client the job of managing the Indians in 1975. It wasn't necessary for Keating to inform Robinson, or even to consult with him. The agent knew what the terms had to be.

The deal was finalized without Keating talking to Robinson, who could, then, honestly continue to deny *he* had talked with Seghi about the manager's job.

Seghi's decision to hire Robinson was explained simply.

"I feel Robby has an uplifting quality about him," said the general manager. "It's the same quality that made him such a great player. He had to overcome so much to reach the top, to become a leader. Because of all the things he's had to go through himself, he knows what it takes and how to impart this to others."

In the game that final afternoon in Cleveland, Robinson was soundly booed again by the fans who were sympathetic to Perry and Aspromonte. He was relieved when the Indians departed for three final games in Boston.

"Naturally, I didn't like it," confirmed the man who had seldom been booed in a major league career that began in 1956 in Cincinnati. "Nobody likes to be booed. I thought it was unfair because I had come to Cleveland to help. All right, maybe I didn't contribute as much as the fans expected, or as much as I hoped. But I tried. I was a victim of circumstances. I didn't come here to take another man's job. I was put into the situation and I didn't like it any better than the fans did."

By the time the Indians reached Boston for those final three games, two things were obvious to all.

One was that, under the lame-duck stewardship of Aspromonte, the players were merely going through the motions, waiting for the season to end. Few could blame them. It was a summer that started with great expectation, was buoyed by increased optimism in midseason when the Indians fought their way into first place, and then collapsed in a heap.

It also was obvious that Robinson would become the new manager, despite repeated denials by Seghi and Robinson that the matter had been discussed by them.

Of course it hadn't. Seghi and Keating made sure of that.

On September 30, after the Indians' 2–1 victory over the Red Sox, Robinson trudged into the clubhouse and, for what seemed to be the millionth time, denied that *he* had reached an agreement to manage the Indians in 1975.

On October 1, Robinson again went hitless in a 7–4 loss to the Red Sox and again denied the same speculation. He still was not lying, for Keating had remained in Cleveland, making sure to stay out of communication with his client.

On October 2, the season ended and Robinson, in his final at bat, delivered his 2900th hit, which also was the 574th home run of his 19-year major league career.

Only then did Robinson provide the slightest clue that, perhaps, he would become the Indians' next manager. His guarded admission required some interpretation, however.

"There's nothing I can tell you except that my plans for going home have changed," he conceded. "Instead of going directly to California from here, I'm going to New York to see a friend."

That friend was Keating.

More conclusive evidence that Robinson was Seghi's choice came in an announcement by Dino Lucarelli, then the Indians' public-relations director, that a news conference "of major importance" would be held at the Stadium in Cleveland the next day.

About an hour after the game in Boston's Fenway Park, Robinson boarded a plane to New York City.

There, Robinson was met by Keating.

Barbara Robinson, Frank's wife since 1961, flew from Los Angeles to Cleveland. "She didn't know for sure until I met her at the hotel that night," related Robinson, "but I think she had a pretty good idea. Ed had alerted her to be ready to come to Cleveland, even though neither told me until later.

"Barbara usually shows her emotions more than I do, but in this case, she stayed very low-key, I think because she didn't want to let her hopes get too high. When I told her, she still didn't get carried away, but she seemed very relieved because of the years of disappointment we'd gone through."

Before Robinson and Keating left LaGuardia, the agent outlined Seghi's offer. It consisted of a one-year contract as player-manager at a salary of $180,000, to include the $173,500 Frank earned as a player in 1974, plus a car and an apartment in Cleveland, the usual transportation costs between California and Cleveland, and an expense account befitting a major league manager.

"The only thing I would have liked," Robinson admitted, "was a contract for more than one year.

"But the big thing was a contract."

Now all that remained was for Keating to coach Robinson on the flight to Cleveland the night of October 2.

"I'll ask you the questions I think you'll be asked tomorrow at the news conference, and you practice answering," suggested Keating.

The two men talked throughout the flight "You're ready," determined Keating as the lights of Cleveland appeared below.

Robinson was. Except for one thing.

"As we got off the plane in Cleveland and walked to the baggage claim area," Robinson related, "we ran into the people we were trying hardest to avoid—the Indians and the reporters who travel with them.

"They were delayed getting out of Boston so that our flights arrived at just about the same time.

"It bothered me; it made me nervous because of what the players must have been thinking—the same things I would have thought if I were one of them—that Frank Robinson was too good to fly back with the team.

"I remember whispering to Keating, 'Dammit, Ed, you'd screw up a one-car funeral.' "

Less than 14 hours later, speculation that Robinson would be the Indians' new manager finally was confirmed.

Then came the questions, many pertaining to several unpleasant episodes from Robinson's past, when he was a naive, sometimes militant, and often confused youth. Now, totally in command of his emotions, Robinson never permitted himself the luxury of indignation, remaining poised throughout the inquisition.

Fashionably and conservatively dressed in a blue plaid suit, pale blue shirt, and dark blue tie, Robinson exuded confidence without brashness. He analyzed each question, generously elaborated his responses, and wove a thread of humor through most of his remarks.

Quickly, thoroughly, major league baseball's first black manager won over those who expected, even those who hoped, he'd stumble and collapse in a heap of rhetorical impotence.

Early in the interrogation, Robinson was asked by a black reporter, "How would you have managed a young Frank Robinson?" It was a meaningful question; the answer could have been loaded with repercussions.

The young Frank Robinson had had more than his share of problems that left lingering, if well-hidden, resentments within the man.

The mature Frank Robinson collected his thoughts and replied with a disarming quip. "My wife says I can't even manage our children," he said.

Then, "How would I have managed a young Frank Robinson?" the mature Frank Robinson repeated and pondered the question. "I wouldn't have been real tough. I would have been fatherly toward him. I would have tried to reason with him."

There was nothing fatherly about the way a frightened, 17-year-old Frank Robinson was introduced to the city of Ogden, Utah, then a member of the Pioneer League, in 1953.

The position in which young Frank found himself was not unusual. His father, Frank Robinson, Sr., and his mother, Ruth, broke up when Frank, Jr., was a baby. Frank, Jr., never knew a real father, though that didn't seem so important early in the boy's life. He was too busy to notice.

The youngest of 10 children raised by his mother, who calls herself Ruth Shaw after the first of her three husbands, Frank grew up in Oakland, California, spending most of his waking moments playing football, basketball, and baseball—especially baseball.

At McClymonds High School, under the tutelage of coach George Powles, the man who was closest to being a father to him, young Frank played with several other future big leaguers—Curt Flood, Vada Pinson, Jesse Gonder, and Willie Tasby, as well as an elongated basketball player named Bill Russell, also destined to become a black leader of men as a coach in the National Basketball Association.

Sports, particularly baseball, were Frank's life, and his morning-to-night, seven-days-a-week dedication resulted in his being signed to a professional contract by Bobby Mattick, then a scout for the Cincinnati Reds, for a $3,500 bonus in 1953.

Robinson was assigned to Ogden where almost immediately he suffered a cruel racial indignity. It was the first of many he'd have to endure and surmount, if not forget, on his journey to the managership of the Indians.

In 1953 integration was just a word to many. The riots and demonstrations—and subsequent achievements—of Birmingham and Selma were still nearly a decade in the future.

Robinson, on one of his first days in Ogden, went to the local movie theater and asked for a ticket.

"We don't serve your kind here," the cashier said coldly. Frank was perplexed. Raised in a predominantly black neighborhood, he grew up with both blacks and whites. Discrimination had not existed for him.

Robinson asked again for a ticket. The cashier said, "We don't serve niggers here."

Now it would outrage Robinson, though he has conditioned himself to fight back by *not* fighting back. Then, bewildered and hurt, Frank withdrew into a protective shell and relied on it for a long time.

"It bothered me, of course," he said, speaking of the incident. "It bothered me so much that I never let anything like that happen again. I stayed in my place. I went only where there was no problem. All I knew how to do then was withdraw."

And play baseball.

On the field, there was no problem for Frank Robinson. "I was natural. . . . I could be myself on the field," he said. "Nothing that happened off the field ever bothered me on the field."

On the fields of the Class C Pioneer League, Robinson was better than almost everybody, black or white, hitting .348 with 17 homers and 83 RBI in 72 games.

Two more minor league seasons followed at Columbia, South Carolina, of the Class A Sally League. In 1954, Robinson was spectacular, hitting .336. In 1955, he struggled with an assortment of injuries and a .263 batting average.

There were more incidents of racial bigotry in the Sally League, but young Frank was learning to cope. "It was the South and I was better prepared for it," he said. "I knew I had to accept what was happening, the name-calling from the stands and all that.

"It was unpleasant, but I turned the unpleasantness into incentive. I made up my mind to do well and get out of South Carolina."

In spring training, 1956, Frank came under the influence of Birdie Tebbetts, the Cincinnati manager, and began to mature.

"If it had not been for Birdie, I probably would not have finished my rookie season in the big leagues," Robinson told the news conference in Cleveland.

Maybe it was the father image Tebbetts projected. Whatever, Robinson developed and holds to this day admiration for Tebbetts.

"Birdie had patience with me when I started poorly, and he stuck with me throughout the season," Robinson said. "He was a great psychologist. He always emphasized positiveness. He had a real low-key approach, which was good."

Under Tebbetts, Robinson emerged from his shell, and went on to be unanimously selected the National League's Rookie of the Year in 1956.

He continued to be an outstanding player for the Reds in subsequent seasons, through Tebbetts' dismissal in mid-1958, Mayo Smith's coming and going in 1959, and into Fred Hutchinson's managerial regime in 1960.

It was under Hutchinson ("a rough, tough, no-nonsense manager," Frank describes him) that Robinson arrived at another milestone that very nearly aborted his career.

To this day he calls it "the turning point of my life."

From 1957 to 1960, overcoming several near-serious injuries causing occasional blurred vision and headaches, and what seemed to be a chronic shoulder ailment, Robinson strung together averages of .322, .269, .311, and .297 while crashing a four-year total of 127 homers.

By the end of 1960, Robinson had become a star, a celebrity, especially in Cincinnati. Trying to live up to that image, he regularly carried large sums of money and became a frivolous big spender.

He also purchased a gun. It was an Italian Beretta .25, to "protect" himself, although, in retrospect, he said, "I bought it because I was 24 years old and not yet a man."

Thus, the groundwork was laid for an incident that occurred on February 9, 1961, in Cincinnati.

On his way home from a basketball game with two friends, Robinson stopped at a drive-in restaurant. After ordering their food, Robinson and his companions became involved in a heated argument with three white customers. Frank still is not sure what precipitated the quarrel, or even what it was about.

Coincidentally, two policemen were parked outside, waiting to be served. They promptly broke up the argument. One of the officers referred to Robinson and his friends as "boys." "When somebody calls a black person 'boy' down South, it's a polite name for 'nigger.' We resented it, and I told the policemen we did," said Robinson.

One of Robinson's friends became even angrier and was arrested for disturbing the peace. It cost Robinson $100 to bail out his friend. Frank had the money in his pocket.

They returned to the same restaurant, in a covert act of defiance with predictable results. As they ate, Robinson and his friends noticed the chef peering at them from the kitchen. According to Robinson, the chef gestured, drawing his right index finger across his throat.

"It angered me very much," said Robinson. "I never was the most even-tempered guy. I know I'm not that bad now, but then, as immature as I was, I let that gesture provoke me."

Robinson leaped to his feet. The chef picked up a butcher's knife.

"I don't think many people in the restaurant saw it because there was a partition separating the kitchen from the dining area," he said. Quickly Robinson drew the gun from the pocket of his jacket. "If you think you're a big man, come on," he shouted.

The chef stopped in his tracks, calling to the two policemen outside the restaurant. Then Robinson compounded his original sin. He lied, denying he had a gun. Of course, the officers found it and arrested Robinson. He was charged with carrying a concealed weapon.

That began a feud between Robinson and William O. De-Witt, then general manager of the Reds, which culminated in another turning point in Frank's career.

Robinson resented what he considered DeWitt's indifference because the general manager didn't personally rush to the immediate aid of his star player. Neither did Phil Seghi, then De-Witt's assistant.

Instead, John Murdough, the club's business manager, was dispatched the following day to help Robinson, a decision still defended by Seghi, and still resented by Frank.

"That's the way DeWitt did things," said Seghi. "Murdough handled those problems. It wasn't a matter of DeWitt being indifferent. It was just a matter of policy. Frank shouldn't have been upset, although I guess he was."

"If it had been handled right by DeWitt, if he had come, or sent someone immediately, I wouldn't have been booked," said Robinson. "But when DeWitt just let me sit, the police took me downtown and locked me up.

"Sure, I'm still resentful, even after all these years."

The incident also affected DeWitt's attitude toward Robinson, an attitude the general manager never was able to change, no matter how Robinson played—and he played very well in subsequent seasons.

The next morning Robinson was released on $1000 bond. Three weeks later, facing a grand jury, Robinson pleaded guilty to carrying a concealed weapon and was fined $250.

It was a minor reprimand. Frank knew it then as he does now. He could have been suspended or even expelled from baseball.

Hutchinson later said to Robinson about the gun incident, "That was a stupid thing you did."

Robinson replied, "It was, but sometimes a man learns from his stupidities." Out of it came a determination to play better than he'd ever played before.

Frank hit .323 with 37 homers and 124 RBI, leading the Reds to the 1961 pennant, and was acclaimed the National League's Most Valuable Player.

That performance helped erase some of the stigma of Robinson's misdeed, except in DeWitt's mind. Relations between the two men continued to be strained, particularly at contract negotiation time. According to Robinson, he never had a peaceful discussion on salary with DeWitt.

Finally, ironically, Seghi took over contract negotiations with Robinson. Of those negotiations with Seghi, Robinson said, "I found him to be like most general managers, but every time I'd leave his office, I'd leave with a good attitude."

Four years after the gun incident, after the Reds had failed four times to win another pennant despite productive seasons by Robinson, DeWitt finally decided to rid the Reds of their "aging" slugger.

On December 9, 1965, as Frank was having dinner with Barbara and son Kevin in their Cincinnati apartment, the telephone rang. Seghi was calling to tell Robinson he had been traded to the Baltimore Orioles for three players.

"I wasn't really resentful; I've always felt being traded is part of baseball," said Robinson. "But I was a little hurt and shocked. I felt sorry for myself. Then I got over it and made up my mind to do the best possible job I could in Baltimore."

It represented another challenge for Robinson, to which he responded splendidly.

Because he did, the deal turned out to be a steal by the Orioles. However, DeWitt was sure it would enhance the Reds' chances in 1966. So did Seghi, who still defends the trade.

"At the time, our club was badly in need of pitching," recalled Seghi. "We felt we had a lot of other good hitters on the club and could afford to give up Robinson to strengthen our pitching. There also was some question about Robinson's throwing, and he did have a lot of injuries, you know."

Shortly after the trade, DeWitt, when called upon to justify the deal, explained with sarcastic simplicity, "Robinson is an old 30 years of age; he has an old body." It has haunted DeWitt ever since.

That indictment further challenged Robinson.

"I very much resented what DeWitt said," admitted Robinson. "Sure, I always had a lot of injuries, but I think they reflect on the way I play the game, not on my physical condition. I play hard, and I get hurt a lot because I do."

In 1966, an even older 31, Robinson became the first man in major league history to win the Most Valuable Player award in both leagues, and the first in 10 years to win the Triple Crown, hitting .316 with 49 home runs and 122 RBI.

The Orioles won the American League pennant and the World Series, with Robinson providing the physical and emotional leadership.

Robinson remained with the Orioles through 1971, leading them to three more pennants, until he was traded to the Los Angeles Dodgers on December 2, 1971, and then to the California Angels on November 28, 1972.

On those occasions the element of shock was missing. Said Robinson, "I knew the Orioles had a lot of good young players they had to make room for, so I told them if I was going to be traded, I'd like to go to a club on the West Coast. As long as I was leaving Baltimore, I couldn't be happier going to the Dodgers.

"But after a year, I wanted to get away from the Dodgers. I wasn't happy with my playing time, or the way I was being handled. I told Peter O'Malley [whose father owns the Dodgers] that if Walter Alston was coming back as manager in 1973, I wanted to be traded.

"In fact, at the time I was traded to the Angels, I was negotiating a contract to play in Japan."

As a member of the Angels in 1973, Robinson found himself playing for a former college coach, Bobby Winkles, who also had long dreamed of being a major league manager.

Winkles, an Angels coach in 1972, achieved his ambition on October 11, 1972. Forty-eight days later, Winkles and California general manager Harry Dalton consummated the trade with the Dodgers for Robinson.

Immediately, speculation began that Robinson was predestined to succeed Winkles when, not if, Winkles should fail. Remember, Dalton was the Baltimore general manager who acquired Robinson for the Orioles in 1965.

"It wasn't bad through most of the 1973 season with the Angels," said Robinson. "I knew there was no way I'd become the manager because I felt I still had a lot of playing time left. I also knew Harry would have told me if he had in mind making me the manager.

Frank Robinson.

Nancy Engebretson, Tucson, Arizona

Frank Robinson and general manager Phil Seghi.

"By the end of 1973, things became very bad. Winkles had a way of doing things that was completely different from what I was used to. I think he was in awe of me, and that created communications problems. We seldom talked."

In 1973 the Angels finished a disappointing fourth in the American League West, even though Robinson, responding to this latest challenge, reached the 30-homer level for the eleventh time in his career. He drove in 97 runs and batted .266 at the age of 38.

The situation created the predictable result. Relations between Robinson and Winkles grew tense.

Robinson went to Winkles to thrash out their problem. Winkles told him, "I know you're a friend of Harry Dalton and if it comes down to it, he'll choose you over me."

"It showed me how small a man he really is," said Robinson.

The next season, 1974, the pressure was on Winkles to improve the team, and the situation worsened. "First Winkles asked me to help him by talking to some of the other players, then he said I was talking to some of them too much," related Robinson.

When Winkles was discharged in June, he issued another indictment of Robinson, claiming it was his inability to handle Frank, not the team, that cost him his job.

"It upset me very much," said Robinson. "It wasn't his inability to handle *me*, it was his inability to manage a ball club."

Once Winkles was gone, it was anticipated that Dalton would choose Robinson to manage the Angels.

"I guess some people thought it would happen, but not me," said Robinson. "I never seriously thought I had a chance." He didn't.

Dick Williams was lured out of retirement by Dalton. "Any time you get the opportunity to hire a man like Dick Williams, you've got to take advantage of it," said Dalton, justifying his choice.

"When Williams was hired, it was like a weight lifted off my shoulders," said Robinson. "I enjoyed going to the ball park again. I wasn't resentful.

"In fact, I had given up my ambition to manage several years earlier. I really did."

At that time, Robinson was quoted as saying, "I'm no longer

considering managing; I'm turning my energies in other directions," though not everybody took him seriously.

"I was serious," Robinson insisted. "I had waited so long and worked so hard, I just thought, 'What's the use?' It seemed like it would never happen. I still *wanted* to manage, but I didn't think I'd ever get the chance. I really did give up."

Not long after the Angels hired Williams, Seghi, now general manager of the Indians, noticed Robinson's name on the waiver list. Circulated periodically, the waiver list is comprised of players available to other clubs for the claiming price of $10,000; if more than one club claims a player, the club lowest in the standings on that date gets preference. The waiver procedure serves two purposes: to sell players deemed expendable and to test interest in certain players, preliminary to arranging a trade. If a player is claimed, the club owning his contract may withdraw him. If not withdrawn, the player must be sold to the claimant.

Seghi claimed Robinson for the Indians on September 5.

Dalton was eager to accommodate anyone willing to take Robinson's $173,500 salary off the Angels' hands. He quickly telephoned Seghi.

"Harry said, 'I see you claimed Robby,'" related Seghi. "I said, 'Yes, I think he can help us because we still have a chance to win this year.' I told Harry I knew the requirement, that Frank had stipulated in his contract the right to reject any deal, and that I thought I could convince him to play for the Indians.

"Then I talked to Frank and we ironed out the details. I made it clear I wanted him because I felt we still had a chance. Nothing was said about managing."

Robinson agreed to report to Cleveland, providing the Indians would sign him to another contract for 1975, guaranteeing a full season's salary at the same $173,500 he was earning in 1974.

Seghi, certainly cognizant of the possibility of Robinson becoming manager, agreed.

Robinson was aware, too.

"I came to the Indians because they met my contract requirements," he said. "I could see a managerial possibility in Cleveland, but I didn't create any threat to Aspromonte. He was under fire before I arrived.

"Yes, I would have been fatherly to the young Frank Robinson," said the mature Frank Robinson as the television lights grew hotter and the cameras alternately whirred and clicked.

Bowie Kuhn nodded approvingly. Lee MacPhail grinned broadly. Barbara Robinson blinked away a tear. Phil Seghi, Nick Mileti, and Ted Bonda leaned back, confident that better things were just beyond the horizon.

Five months later Robinson would be meeting with his team for the first time. It would be spring training in Tucson, Arizona, and he would have his opportunity to handle men, to *manage*.

2. *"It Was Frank's First Test"*

TUCSON, ARIZONA, Feb. 24—During the ensuing five months Frank Robinson was in such constant demand as a speaker that he often said, "I'm anxious to start doing. I'm tired of talking."

Nothing was much different upon his arrival in Tucson, Arizona, February 24, for the beginning of spring training and his career as the Indians' new manager.

Robinson was greeted by the expected swarm of reporters, and those looking for controversy were not disappointed, though Robinson's initial problem—recurrence of trouble with Gaylord Perry which erupted last September 27—didn't surface immediately.

Meeting with the first wave of reporters, Robinson said disarmingly, "I enjoy talking baseball. My toughest time is when you guys run out of questions. The only time I get resentful or uptight is when I think somebody is trying to back me into a corner with a question I think is unfair.

"Looking back at the winter, I can recall only once that I was asked a question I resented, and it wasn't really the question that bothered me. It happened in New York. One writer asked me what I think is the most important thing about running a ball club, about managing. I started to answer, 'Winning. . . , ' but he broke in and said, 'The number one thing you've got to handle is the press.'

"At first I didn't believe he was serious. Then I realized he meant what he was saying, which was okay if that's what he thought. He kept arguing, and that's when I took offense. His point was that the press can keep a manager around much longer than he otherwise might last. I said, 'Sure, it makes it easier for a manager if he gets along with the press, but that's not the number one thing to worry about. Winning is the most important thing.' "

Milt Richman, sports editor of United Press International, was that writer. Shortly after Robinson related the incident, Richman appeared in Tucson.

According to Richman, "I didn't try to back him into a corner, and I wasn't trying to be a wise guy. I was serious. I know a lot of cases in which a manager's job was protected by the writers. Casey Stengel with the Mets was one. Stengel with the old Braves was another. He told a lot of funny stories and kept the writers satisfied. That's what I meant.

"I didn't know Frank was upset. One of the things I told him was, 'I know a manager who was *hired* by the press—you.' He didn't say a word to that. When I saw him this morning, I asked him, 'What will be the toughest thing for you to do as a manager?' and he replied, 'Handle the press.' "

Robinson was aware that the entire country would be watching him more closely than other managers, other managers who are white.

"I have no apprehension about the attention," he said. "All managers get second-guessed. I can handle it. I hope the attention I'll be getting won't turn into a circus atmosphere because I wouldn't want to have anything interfere with what the players have to do."

As for his intention of being a player-manager, he said, "I haven't lost my eagerness to play. I want to play and I will, but how much depends a lot on how well the other guys are doing. My personal goals [3000 hits and 600 homers] are important to me, but I won't put them above the welfare of the team."

As anticipated, Robinson was questioned regularly about George Hendrick, whose animosity toward Ken Aspromonte was a common subject among Cleveland fans in 1974.

"Everywhere I went this winter people asked me about Hendrick," said Robinson. "I told them all the same thing I'm telling you now. George has the potential to be a superstar, and all I'm going to do with him is no different than anyone else has done who managed him. That is to tell George how I want the game played. I'll ask him to give me his 100 percent, not mine, not anyone else's, just his. That's all I will ask of any of my players."

That's how Robinson played the game himself. "On a 1-to-10 scale of playing hard," he said, "I'd rate myself a 10." It was neither a boast nor an apology. "I believe you should do everything to win short of hurting someone deliberately. If you're going into a second baseman, let him know you are going to knock him down, bump him or do something every time, and he's going to be thinking about you every time."

Robinson also made it clear he wants a knockdown pitch—thrown under a batter's chin to force him away from the plate—when the situation calls for one. "I will order it, and it better be thrown. I don't believe in throwing at batters' heads, although mine was a target enough times, but I want it known we will protect our people. If our guys get knocked down, we will retaliate. They don't play football halfway, and nobody criticizes them, and baseball shouldn't be played halfway either."

Robinson further revealed his 100 percent philosophy in his remarks against fraternization on the field between players of two clubs. "You can't inquire about an opponent's family and then knock him down," he said.

Often, too, Robinson was asked—and readily talked about—how he would be evaluated as a manager, and whether his performance would warrant his being rehired at the end of this first season.

For Frank Robinson to be a successful manager, he must do much more than survive. If the Indians surmount the odds against them and win the pennant, there'll be no doubt of his ability to manage. Anything less than a pennant, even a better than .500 finish (which the Indians have not achieved since

1968), will indicate only that he has the ability to manage in the major leagues.

Robinson himself offered a more subtle measurement. "I won't judge my success necessarily on the standings, but on how much I am able to get out of my men. I'll know that myself."

Short of winning a pennant, will others be that perceptive? Particularly others like Ted Bonda and Phil Seghi? "I don't know," replied Robinson. "I'll just have to take my chances."

When the time for donning uniforms for the first time in 1975 finally arrived, Robinson denied any anxiety, though he admitted, "Maybe I will be nervous on March third or the thirteenth or April eighth, but right now I don't feel any different than I ever have."

He referred to, first, the reporting date for the entire squad, second, the initial exhibition game in which he'd be managing for the first time against another major league team, and third, Opening Day in Cleveland.

In meeting with his players, Robinson outlined the few rules he would impose which "will be strictly enforced," he warned.

"The first thing, rule number one, is that every minute we're on the field we'll be running, not walking, and that will include Frank Robinson, the player," said Robinson, the manager.

"We'll have a two o'clock curfew in spring training, but none once the season begins. Telling grown men to be in bed at a certain time is ridiculous. Anybody who wants to break curfew will do it anyway. If somebody abuses the privilege, I'll clamp down on individuals, but I don't believe in penalizing everybody because of a few."

Robinson was to be proved wrong in his no-curfew attitude. He also faced his first challenge of authority following the initial workout, after which veteran pitcher Fritz Peterson commented breathlessly, "Not only was that the toughest first day of spring training I've ever gone through, it also was the first time I ever saw a manager sweat in spring training."

Some expected grumbling began in the corners of the clubhouse almost immediately, fostered not only by the amount of sweat expended in the workouts, but also by two trades the Indians made the first few days.

First baseman Boog Powell and left-handed pitcher Don Hood were acquired from Baltimore in exchange for catcher Dave Duncan. Then another left-handed pitcher, reliever Dave LaRoche, came from the Chicago Cubs for pitcher Milt Wilcox.

Pitchers Gaylord and Jim Perry wondered about the wisdom of giving up Duncan, an excellent receiver but weak hitter, leaving the catching chores to John Ellis and rookie Alan Ashby. Several other pitchers were fearful that the arrival of Hood and LaRoche would jeopardize their chances of keeping their jobs on the staff.

But Robinson shrugged away the doubts, as did Seghi. "I want us to develop a feeling of togetherness on the field, in the clubhouse, and off the field," said Robinson. "I mean, on the field I want to see guys pulling for each other, sacrificing themselves for the good of the team. In the clubhouse I don't want to see pitchers here, catchers there, infielders in that corner, outfielders in another corner. I want the guys to get together. When the game is over, it's not necessary to invite a teammate to your house for dinner, but I like to see five or six or seven fellows going out together when we're on the road. I like a family relationship. Every winning club I've ever been part of has been together."

Almost simultaneously, Gaylord Perry's complaints about Robinson's grueling conditioning program betrayed the *lack* of togetherness.

"I'm nobody's slave," he said defiantly, referring to the requirement that everyone run 15 times from foul line to foul line rather than the traditional short sprints most teams employ and most pitchers prefer.

"I've got to run sprints, and I will whether Robinson likes it or not. It's my way of getting in shape, to pitch for this club or a club I might be traded to. I want to work out in the infield, too. I am proud of my fielding, but they don't want me to take grounders and that bugs me.

"Another thing I don't like," continued the veteran pitcher who won 21 games in 1974, "is this running backwards they want us to do. I've never run backwards in my life. Not for anyone and I'm not about to start now. Pitchers are different. We don't do a lot of long running. We run short, covering first base

Nancy Engebretson

Frank Robinson on the first day of spring training.

Nancy Engebretson

Frank Robinson, Gaylord Perry (running backwards)—see page 38.

and things like that. That's why sprints are important. Let the other guys run foul line to foul line if that's what Robinson wants. But let us pitchers run sprints. At least let *me* run sprints. I'm not training for a marathon race, and I'm not about to let some superstar who never pitched a game in his life tell me how to get ready to pitch."

Gaylord's older brother Jim agreed, though with less temerity. "We may have a staff of pitchers who can run, but who's going to pitch for us? I know how to get in shape after all these years. I don't need somebody telling me, and I especially don't need somebody watching me every minute," said Jim.

Robinson was clearly unwilling to grant special privileges.

"Nobody establishes his own training program on my club," he said. "I want everybody to feel the same; I want to have a rookie look up from what he's doing and see a veteran like Gaylord Perry doing the same thing. That's important."

When asked if he, Frank Robinson, superstar, had been permitted to establish his own training routine before becoming manager of the Indians, he acknowledged, "Yes, I had some special privileges, but I never asked for them. Though I was granted some privileges, I never took advantage of them."

As he talked about managers, Robinson made clear that Walter Alston, his manager with the Los Angeles Dodgers in 1972, was one for whom he felt less than deep respect.

"I once said Walter Alston is not my kind of manager," said Robinson. "He didn't communicate. Nobody knew his job from one day to the next. Alston never recognized that some players are better than others. He was not on top of the game like some other managers I've played for, guys like Earl Weaver, Birdie Tebbetts, Fred Hutchinson.

"I'm different from Alston because I'm a different personality. I'm not the type to sit and be quiet when something bothers me. I think it's good to get some things settled right then and there, and then forget them. I think it's important for a manager to do that, not necessarily to establish authority, but to establish the fact that we're all doing this together."

This was the background for Robinson's first test, his first confrontation with one of his players, though it wasn't his first confrontation with Gaylord Perry. Neither would it be his last.

The first three days of spring training Gaylord grumbled outwardly and seethed inwardly. "The way this place is run is really chicken----," the ace pitcher said several times. "If it's going to continue, I want to get out."

Perry performed the running exercises as prescribed by Robinson, but with little enthusiasm. He did other things in the program halfheartedly, too, in Robinson's opinion. Finally, Robinson had enough.

"I called Gaylord into my office," Robinson related later, "and invited him to sit down and talk. I said to him, 'Gaylord, is there anything bothering you? Is there anything you want to get off your chest? If there is, let's have it now.'

"He said there wasn't anything he wanted to talk about, so I told him, 'Well, there's something bothering me and I want to get it off my chest.'"

Robinson told Perry he didn't like the pitcher's attitude. He didn't think Gaylord was working as hard as he should. "I told him I thought he should be setting a better example."

Perry offered little in rebuttal. "I just felt it would be better if I didn't say anything," he recounted. "He's the boss. I let it go at that."

The more Gaylord thought about the reprimand, the more he burned. He dressed in silence, then went to Seghi's office. "I really intended only to talk about getting some new arch supports for my baseball shoes," he said. "I talked to Seghi about the shoes, and then all of a sudden I found myself talking about what happened between Frank and me. I finally told Seghi, 'Maybe it would be better for all concerned, for me, for Frank, and for the club if you traded me.'"

Seghi soothed Perry. "Don't worry about it, Gaylord. We'll get this settled."

It might have ended there had not this writer learned of Robinson censuring Perry. "What about Gaylord's problem with Robinson?" Seghi was asked. "I understand he wants to be traded. Is that correct?"

Seghi, visibly upset, tried to shrug off the question. "Oh, I hear that kind of ---- from a lot of guys every spring," he said. "Why are you trying to make something big out of this? Why must you guys always go around looking under the rug for controversy? Frank has a program to run and everybody is expected to adhere to that program. That includes Gaylord Perry. I'm backing my manager 100 percent. There's no way I'm going to trade Gaylord because of this. I've already told him so. That's all I'm going to say."

Seghi, his pipe trailing a cloud of blue smoke, abruptly ended the conversation, striding away in the direction of the field where Robinson was observing batting practice. Seghi called the manager aside and it was then, for the first time, Robinson learned that Perry had gone to the general manager and "suggested" he be traded.

Seghi instructed Robinson to attend another meeting with Perry, this one in the general manager's office, for the purpose of "clearing the air."

It took about an hour. When the three men emerged, all were smiling, but lingering resentments remained with each.

In the schedule for the following day's activities, Robinson changed the running program for the pitchers. They would now run 15 sprints. "It's something I planned to change in another day or so, anyway," shrugged Robinson. "But as long as some of the pitchers feel so strongly, there's no reason for not making the change now. If it makes them happy, that's fine."

Robinson also admitted, "Am I disappointed? Yes, that's the right word. I would like to think we, Gaylord and I, could have settled this thing between ourselves. But I am happy to have a man working upstairs who cares enough to step in."

If Robinson was happy that Seghi stepped into the squabble, baseball commissioner Bowie Kuhn was not and said so in an informal, chance meeting with a newspaperman. "I was sorry to see Seghi get into the confrontation between Perry and Robinson," said Kuhn. "I thought he should have let them settle it themselves. That's the second run-in between those two."

Kuhn did not realize he'd be quoted. When he was, in the - *Tucson Daily Citizen,* Seghi was infuriated. "I can't believe the commissioner would be so stupid as to say something like that," snapped Seghi. "But don't quote me until I talk to him and make sure he did."

Fifteen minutes later Seghi strode into the press room of the Indians' headquarters and declared tersely, "I have a statement to make. I called the commissioner and expressed my distress, my amazement, my shock at his comments relative to what I feel was and is an intrafamily matter and not the concern of the commissioner. I respect Mr. Kuhn's right to have a view on the matter, and I told him so. But to make a public comment like he did is unbelievable to me. He told me he felt I was completely justified in being disturbed."

As for Robinson's change in the program, Gaylord did not consider it a concession to him. Robinson insisted it wasn't, but most of the players thought otherwise. So did most of the general managers of opposing clubs; many immediately called Seghi, offering to help solve the problem by taking Perry off the Indians' hands.

Seghi scoffed but conceded privately, "It was Frank's first test."

Harmony returned for a while as Gaylord went grimly about his business, declining to comment on his problem with Robinson.

Seghi, whenever asked, called the matter "ancient history."

Robinson maintained, "It's over with and settled."

When trade rumors involving Perry persisted, Seghi was dismayed. "My thinking on trading Gaylord Perry is no different than it was before," he snapped. "I'm not marketing Gaylord, and he won't be traded unless someone makes me an offer that's too outstanding to refuse."

Later, Seghi protested further. "Everybody is implying that I'm sitting on a powder keg. Incidents like this occur every spring. They always have and they always will. Why don't you let it die?"

When it was suggested that the two strong-willed men, Robinson and Perry, probably will have trouble again, Seghi countered, "That's like someone coming to me and saying, 'Hey, Phil, I think somebody is going to shoot you next July.' Progress always portends problems, and we're making progress. What you're all doing is the same as a doctor sewing up a cut, and then continually pulling it open to see if it's healing. Why don't you let this heal?"

Although many clubs talked with Seghi about a deal for Perry, only the Boston Red Sox persisted. Haywood Sullivan, their vice-president in charge of player personnel, arrived shortly after the exhibition games and began to scout Gaylord and discuss a possible trade.

Sullivan readily admitted an interest on behalf of the Red Sox in Perry, and early reports indicated they were offering pitcher Roger Moret, second baseman Doug Griffin, and outfielder Bernie Carbo. When the Indians insisted on receiving more pitching, Sullivan's offer was changed to include Moret, either rookie pitcher Steve Barr or Dick Pole, and either Carbo or Griffin.

Seghi, while claiming he wasn't trying to trade Perry, continued to negotiate with Sullivan. On one occasion he confided, "If they [the Red Sox] want me to rape them, I will. But I'm not going to trade Gaylord unless I can get everything I want for him." He wanted Moret and another starting left-handed pitcher, Bill Lee, and shortstop Rick Burleson, which quickly scared off Sullivan. "We like Gaylord, but not as much as Seghi thinks we do," he said, scurrying back to Florida and killing, for the moment at least, speculation that Perry would be traded.

A few weeks into spring training Robinson announced that shortstop Frank Duffy and Hendrick would serve as cocaptains of the Indians. The qualifications, Robinson said, were "knowledge of the game, personality, and temperament, plus not being afraid to speak up to a player.

"It also requires good judgment," he added. "A captain must be able to handle the responsibilities and still be able to play the game well, to handle his own position well. My captains will be like extra coaches, working coaches on the field. They'll do more than just take the lineup to the plate. They'll also be something of a buffer between me and the players. A lot of times a player would rather go to a captain, a fellow player, than take his problems to a coach or to the manager. I don't want my captains to be spies, but I want them to be active coaches."

Of his choices of Duffy and Hendrick, one white, the other black, Robinson said, "I wanted two guys who play every day, who know the game and have leadership qualities. Also guys who are in the middle of things, as the shortstop is in the infield, and the center fielder is in the outfield.

"I think, too, the cocaptains will widen the avenues of communication on the club," Robinson added.

Some outside observers interpreted the move as one that

Nancy Engebretson

Cleveland's 1975 cocaptains, shortstop Frank Duffy (left) and center fielder George Hendrick.

could create a division between the black and white players, defeating Robinson's goal of togetherness. Others, including many fans, felt Robinson's choice of Hendrick meant he'd cater to the center fielder just as he insisted he would not cater to Gaylord Perry.

The appointment of the cocaptains caused no great stir among the players, though Gaylord Perry remarked, "It's something that should be earned, and in my opinion neither Duffy nor Hendrick has earned it. Neither one is a leader yet."

Then Gaylord recalled with bitterness the final game of the 1974 season. "I wasn't scheduled to pitch, and there was no good reason for my doing so," he said. "But the man [Aspromonte] asked me if I would. I said yes. But the center fielder [Hendrick] and the shortstop [Duffy] didn't play. They were too tired, I guess. I was tired, too, but I went out there when the man gave me the ball. The other two guys didn't. I haven't forgotten.

"A couple of double plays weren't made that Duffy might have made. They cost me a couple of runs, and I lost the earned run championship," said Gaylord of the final game the Indians won in Boston, 8–6. He finished with a 2.51 ERA while Catfish Hunter, then with Oakland, had 2.49.

Hendrick had been penciled into the lineup for that final game of 1974, but refused to play and left the clubhouse about an hour before the teams took the field. His refusal to play was the result of something that had happened 12 days earlier in New York on September 20, a 5–4 loss charged to Perry.

Gaylord thought Hendrick should have caught a ball that fell for the hit that drove in the Yankees' winning run in the sixth inning. After the game Perry complained to Aspromonte that he didn't want Hendrick playing center field again when he was pitching. So, in Perry's next two starts, Hendrick was on the bench. George knew why. Before the final game, after Hendrick was listed as a starter, Aspromonte asked Gaylord to pitch. This time Hendrick took himself out of the lineup and went home.

Relations between Gaylord and Hendrick in the spring were cordial, but the pitcher harbored resentment from last season and there remained an undercurrent of unrest, because other players were aware of the situation.

In a further effort to clear the air and keep it so, Robinson held what he said would be the first of many rap sessions in which all the players were invited, even urged to air their complaints.

"I told them, 'If you've got anything on your mind, anything at all, let's hear it now and talk it out," Robinson reported. "I want to exchange ideas. If some of the guys don't agree with the things we're doing, I want to know it so I can change the program, or defend the things we're doing.

"This is something I thought about a long time ago and decided if I ever became a manager, I'd try. We'll do it again when the occasions permit, and I think the next time the guys will speak up more freely. This time I think they might have been self-conscious. Only about six questions came up, and all of them related to travel plans for the coming season ."

Gaylord Perry was among those who had nothing to say. "I guess those kind of meetings are good, but I've learned that it's sometimes better not to do any complaining," he reasoned.

Robinson used the rap session as an example of his intentions to be an unorthodox manager.

"There are a lot of so-called traditional things I don't necessarily agree with," he said. "I'm not going to be a manager who manages strictly by the book. Another thing, when we lose a game, I don't want my players coming into the clubhouse with their chins hanging down against their chests, like the world was about to end. I don't want them laughing and joking either, but I want them to talk, to discuss what went wrong. Not the play that lost the game, but how we could have improved other aspects of our play.

"I also don't agree with the 'rules' that say a team shouldn't play for a tie when it's on the road. That kind of thinking is ridiculous. Heck, you've got to tie the game before you can go ahead, so why shouldn't you play for a tie anytime, on the road or at home?

"It's the element of surprise, mainly, that justifies my plans to be unorthodox. Like once in Puerto Rico I pulled the hit-and-run with the bases loaded. It caught everybody by surprise. That's what I mean."

When he was asked how the bases-loaded, hit-and-run play worked out, Robinson replied, "I was afraid you'd ask."

Another Robinson innovation in spring training was the hiring of Maury Wills, the onetime major league champion base stealer, as a special instructor on baserunning. When he reported, Wills promised to help the Indians win 10 to 15 games they wouldn't otherwise win. He spoke with deep respect for Robinson.

"My admiration for Frank is one of the reasons I'm here, but the fact is, I used to hate him as a player," said Wills. "I hated him because he was such a fierce competitor; he'd do anything to win. He didn't like me either, for the same reason, I guess. But we respected each other. In my opinion, he is the most courageous player I've ever seen.

"I guess I can tell this story now that it's so old. It happened in 1961 when I was with the Dodgers and Frank was with the Cincinnati Reds. We were leading by a run or two late in the game and Frank came to the plate with a runner on first and one out. Walter Alston stood on the dugout steps and held up four fingers, the signal to intentionally walk Frank.

"Don Drysdale, who was pitching for us, called the catcher, John Roseboro, out from behind the plate. They talked for a few seconds, then Roseboro went back to the plate and got into his crouch.

"Drysdale's next four pitches were right at Frank's head, and each time he got off the ground, he stepped closer to the plate. What a way to intentionally walk a batter! I don't remember how we got out of the inning, but I was very glad I didn't have to make a play on Robinson."

Later, Robinson confirmed Will's story and provided more insight into his personality. "I was mad inside at Drysdale, but I refused to show it because I knew that's what he was trying to do, upset me. By upsetting me he knew I couldn't play at my best, so I just refused to let it bother me."

Through most of spring training, at least until the exhibition schedule got under way, and partly because of Robinson's early problem with Perry, there was not much levity in camp. A visiting writer asked one morning, "Is it me, or isn't anybody around here having any fun? Why is it so grim?"

The character of the Indians' organization has long been one of solemnity, possibly because baseball in Cleveland has been financially unstable. Since 1958 there have been threats to move the club elsewhere (on at least two occasions plans were formulated to transfer the franchise, first to Minneapolis and then to Seattle) and as many countermeasures by civic leaders to "save" the Indians.

The structure of the partnership that controls the club contributes to the grimness. At the time of Robinson's hiring no fewer than 42 individuals owned stock, and many of the partners openly feuded with each other, making it difficult for the officers and employees to remain neutral in situations of impending crisis. The result is an atmosphere of inhibition.

Another factor in the development of the humorless personality of the organization relates to Gabe Paul, who assumed control of the Indians in 1961 after a long career at Cincinnati and a brief stay at Houston. He left Cleveland in January 1973 to join George Steinbrenner III and others who purchased the New York Yankees.

To Gabe Paul, baseball is a way of life. To people who are employed by Gabe Paul, baseball *must* also be a way of life. In Cleveland he was referred to (behind his back, of course) as "Pope Paul." The only time the "Pope" sincerely smiled was when the Indians won, which was less often than when they lost.

Seghi succeeded Gabe Paul as general manager of the Indians after coming to Cleveland as farm director in November 1971. He worked for Gabe at Cincinnati from 1956 until Gabe left five years later. Their personalities are remarkably similar, including their total dedication to baseball. Thus, the departure of Paul and the ascendancy of Seghi represented merely a change of command, not a change of attitude, disposition, or method of operation.

Because of that grimness, that total dedication to winning in the face of losing, writers covering the club often are made to feel like intruders.

Once the exhibition schedule got under way, conditions improved if only because some of the boredom was alleviated. "Everyone is eager to get started, to *play*, even if the games here don't mean anything," said Robinson.

There was no doubt about his eagerness. Robinson said, "I feel the same way I did as a player, nervous and fidgety until I went to the plate for the first time. Then I was okay. Then I was myself again."

When he went to the plate on March 13, it was to carry the Indians' first lineup of 1975 to the umpires. Robinson had it ready 24 hours in advance. "It's probably the twenty-fifth combination I've put together since spring training began," he commented.

"I'd love to win every game we play here. I hate to lose at anything, even when I play cards with my children. But I know we've got certain things to do which, in the long run, are more important than winning now. We've got to find out who can help us the most. I've got some pretty good ideas, but I want to make sure. I also want to make sure we're fundamentally sound. We'll probably emphasize winning more in the final week, but for now, there are other things I want to see and do."

His managerial debut, against the San Francisco Giants, resembled something out of Hollywood. Robinson was wired for sound by NBC-TV camera crews. Two hours before game time, photographers, writers, broadcasters, and the usual throng of well-wishers surrounded him at every turn, backing him into every corner.

The clubhouse, usually noisy, was silenced by the television director as Joe Garagiola interviewed Robinson. The players of both teams seemed to be merely extras: the clubhouse, dugout, and field were the set. The star, of course, was Frank Robinson.

"Robinson, take one, roll it!" commanded the director.

"This being your first day as a major league manager managing against another major league team, what are your thoughts?" asked Garagiola.

"My feelings are that this is the end of a long road, but the sacrifices were worthwhile to get here. I also have a feeling of gratefulness to all the people, black and white, who made it possible, the sacrifices of all the black players before me, and especially to Jackie Robinson, who's in my thoughts almost every time I put on a uniform. My only regret is that Jackie couldn't be alive to see this happen.

"My thoughts also are of my wife, who has been father and mother and counselor to my children while I've been gone, trying to make this day possible. She made it easier for me with her sacrifices."

"That's great, Frank! Well done!" said the director. "Now, let's do it again." Robinson did it again.

During the ceremonies at home plate, witnessed by 4071 spectators at Hi Corbett Field, Robinson shook hands with the umpires and Wes Westrum, the manager of the Giants, who "congratulated me and wished me luck," reported Robinson.

The predicted nervousness did develop. "I was all right until the game actually started, then my heart began beating faster and faster, louder and louder," recalled Robinson. "I'm sure the microphone they planted on me picked it all up. The nervousness never completely went away, although there were times I forgot about it. But it kept coming back. I think it's because I was so determined not to foul up, not to miss anything. I knew this was just a dress rehearsal, it would continue until Opening Day in Cleveland, at least."

Robinson did foul up in that exhibition opener.

In the tenth inning, with the score tied, 4–4, he summoned LaRoche, a southpaw, to pitch to left-handed batter Ed Goodson. There were runners on first and second with two out.

What Robinson didn't know, he admitted later, was that Goodson had been practicing all spring to be a switch-hitter. He batted right-handed against LaRoche and lined the first pitch into right center field for a two-run double that broke the tie and won the game for the Giants, 6–4.

"I got caught this time," confessed Robinson. "Sure, I'm sorry we lost. Losing takes some of the edge off my first game. But I'm not disappointed. Disappointed means you're not satisfied. We're here to get some work in, to learn some things, and to see what we can do in certain situations.

"Don't judge anybody or anything by what you saw today."

Between that loss and an 11-6 victory over the Oakland A's on April 5, the Indians won nine games and lost eight prior to their breaking camp and returning to Cleveland for the April 8 opener against the New York Yankees.

Robinson made his 1975 debut as a player in the Indians' eighth exhibition game, on March 23, against Milwaukee. He flied out, then walked and retired to the dugout. Between then and the end of spring training, Robinson appeared in only five games, getting three hits in nine official at bats for a .333 average with four runs batted in.

He called spring training "very satisfying, all things considered."

Through it all trade rumors involving Gaylord Perry periodically arose, though nothing of substance actually developed. Perry and Robinson were overtly cordial to each other, but there was reason to believe they remained antagonistic and suspicious.

Through it all, too, Robinson was both praised and criticized; he had his first of what were to be many altercations with an umpire; there was at least one more incident that raised doubts about his insistence upon the Indians experiencing "togetherness"; and he displayed an otherwise unrevealed (perhaps unknown even to himself) sense of compassion when it came to cutting players from the roster.

On March 15, when the Indians visited Yuma, Arizona, for a two-game series with San Diego, E. J. (Buzzie) Bavasi, president of the Padres, made a point of congratulating Robinson. "I wished him luck and all that," said Bavasi. "I've always liked Frank and I think he'll do a good job as manager, and I told him so. There was something else I wanted to tell him but didn't. I wanted to tell him I wish he hadn't knocked Walter Alston the way he did in the *Los Angeles Times* the other day. Then I thought, What the hell, keep out of it. I think the reason Frank said what he did about Alston is that he resented not getting special treatment from Alston in 1972 like he did everywhere else, especially in Baltimore. I didn't think what Frank said about Alston was fair."

What Robinson said about Alston also was not complimentary. "I didn't think the Dodgers would ever win again as long as Alston was the manager unless the players decided to do it on their own, which I'm sure is what happened last [1974] year," Robinson was quoted in the *Times*.

"It was my feeling that Alston had reached a point where he was satisfied simply to produce a contender. He never made any attempt to motivate, to pump up the team, to instill confidence. He never chewed us out. We'd sit in clubhouse meetings and all of us would be hoping that this would be the time he'd let us have it, that he'd light a fire. By the time the meeting was over, he'd have ended up almost apologizing to us. His favorite saying was, 'Well, no matter what happens this year, I can go back to Darrtown with enough shells for my shotgun.' I mean that shows he was satisfied. I can't say for sure that team could have won a pennant [it finished third in 1972, 10½ games behind Cincinnati], but it could have been much better than it was.

"It wasn't all a matter of motivation. I didn't think Alston was on top of the situation on the field. There were several instances when things happened and instead of reacting like this [Robinson snapped his fingers], he didn't react until several moments later.

"I remember a game in St. Louis when we had the bases loaded and Willie Davis swung at a 3-and-0 pitch and popped it up to kill the rally. A few seconds later Alston jumped off the bench and asked us, 'What was the count?' I mean there's no way Earl Weaver would ever have to ask what the count was.

"That was the first game of a doubleheader, and between games Alston had a clubhouse meeting where he came down on the entire team. Instead of ironing it out with Davis in his office, he penalized the entire team by saying that none of us was to swing at a 3-and-0 unless we got a green light. Well, when you penalize all 25 because of what one did, you tend to drive the entire team into a shell."

The next day, during another game with the Padres, a rookie umpire named Paul Maltby told Robinson, in no uncertain terms, to "shut up."

In the fourth inning, second baseman Jack Brohamer was called out on strikes by Maltby. Brohamer argued, then returned to the dugout. But Robinson continued to taunt the umpire. Finally, Maltby tore off his mask and ran to the edge of the Cleveland dugout, shaking his fist in anger at Robinson. "Shut up or get out of here!" Maltby warned the manager. Robinson shut up.

"I remember Maltby from Puerto Rico, and I'm sure he remembers me," said Robinson. "We had some problems down there, too." Robinson had said earlier, "I don't want my players to do a lot of arguing with umpires. I'll tell them, 'If you've got a beef with an umpire, let him know. Get it over with, and then forget it.' I don't want my team to be known as a bunch of crybabies because it will come back to haunt us. Don't let umpires tell you they don't talk to each other about teams and players. They do. It gets around the league and pretty soon you don't get the close calls. I don't want that to happen to us."

Those words became significant later.

When the Indians left Yuma that day, with Robinson still scowling, partly because of the loss to the Padres but mainly because of Maltby's admonition, they traveled to Palm Springs, California, in two chartered buses. In the first, along with Robinson and Seghi, were coaches Harvey Haddix and Jeff Torborg and 18 or 20 players. Haddix and Torborg and the 18 or 20 players are all white. In the second bus rode coaches Tom McCraw (a player-coach) and Dave Garcia, accompanied by the rest of the players on the squad. McCraw is black, Garcia is of Spanish descent, and all but a few players with them are black or Latin.

Wasn't that strange, Robinson was asked, particularly in view of his desire for more togetherness?

"No," he replied stoically. "I don't know why or how it happened that way, or what the circumstances were. I guess everybody just paired up with friends to play cards or talk. I'm sure not going to worry about what they do on the bus. It's the same as guys choosing roommates. It's their choice and I have nothing more to say about it."

In Palm Springs, March 18, in a game against the California Angels, George Hendrick committed his first sin. In the sixth inning he lined deep to right field. The ball sailed over the head of the right fielder and thudded against the fence. It should have been a triple. Hendrick trotted around first base and halfway to second: with a last-moment burst of speed and long slide, he beat the throw for a double.

Robinson was asked if he found fault with his cocaptain's running. "For now I'm giving George the benefit of the doubt, but I plan to sit down and talk to him to find out what he was thinking," the manager replied.

But one of the players wondered. "Hendrick is doing the same thing he did last year when he cost Aspromonte his job," he said. "The manager said he's going to talk to him? Nobody's going to talk to him. The guy who should have done something last year was the general manager [Seghi], but he didn't. Nobody will talk to George about it now. They're all afraid of him."

Robinson did talk to Hendrick. "I asked George, 'Why didn't you run hard?' He told me, 'I thought the ball was out of the park. I didn't think it would hit the fence.' I was satisfied with his explanation, though I told him not to let it happen again. He told me it wouldn't.' "

The manager also was annoyed by the questions. "Just because it's George Hendrick, everybody is watching every move he makes," he said. "As far as I'm concerned, George has been playing super this spring. There have been at least two other instances of guys not running hard after they hit pop flies, but nobody asked me about them. Why not?"

The writers' only answer was that they hadn't noticed the others, which proved Robinson's point.

A few days later the Indians played the Milwaukee Brewers for the first time and Hank Aaron spoke earnestly as a fellow black man who can understand the pressure Robinson is enduring this season.

"I don't think it'll bother Frank one bit," said Aaron. "It's something he has to anticipate. The best thing Frank can do is cooperate with everybody who makes demands on his time. He's a terrific competitor and I'm sure he'll do an excellent job of managing the Indians. A manager's success depends upon the kind of players he's got. Even I could manage the Oakland A's and win with all the talent they've got." How about the Indians? "I don't know," replied Aaron, chuckling.

Asked what he thinks will be Robinson's biggest problem, Aaron said with another chuckle, "It already seems to be Gaylord Perry, from what I've been reading. But to me, it proves a point. If every little dispute Frank has with a player is blown out of proportion, that's going to be his biggest problem. It's unfair. If Gaylord had a dispute with a veteran white manager like Walter Alston, it probably would've been handled as just one of those things that happens on every club.

"That's the kind of thing that might stand in the way of Robby being a successful manager: not the way he manages or handles players, but the way it's all reported by the press."

George Scott, the Brewers' hulking but adept first baseman, is another who swears by Robinson.

"If it weren't for Robby, I wouldn't be a $100,000 player today," said Scott, who commanded a $105,000 salary from the Brewers in 1975. "After I had a bad season in 1968, my confidence was shattered. I lost everything. I played that winter for Robby and he worked with me every day, in every way. He gave me a completely new attitude. He turned my career around.

"Sure, there'll be some guys over there who'll give him some problems, but Robby can handle them, and he'll handle them with a lot of class."

The Oakland A's made their first visit to Tucson on March 28; the day was rainy and cold, but that was only one reason Bobby Winkles, one of their coaches, spent most of his pre-game time in the clubhouse. Winkles does not regard Robinson as one of his favorite people, and vice versa.

"I don't particularly want to see Robinson," said Winkles as he waited for the game to start. "If I do, we'll probably speak, but just to say hello, and I wouldn't go out of my way to do it, just as I know he wouldn't go out of his way to speak to me. I'd be lying if I said anything else. But I wish him luck, I really do. I think he'll make a good manager because he is a good baseball man. Can he get along with the players? I don't know how important that is as long as he's respected by the players, and I think he will be.

"What Robinson said about me after I was fired by the Angels is his business. I'm not holding any grudges. I lost the job on my own. Robby didn't get me fired. I just wasn't my own man like I should have been. If I ever get another managing job, I'll be different.

"What's funny, well, not really funny, but ironic, is that Robby is going into the same kind of situation I was in. He's the first black manager, and I was the first college coach to go directly from a campus to a big league manager's job. I was a national guinea pig, and so is he. Everybody wanted to interview me, just as they all want to interview him. It's tough. I hope he can handle it better than I did.

"When I was fired I was really hurt and I said some things I shouldn't have said, some of them about Robby. After a day or two I got over it because, I think, I am a big enough man. If I get another chance, I'll be the boss. I was just a rookie, but I won't be the next time."

Later that afternoon, the sun came out and the Indians and

A's played a game, won by Cleveland, 9–8, after relievers Tom Buskey and rookie Dennis Eckersley blew a 7–3 lead in the ninth inning. Even so, as it turned out, Robinson saw something in Eckersley's performance that convinced him the kid was good enough to pitch in the big leagues this year.

Perry, however, was critical of the way Eckersley was rushed into the game.

"Throwing a kid like Eckersley into a situation like that was as stupid and unfair a thing as I've ever seen," said Gaylord.

After Eckersley's brief stint on the mound, in which he gave up a hit, two walks, and two runs in one-third of an inning, Robinson called the rookie into his office. "I thought Robinson was going to tell me I was going back to Oklahoma City. I was really scared."

Robinson had something else in mind. "I just wanted to talk to the kid while everything that happened was fresh in both our minds," explained the manager. "He tried to be too fine. He should have been more aggressive. A relief pitcher cannot afford to miss like he did, and I wanted to be sure Eckersley knew it."

Was part of the problem perhaps that Eckersley wasn't aware he was scheduled to pitch in the game?

"I don't know," replied Robinson. "He wasn't scheduled to pitch, but we needed somebody in a hurry and he just happened to be loosening up. You might say he was in the right place at the right time. I liked what I saw of him. He's got some guts. He's got poise. I told you at the beginning I'm more concerned with seeing what a kid has than I am with winning or losing, and I liked what I saw this kid do."

It turned out that the 20-year-old Eckersley, who was not deemed ready when spring training began, earned a place on the roster despite his inexperience—after only three minor league seasons.

The day the roster was cut for the final time, bringing it down to 25 players, Robinson said, "I kept hoping the game we were playing would never end because I didn't want to do what I knew I had to do. It was tougher than I thought it would be. Whatever you say isn't adequate. It doesn't make them feel any better. I never went through that as a player, but I know how the guys felt. I can't say I felt worse than they did, but I know I felt bad, real bad, for all of them."

Finally it was time to go home, back to Cleveland and Frank Robinson's official debut as major league baseball's first black manager.

Asked to rate his team's chances in the coming pennant race—which will have a great bearing on his chances of being rehired as manager of the Indians—Robinson said, "I guess, realistically, I'd have to rate the Baltimore Orioles and New York Yankees as cofavorites. Don't misunderstand me. I'm not selling us short. If we play up to our potential and execute the way we should, we can win it, I really believe that. I'd say the odds on us should be something like 3 to 2. I'd put the odds on the Boston Red Sox at 5 to 2, the Milwaukee Brewers should be about 9 to 2, the Detroit Tigers something like 20 to 1.

"Offensively, we're better than both Baltimore and New York. Defensively, the edge should go to the Orioles, but I like our club in the field better than the Yankees. As for pitching, Baltimore and New York, overall, have an edge on us; but if the right things happen, our pitching would be good enough to win."

By "right things" Robinson meant an improvement in the bullpen and good seasons again by Gaylord and Jim Perry, with Fritz Peterson regaining his 1972 form when he won 17 games, and Don Hood doing as well as expected (or hoped).

On the flight to Cleveland, Robinson spoke with more optimism about the coming season. With Opening Day against the New York Yankees only 48 hours away, Robinson pronounced the Indians "as ready as we can be."

He insisted he was not disappointed by anything that happened but admitted, "I wish the relievers would have come as fast at the end of spring training as the starting pitchers did." Robinson predicted "at least a .500 record," but stressed, "I'll be very disappointed if we don't do better." Of his celebrated squabble with Gaylord Perry: "I think we're better because of it." Most of all, he was pleased by the attitude of the players. "It was excellent from beginning to end."

He was asked whether the pitching staff was questionable in his mind, as it was to some.

"No. The addition of Don Hood and Dave LaRoche, and Jim Kern and Dennis Eckersley will make us better. The Perrys show no signs of breaking down, and I feel as strong as ever that Fritz Peterson will win between 15 and 20 games. I'm not sure yet who will be our fourth starter, but we'll need only three the first three weeks, so we've got time to decide."

Robinson defined the Indians' strengths and weaknesses: "Our offense will be strong. Our defense will be good. As for pitching, we have enough if everybody does his job. I definitely feel we could have three 20-game winners on the staff in the Perrys and Peterson. Our catching is fine. Alan Ashby is going to surprise a lot of people. John Ellis will do most of the catching, but Ashby is going to play a lot."

His thoughts on managing, Robinson said, "are that it's much more involved than I expected. Much more because there are so many little things I didn't anticipate. It'll be better now that the season is starting. Playing the game is the easiest thing for a manager."

Is he beginning to feel the pressure?

"Not yet because I'm too busy thinking about other things. I'm too busy to be nervous. I'll probably start to get, well, anxious along about Monday night or Tuesday morning, when I start thinking more about the opener. Then it'll be over, I hope. Then we can just concentrate on playing."

One other thing Frank Robinson is eagerly anticipating, he admitted. "I'm looking forward to the day, I hope by midseason, when people will stop writing, 'Frank Robinson, baseball's first black manager,' and just write, 'Frank Robinson, manager of the Cleveland Indians.' It's a fact; it's happened. Save the identification for my epitaph."

3. "Like Alice in Wonderland"

CLEVELAND, OHIO, APR. 8—Cleveland Municipal Stadium did not collapse in a heap of rubble when manager Frank Robinson carried his first lineup card to the plate and handed it to umpire Nestor Chylak. The Stadium did shudder ever so perceptibly under the thunderous cheers of 56,715 baseball fans when player Frank Robinson smashed a home run in his very first time at bat. It was, without a doubt, one of the most dramatic moments in baseball. As the ball arched higher and deeper to left center field, the fans stood as one, roaring approval. The Yankee pitcher, Doc Medich, reached for another ball, trying to shrug off the ramifications of what had just happened.

"It gave me goose bumps and it took all the pressure off the rest of us," said Boog Powell, who homered later in the game, ensuring the Indians' 5–3 victory.

Thrilled, too, was winning pitcher Gaylord Perry, who was the first to leap out of the Indians' dugout to greet Robinson after his home run. And when the game ended with another

Paul Tepley, Cleveland *Press*

Frank Robinson on opening day, April 8, 1975.

Outfielder John Lowenstein (left) congratulating Frank Robinson
after Robinson homered in his managerial debut, April 8.

standing ovation, Robinson was the first to greet Perry coming off the field. Both times the men embraced: the white, Southern-born pitcher and the black manager.

"Any home run is a thrill, but I've got to admit this one was a bigger thrill," confessed Robinson, whose office was packed with writers, broadcasters, and cameramen after the dramatic debut.

For the record, Robinson delivered with the count at 2 and 2, on the eighth pitch by Medich. The first two were quick strikes. Robinson fouled off the next two, two more were wide, then another foul, all preceding the homer. When Robinson reached the plate and before he was mobbed by his players, he doffed his cap. "That was for my wife." Barbara was seated with son Kevin and daughter Nichelle in the loges behind the plate.

The homer made general manager Phil Seghi, the man who hired Robinson, something of a prophet.

"Phil suggested to me this morning, 'Why don't you hit a homer the first time you go to the plate?' " related Robinson. "I told him, 'You've got to be kidding.' "

Later, Seghi said, "I might have suggested he hit a homer, but I never dared dream he'd do it. I should have. Knowing Frank, I shouldn't be surprised by anything about the man's ability to rise to an occasion. Frank Robinson doing the unusual is only usual for him."

Robinson admitted he could hardly believe what happened as he toured the bases to the cheering of the crowd.

"At first there was nothing running through my mind really," he said. "But by the time I got to third base, I thought to myself, Wow, will miracles never cease?"

It was, Robinson said, "The single most satisfying thing that happened, other than winning. Right now I feel better than I have after anything I've done in baseball. Take all the pennants, the personal awards, the World Series, the All-Star games, and this moment is the greatest."

He also spoke of the crowd. "It was unbelievable. If I could have asked God for a good day, I never would have asked for something like this and expected it to happen. Everything was all I could ask for."

It was almost all Rachel Robinson could ask for, too. Jackie Robinson's widow was invited by the Indians to throw out the ceremonial first pitch. In her pregame remarks, Rachel Robinson said, "I want to say I'm proud to be here, and I want to congratulate you for honoring yourselves by being the first to take this historic step." And later, "I've wished, since I was asked to do this, that Jackie could be here, and I'm sure in many ways he is."

Mrs. Robinson continued, saying she was "heartened by this symbol of progress," but said Jackie had always hoped it would happen sooner. "I hope this is the beginning of a lot more black players being moved into front office and managerial positions and not just having their talents exploited on the field."

When asked if Frank Robinson's success—or failure—as a manager might have any bearing on the hiring of other blacks as managers, Rachel Robinson replied softly, but with some defiance, "Why should it? White men have failed as managers, but it has not harmed the chances of other white men."

Barbara Robinson, when introduced at a luncheon, stood alongside Rachel Robinson and delivered a short and simple speech. "If it were not for Rachel and Jackie, I would not be here today."

Bowie Kuhn also spoke during the pregame ceremonies. "This is an historic day in baseball and I am happy on behalf of baseball to bring its greetings to Frank Robinson and the Cleveland Indians . . . to bring our congratulations to the management of the Cleveland Indians Baseball Club. We hope you have a great season in Cleveland."

Yankee manager Bill Virdon came up with the best postgame remark. Smiling and pleasant despite the defeat, Virdon observed wryly, "Well, I guess this makes me the answer to one of those trivia questions. Who was the losing manager the day a black man managed for the first time in the big leagues?"

Seghi, beaming with pride, proclaimed, "There wasn't one single disappointment for me, not one. It was the kind of a day, the kind of a game you only dream about, like Alice in Wonderland."

APR. 9—All the members of the Indians' family basked in the afterglow of the Opening Day success, including Frank Robinson, albeit reluctantly.

"I'd rather look ahead than behind . . . but I'm still perfect," he quipped. "I still haven't made a single mistake." Nobody argued.

"The only times I got excited, I mean really excited, were at the beginning when they played the national anthem, and at the end when the fans were cheering so loud. I couldn't believe the noise they made."

Robinson spoke without emotion of the game itself.

"Actually I had no tough decisions, although I came close twice." Both involved whether Gaylord Perry should remain in the game. In the second inning, Ron Blomberg and Graig Nettles led with singles. Ed Herrmann flied out, the runners advanced and scored on a double by Chris Chambliss. When Thurman Munson singled for another run and a 3–1 Yankee lead, Robinson sent a hurry-up call to the bullpen.

"If they'd have scored another run, I would've had to get Gaylord out of there," said Robinson. But the Yankees didn't.

In the ninth inning, after Herrmann's one-out single, Robinson hurried to the mound for a conference with Gaylord.

"I just told him not to give Chambliss a pitch he could pull, hit out of the park," related Robinson. "I said, 'If he hits it, don't let him pull it.' " Chambliss then pulled a long fly to right. "I said to myself, 'Holy smokes, it's out. Oh, no!' I really thought it was gone." Right fielder Charlie Spikes backed against the fence and plucked the ball out of the air. Perry retired Munson to end the game. "It was a great effort by Gaylord," said Robinson.

Robinson, while insisting he's not a collector of mementos, saved from the opener not only the ball he hit for the homer but also the first pitch of the game by Perry.

"I tossed it out for Frank. I thought he'd appreciate it," said Gaylord.

Did that gesture by Perry help ease the tension between the two men?

"Can't you guys let anything fade away?" Robinson asked, not unpleasantly. "I just didn't think Gaylord was putting out 100 percent. I talked to him and I felt there was a change after that." Are their wounds healed? "I can't look inside Gaylord's head, but as far as I'm concerned, it's all over.

"At least it'll be all over as soon as you guys stop writing about it."

Paul Tepley, Cleveland *Press*

Commissioner Bowie Kuhn (right) wishing Frank Robinson good
luck before Robinson's managerial debut.

William A. Wynne, Cleveland *Plain Dealer*

Commissioner Bowie Kuhn addressing a crowd in Cleveland Stadium opening day, April 8, 1975.

While further exchanging quips with reporters, Robinson revealed his plans—"they're irrevocable"—to quit baseball completely in 1980, no matter how successful he is as a manager.

Jesting that his decision would solve the "problem" of how to fire the first black manager, Robinson said he would manage for only five years, "if I last that long."

His reason? "I want to relax and enjoy life. It's a decision I made this spring. Nothing prompted it, I just decided. It's not the managing, it's the [baseball] life itself."

At the moment Robinson was asked if he had informed Phil Seghi of his planned retirement, the phone at the manager's elbow rang. He picked it up and, with a grin splitting his face, said, "I didn't mean it, Phil, I really didn't."

Also irrevocable, Robinson insisted, is his intention of playing no more than one season "no matter what."

But what if, in 1975, Robinson gets 99 more hits for a career total of 2999, and 25 more homers, for 599?

"Then I'll be the only man in baseball history with 2999 hits and 599 homers. That's not a bad distinction, is it?"

The most demanding of his duties to date, he asserted, "are all the interviews, everywhere we go," and the toughest task "was every time I had to cut players from the squad . . . it never got any easier."

Robinson said of his duties as player-manager, "I don't think managing will be as difficult as it would if I played in the field, on defense. The hardest part of all will be to keep myself in shape to play."

So now that the opener is out of the way, what is Robinson planning for an encore?

"An encore?" he asked. "All I can promise is that I'll show up for the next game."

For now it was enough for Cleveland baseball fans.

4. *The Shakedown Cruise*

MILWAUKEE, WISCONSIN, APR. 11—Henry Aaron was welcomed home prior to the Brewers' opener against the Indians, but two lesser known players stole the spotlight in Milwaukee's 6–2 victory. Johnny Briggs homered and singled and Pedro Garcia delivered a key double in the sixth inning to spoil the Indians' and Frank Robinson's perfect record.

"I really thought we'd win them all," quipped Robinson after the loss, charged to Jim Perry. Ironically, the winning pitcher was Billy Champion, the right-hander the Indians sought for outfielder John Lowenstein in trade all winter. Robinson, the Indians' designated hitter, went hitless in three at bats, walking once.

What troubled Robinson more than the defeat was the improper execution of fundamentals in the sixth inning. The Brewers attempted a double steal. The Indians were unsuccessful in retiring even one runner, setting the stage for three final runs that turned a close game into an easy victory for Milwaukee.

"The thing that bothers me," said Robinson, "is that we worked so much on that play in spring training. Hammer [Jack Brohamer] just didn't do the right thing. Because we couldn't get even one of their runners, it meant the difference of three runs, and three runs, from 3–1 to 6–1, turned the whole game around in their favor."

Did Robinson feel slighted because he wasn't the center of attention, because the fans came out to welcome Hank Aaron back? "No, it was a relief."

APR. 12—Frank Robinson lost his first argument with an umpire, and the Indians lost their second game of the season, 6–5, to the Brewers. The Indians' ninth-inning comeback, when they nearly salvaged the game, was short-circuited by a contested interference ruling by umpire Nick Bremigan.

After George Hendrick opened the ninth with a home run that cut the Indians' deficit to one, Charlie Spikes lofted a foul near the field boxes alongside the Milwaukee dugout. Brewer catcher Charlie Moore pursued the ball, but stumbled at the last moment. At the same time, a fan leaned over the railing and deflected the ball. Bremigan immediately ruled Spikes out. Robinson barged onto the field to dispute the call. He lost.

"Bremigan said, in his judgment, Moore would have caught the ball," related Robinson. "There was nothing more I could say when he came up with the judgment line. But Bremigan took the bat out of Spikes's hands, and Spikes is the kind of hitter who could have tied the game with just one swing."

Throughout the argument Robinson—nose to nose with Bremigan—kept his hands in his jacket pockets as he bumped the umpire around the plate area. "I kept my hands in my pockets," he explained later, "because my hands were cold."

The basis of Robinson's argument was twofold. "First, Moore was not in position to catch the ball. Second, the other umpires should have helped Bremigan. I asked them, but they wouldn't. I don't know why Art Frantz didn't say anything, but I think I know why Larry McCoy stayed out of it." Crew chief Jerry Neudecker remained aloof at his position at second base.

"McCoy and I had our problems in Puerto Rico several times. I don't think he wanted to get into it with me." Robinson's logic made sense—except in this case it was not Larry McCoy but Jim McKean.

In the second inning Boog Powell hit his second homer of the season. The first baseman was pleased. "I don't know the reason I'm doing so well . . . except that it's a completely different atmosphere around here. Maybe that's the key, that and not having to worry about my job, knowing that Frank's going to play me tomorrow no matter what happens today. This is the best start I've had since 1963. Normally, a good start, no, a great start for me is to be hitting .250 in May."

When a writer commented, "Fritz Peterson didn't pitch very well, did he?" Robinson glared. "Don't try to get me to knock my players."

APR. 13—Gaylord Perry stopped the Brewers and blanked Hank Aaron as the Indians evened their record by beating Milwaukee, 3–1. In the ninth inning, John Lowenstein homered to tie the score, George Hendrick and Charlie Spikes singled, and John Ellis doubled for the winning runs. Perry is 2–0.

Left fielder Oscar Gamble pulled a hamstring muscle and now the Indians have two regulars sidelined: Gamble and shortstop Frank Duffy, who's still nursing a rib-cage muscle torn during spring training.

On the flight to Cleveland, John Ellis and Charlie Spikes quarreled. Ellis objected to Spikes playing his portable phonograph so loud. "Get yourself earphones so the rest of us don't have to listen to the crap [hard rock] you're playing on that thing."

"You don't have to pay attention if you don't like it," responded Spikes. They glared. Frank Robinson, sitting a few seats ahead of Spikes and Ellis, ignored them. Sometimes it's the best way.

CLEVELAND, OHIO, APR. 15—While the Indians worked out today, the weather changed from bad to worse. Phil Seghi was pleased. Last December Seghi unilaterally postponed a two-game series with the Detroit Tigers, tentatively scheduled for today and tomorrow. That left both teams idle for four days.

"I knew the weather would be lousy," chortled Seghi. "I

checked the *Farmer's Almanac.* If we had played the Detroit series, we wouldn't have drawn anybody. The weather in April in Cleveland is just too bad. It makes sense to me."

Not to Detroit general manager Jim Campbell, however, who was furious at last December's decision. He forced a rules change to prevent such a thing happening again without the mutual consent of the two teams involved. He's still angry.

APR. 16—It was a beautiful day for a ball game.

Harold Bossard, the chief grounds keeper at Municipal Stadium, crossed the field to where Phil Seghi sat watching the Indians practice.

"Hey, Mr. Seghi, whatever happened to your *Farmer's Almanac,*" teased Bossard. The general manager, who's seldom speechless, had little to say.

Frank Robinson didn't like the long layoff. "No way I would have agreed to it if I had been asked. But I wasn't asked."

Jim Campbell phoned Seghi, but Phil was gone from the office. It was such a nice day, by that time he probably had gone fishing.

APR. 17—Ted Bonda, Phil Seghi, and Frank Robinson spoke before the Shrine Luncheon Club today. All the players were in the audience.

Bonda was cheerful. "Last year people were saying we were almost bankrupt, but here we are, a year later, looking forward to a good season. Everything looks brighter, thanks to the team put together by Phil Seghi and managed by Frank Robinson."

Applause.

Seghi was proud. "No longer do we have an atmosphere enshrouded in gloom and doom. One big reason is the presence of Frank Robinson. He is our manager today because I thought he was the strongest man in America to get the job done."

More applause.

Robinson was sincere. "One thing I'm especially pleased about is the attitude of our players. Throughout spring training we tried to mold them into a team, not a group of individuals, and we have."

Much more applause.

"The most difficult days of my life were when we had to trim the roster, but that's a good sign because now there are people down below we know can play up here, and the people up here cannot get complacent. We know our farm system is starting to pay off. I think we have an outstanding team, although I'll promise only one thing: that we'll be an exceptionally well-drilled team that knows how to play the game, and that we won't stand still. I think we have the pitching to carry us. Pitchers mature late, you know, and our top three guys, Gaylord and Jim Perry, and Fritz Peterson, all keep themselves in great shape. Our bullpen is improved, too, and I think it'll be a good one."

Standing ovation.

APR. 18—The Wahoo Club, a group of Cleveland baseball fans, held its first meeting of the season today. Frank Robinson was the guest speaker.

He said, "We accomplished in spring training what we set out to accomplish, to come home with the best-conditioned team possible." The fact is, however, pitcher Fred Beene pulled a back muscle and infielder Angel Hermoso hurt his right knee, injuries that sidelined the two players. And Frank Duffy and Oscar Gamble can't play though they're not on the disabled list.

The Indians lost for the third time and Gaylord Perry for the first time, 5–1, to the Milwaukee Brewers. Hank Aaron, Gaylord's longtime foe, delivered his first American League homer in the sixth inning. Darrell Porter and Johnny Briggs also homered off Perry, who was replaced in the eighth inning by reliever Tom Buskey. Robinson sent pitching coach Harvey Haddix to the mound to make the change and Gaylord stalked off, obviously upset.

Later, Robinson explained with what he hoped were soothing words. "Gaylord threw the ball well. It's tough to pitch without any runs, and I think Gaylord himself will tell you he made bad pitches to the guys who hit the homers. When I took him out, I had made up my mind, one more run and we had to make a change. Gaylord made a great pitch to Aaron, but he blooped it for a single and the run came home. I had to take him out, even though it was a good pitch. I couldn't concern myself with *how* the run came in, all I could concern myself with was that the run *did* come in."

Gaylord admitted he made three bad pitches. When asked about Robinson's decision to bring in Buskey, Perry snapped, "I just work here."

John Ellis didn't approve either. "They're second-guessing the hell out of us, Gaylord and me, between every inning," grumbled the catcher. "It's awful. Haddix and Robinson come to me every inning and say, 'Tell Gaylord to pitch this guy and that guy different.' But Gaylord has been pitching the same way for three years and he's won 20 games each year. How the hell can you second-guess that?"

The Indians also lost the services of Boog Powell, their best hitter, for about a week. Boog was hit on the right elbow by a pitch from Pete Broberg. "When I picked up the pitch, it was right here," said Boog, holding his hand about a foot away from his right ear. "I threw my arm up and the next thing I knew, I was on the ground and my arm and hand were numb. At first I didn't really know where I got hit. Then, when I realized it was on my elbow, I was relieved, even though it hurt like hell."

APR. 19—Prior to today's game, another loss, 3–0, to the Brewers, Frank Robinson made a request of this reporter.

"I want to ask you not to play me against my pitchers," he said. "I don't think it's fair for you to ask me why I took out a pitcher, and then go to him and ask if he was unhappy about being taken out. It's a negative question and the only answer you can get is a negative one. What do you expect the pitcher to tell you, that he was ready to come out? Of course he won't."

Robinson was told, "It's difficult to honor your request, for several reasons. One is that, usually, asking the pitcher about being taken out of a game is a pertinent question. Another reason is that, if I don't ask, somebody else certainly will."

"Okay, then, I'll ask the rest of the writers and see what they say," said Robinson.

During the game Jim Perry was victimized by a couple of windblown hits that center fielder George Hendrick ordinarily would have caught. In the ninth inning Harvey Haddix went to the mound to change·pitchers.

Jim took a vicious swipe at the turf in his second step toward the dugout.

Later, Perry, who first took sanctuary in the trainer's room, spoke of his frustration to a newspaperman without being asked.

"I'm no rookie and I think I at least deserve the privilege of being asked if I still feel good, and how I'm throwing the ball. But I wasn't. I was out there busting my butt, trying to win, and here comes Harvey to tell me I'm through. He didn't say anything to me except, 'We're bringing in Buskey.' I would have been honest with him, but I didn't get that privilege. Hell, I'm a veteran.

"At this rate, Harvey will be hated by all the pitchers by the time the season is half over. Every time he comes to the mound, you know you're gone, without any questions about how you feel. You can't take it out on the pitcher in a game like this one. It was tough because of the wind. I don't blame the other guys, but I shouldn't be blamed either."

Also in the ninth inning Robinson the manager sent Rico Carty to the plate to bat for Robinson the player. Carty grounded into a game-ending double play. It was the first time since 1957, when Frank Robinson was only a second-year major leaguer, that anyone batted for him except because of an injury. Said Robinson, "I thought Rico could do a better job."

After the game the black community in Cleveland held a dinner dance honoring Hank Aaron and Robinson. It was oversold, and displayed unfortunate racist overtones. Among those who attended were Bowie Kuhn, Cleveland Mayor Ralph J. Perk, Ted Bonda, Phil Seghi, and players Ed Crosby, Alan Ashby, Don Hood, Frank Duffy, Gaylord Perry, Leron Lee, Oscar Gamble, Rico Carty, and Angel Hermoso.

In his speech the Reverend Jesse Jackson of The Southern Christan Leadership Conference contended that black players have been and are being exploited by whites, including sportswriters. He pronounced at the onset, "Frank Robinson is not a black manager! He is a manager who is black!" and insisted, "Frank Robinson is not on trial, baseball is on trial!"

When asked for his reaction, Robinson said guardedly, "The problem, I think, is a matter of impatience. I wish people, all people, could be more patient."

APR. 20—Frank Robinson's first duty today, prior to a 7–4 victory over the Brewers, was to call Jim Perry into his office.

"It wasn't a reprimand, we just talked," explained Robinson. "It was no big deal, but I feel that nobody on the club should show up his manager, coaches, or teammates. It's like I told the guys in spring training. 'Don't show me up. Don't drag me through the papers. If you do, I'll do the same to you.'

"I'm not trying to muzzle my players, but . . ." he shrugged. "One of the most important things a team can have is togetherness. All of us, the players as well as the manager and coaches, are trying to do the best we can to win. Nobody should lose sight of that."

Jim wouldn't talk at first but later acknowledged the meeting. He didn't consider it a reprimand either, nor did he reveal much of their conversation.

Gaylord got a kick out of the incident. "All the guys were asking me this morning, after reading the paper, if I put on Jim's shirt and pretended to be him. They know Jim doesn't talk that way, but I do," chortled Gaylord.

On the three occasions pitching changes were made today, Robinson himself went to the mound.

It seemed significant that Robinson rather than Harvey Haddix made the changes, but the manager sloughed off the suggestion. "I just felt I should go out there myself," he said.

Immediately after the game, when reporters entered his office for the usual postgame critique, Robinson referred to Jim Perry's complaint. He made a request that indicated his naïvete, his inexperience as a major league manager.

"I want to ask you guys to do me a favor. I want to ask you guys to agree, all of you, *not* to ask my pitchers, 'Do you think you should have come out of the game?' It's the kind of a question that can produce only negative results."

Richard Bilotti of the Associated Press volunteered a reply. "I'm afraid I can't agree to that for several reasons. One is I consider that question pertinent in almost every case and I believe I'd be derelict in my duty if I agreed not to ask it. I also

am afraid such a thing, such an agreement, could set a danger-
ous precedent. It might be the first of similar requests by you,
and if we agreed to this, we'd be more obligated to agree to other requests by you."

Robinson smiled. "Okay, if that's the way you feel, forget it.
I was just asking for a favor, but if you don't agree, well, okay.
But wait until you ask for a favor." Nobody considered it a
joke.

DETROIT, MICHIGAN, APR. 22—While the Indians were being
embarrassed by the Detroit Tigers, losing again behind Gaylord Perry, 6–1, Frank Robinson displayed his class. A few Tiger fans behind the Indians' dugout jeered George Hendrick
with some intense abuse. Finally, outfielder Leron Lee exploded in anger and shouted back at the fans, challenging them to
meet him and Hendrick after the game.

Robinson interceded, speaking to the fans in calm tones.
"Look, fellows, you have a right to root for your club and get
on us. But I cannot be responsible for what my players say and
do back to you. Try to look at it that way."

The hecklers quieted. Later, one of them said, "We were
razzing Hendrick pretty good. There were six of us. Then the
other player [Lee] exploded and Robinson came over. He was a
perfect gentleman. He said to think of the women and children
sitting around us. It was such an intelligent and sensible response, nobody said a word the rest of the game. Robinson's
charm took the air out of everybody."

What made Robinson's response even more impressive was
that the Indians were playing poorly. Hendrick failed to catch
a routine pop fly hit by Ron LeFlore in the fifth inning, after
the Indians had taken a 2–0 lead. There were two out and the
Tigers had two on base. Both runners scored, and, before Perry
was able to get the third out, there were two more hits, one a
homer by Willie Horton. The Tigers had a 5–2 lead that was
never threatened.

Robinson didn't openly criticize Hendrick. Neither did Gaylord Perry. But both found fault with the official scorer for calling the pop fly a two-base hit, making all five runs earned. In so
doing, Robinson and Perry were saying Hendrick should have
made the catch.

"That was the whole ball game right there," said Robinson. "George got to the ball, he got his glove on it, so he should have caught it. I will talk to him tomorrow, just to find out what happened. I'm sure he'll tell me he should have caught it. It was a hometown gift hit. It was not a legitimate hit."

After the game, Perry waited in the dugout for 15 minutes with John Ellis. They were subdued when they arrived in the clubhouse.

"It seems like everybody is ganging up on me," Gaylord said softly. "I had very good stuff, but when I jammed 'em with a pitch, they hit it off their fists, and when I pitched 'em away, they hit it off the end of their bat. It seemed like they always hit it where we weren't. I can't even get mad at the umpire. He called a pretty good game."

As the reporters continued to probe, Perry added with resignation, "It's best not to get upset." He turned and headed for the showers. Robinson excused himself from another group of reporters and intercepted Gaylord. The manager shook the pitcher's hand and commended his performance. Perry's only reply was, "Thanks, skipper."

Hendrick, always reluctant to talk to writers, showered and dressed hurriedly. Before leaving the clubhouse, he was asked about the play that lost the game.

"How did you see it?" Hendrick asked. The reporter told him. "Okay, then, just write it like that." He walked away.

APR. 23—Danny Carnevale, the Indians' special assignment scout, sat in the lobby of the Pontchartrain Hotel, quietly observing the players as they walked through. Suddenly, Carnevale asked this writer, "I've got a question maybe you can answer. Doesn't anybody on this club ever laugh or joke around? Why is everyone so grim? Nobody needles anybody and that's unusual. There should be some humor, some light-heartedness, some fun. Is it always like this with these guys?" Yes, come to think of it. "Why?" That's a good question.

Before the game, a 4–3, rain-interrupted victory for the Indians and Jim Perry (with relief help), coaches Dave Garcia, Jeff Torborg, and Tom McCraw held a meeting with most of the infielders and outfielders.

"It was McCraw's idea to talk about some things," said

Marvin M. Greene, Cleveland *Plain Dealer*

Charlie Spikes (left) and Gaylord Perry.

Courtesy of the Cleveland Indians

Frank Robinson and Gaylord Perry (right).

Garcia. "It really was a reminder of some of the fundamentals we worked on in spring training. What happened yesterday [-George Hendrick's failure to take charge in the outfield] wasn't brought up specifically, but it was covered in general."

About an hour later Frank Robinson conducted a meeting involving all the players. "We just went over the Tigers' hitters and how we want to pitch to them. Don't read anything else into it," advised Robinson.

Jim Perry was taken out in the sixth inning, just before a 65-minute rain delay. He was replaced by Don Hood after two homers cut the Indians' margin to one run. This time Jim left peacefully. "The problem was," he said, "that it was raining so hard, I couldn't keep my hand dry. I couldn't find a dry place on my uniform to wipe."

Jack Brohamer's two-run homer in the fourth inning provided the margin of victory. Afterward, a Detroit radio announcer entered the Cleveland clubhouse to interview Brohamer, who also had a close call in a fielding collision with Charlie Spikes.

"Are you all right, Jack?" the broadcaster asked a player he thought was Brohamer.

"Oh, sure. I'm tough. I don't get hurt easily."

"What kind of a pitch did you hit?"

"It was a hanging slider. It was a big thrill for me to see the ball go into the upper deck."

"Thanks a lot and good luck to you, Jack."

"You're welcome," said John Ellis, trying hard not to laugh.

Maybe Ellis heard what Carnevale said this morning.

BALTIMORE, MARYLAND, APR. 25—The Indians' game with the Baltimore Orioles was postponed by rain. Jerry Hoffberger, owner of the Orioles, dropped by the Lord Baltimore Hotel to chat with Frank Robinson. They're close friends since Robinson sparked the Orioles to four American League pennants and two World Series championships.

Robinson was not around, but Hoffberger was willing to talk about him instead of to him.

"Frank is going to be a helluva manager," predicted Hoffberger. "But it'll be difficult to measure his success in wins and losses because the Indians aren't that good a club. If Frank were managing our club, it'd be different. If we didn't have the guy we've got [Earl Weaver], we would have been interested in Frank to manage the Orioles, but our guy is the best in the business."

Phil Seghi snorted when he heard Hoffberger's remarks. "If Hoffberger thinks so much of Robinson, why didn't he *ever* - talk to him about managing? Robinson went to Baltimore in 1966 and Weaver wasn't hired until the middle of 1968. If he thought so much of Robinson, why didn't he hire him before I did?"

Seghi also had some other things to say. He indicated growing concern about Jim Perry, expressed the fear that Gaylord might "break down," and again lamented the trade he wasn't permitted (by Ted Bonda) to make in October 1973 which would have sent Gaylord to the Boston Red Sox for three pitchers—John Curtis, Lynn McGlothen, and Marty Pattin.

"If we had those guys, we'd be in great shape today, but now I can't make that kind of a deal for Gaylord because everybody is worried about his age. The same with Jim. I can't even *give* Jim away. I'm afraid we're going to be stuck with both of them," said Seghi.

APR. 26—Even Phil Seghi thought Frank Robinson blundered as the Indians split a doubleheader tonight—and maybe the manager did, though his subsequent explanation made sense.

The Indians won the opener, 3–0 on a five-hitter by Gaylord Perry, but lost the nightcap when the Orioles rallied for two runs in the ninth inning. It happened after Dick Bosman retired the first two batters to advance to within one out of a 2–1 victory. However, the Orioles came to life on back-to-back singles and, clearly, a pitching change was in order.

Earl Weaver tried to influence Robinson by sending left-handed pinch hitter Jim Northrup to the plate, though he also had Tommy Davis, an even tougher right-handed hitter, in abeyance. Robinson called upon Tom Buskey, a right-handed reliever, and when he did, Seghi slapped the counter in the press box and cursed. Obviously the general manager disagreed with Robinson's choice of pitchers.

Northrup complied by bouncing a Buskey pitch routinely toward third base. Buddy Bell moved over to get the ball for the third out, but at the last moment it skipped low and darted past the third baseman, into left field for a single that scored the tying run.

Al Bumbry, another left-handed batter, came to the plate next and Robinson still disdained a left-handed pitcher, still avoiding the substitution of Davis. Buskey pitched to Bumbry, who lined a single to produce the winning run.

In the somber Cleveland clubhouse, Robinson declared, "We did everything right except win. Buskey is a sinker-ball pitcher who makes them hit the ball on the ground. He did his job; the ball Northrup hit just didn't come up the way Bell expected."

Robinson played the first game and received a standing ovation from the Baltimore fans who remember him well. Although he took himself out for a pinch hitter (Leron Lee, who struck out) in the eighth inning, Robinson delivered two hits.

Obviously, Weaver doesn't know how to pitch to Robinson. "Sure he does, but Earl wasn't pitching," replied the Indians' manager. Weaver and Robinson spoke briefly during the pregame exchange of lineup cards, shook hands, and laughed before the meeting ended. "Earl said to me," related Robinson, "'I hear you're doing a good job, but it can't be so good, your record is only 4–5.' I told him, 'That's right, but you're supposed to be the best in the business and your record is only 5–5, so I can't be doing so bad.'"

APR. 27—Jim Perry's first pitch in today's game spoke loudly for what was to follow. Al Bumbry lined it into the left-field corner, Ken Berry's error gave him an extra base, and five minutes later it was all over for the Indians. Before the inning ended, the Indians committed another error, the Orioles scored three runs and won, 6–1. Frank Robinson was very angry.

For the first time the manager locked the clubhouse and scolded the Indians for their lethargic play, threatening fines if it continues. "I haven't gotten tough until now," he said. "I've been as nice as can be, but we played miserably and it has got to stop. I'm starting with words. I don't like to take a guy's money, but I will if I have to. It's not a lack of desire; it's more a lack of concentration, a nonchalance, and I won't stand for it."

Most of the players agreed the lecture was deserved. "Frank told us we're playing like horse----, and he's right," said one.

Robinson also had harsh words with the umpiring crew—Jerry Neudecker, Jim McKean, Art Frantz, and Nick Bremigan—and almost was ejected for the first time. Robinson was angered by Bremigan's refusal to reprimand Orioles' catcher Elrod Hendricks for slamming his helmet to the ground after being retired in a close play at the plate. A reprimand would have cost Hendricks a $100 fine.

"I went to McKean first and asked if he saw what Hendricks did," testified Robinson. "McKean said he did, but that only the crew chief [Neudecker] could make such a ruling. I went to Neudecker and he said he didn't see what happened. I told Neudecker to ask McKean, but he wouldn't. Nobody would make a decision; they all kept passing the buck. That's why I got so mad." (Later Neudecker and Robinson would clash again, even more heatedly, in what would be Robinson's first serious breach of conduct as a manager.)

Neudecker admitted Robinson came close to being ejected for his argument concerning Hendricks' action. "It wasn't for abusive language, it was that he wouldn't quit arguing," said the umpire. "Finally I told him, 'Frank, you've been here too long. I'm going to walk away, don't follow me or you're through.'" Robinson stalked off the field.

Later, as Robinson was leaving his office, he was called on the telephone by Elrod Hendricks, a friend who had played for Frank six seasons in Puerto Rico.

"'That's gratitude,' I told Robinson," related Hendricks. "I said to him, 'After all the years I played for you at Santurce, why do you want me to get fined? You know I don't have $100 to throw away.' But that's the way he is. It proves what I've always said about Robinson. Once the game starts, he gets mad at even his best friends. The whole game he was screaming at me, trying to get me mad, but I learned from him not to."

As Robinson talked on the phone to Hendricks, a smile crossed his face. "You're right, Elrod. I'm not mad at you anymore, but you shouldn't get mad either."

❋ ❋ ❋

NEW YORK, NEW YORK, APR. 28—New York sportswriters are a strange breed. They find it difficult to believe that reporters anywhere else could possibly interview baseball's first black manager with any degree of competence.

Larry Merchant of the *New York Post* confidently entered Robinson's office at Shea Stadium, apparently expecting to be greeted royally. He was virtually ignored for 10 minutes. Finally Merchant asked, "Why do you put those two strips of tape on your wrist?"

"So that when I'm in the dugout and want to wave to my outfielders, they'll be able to see my hand," replied Robinson with a straight face. Merchant dutifully noted the reply.

Another writer suggested, "You seem anxious *not* to play. Is that an accurate observation?"

"No," said Robinson, "it's just that I put managing ahead of playing, but some people are putting it the other way around."

Will the Indians be in the race for the division title? "We are in the race. Turn the standings upside down and you'll see we're leading."

They lost to the Yankees, 6–1, in another lackluster performance. Fritz Peterson was knocked out in the first inning, facing only five batters, four of whom hit the ball safely and hard. Later Peterson was upset because, "I stunk up the place, and I really wanted to beat those guys." "Those guys," the Yankees, were Fritz's teammates until he was traded to Cleveland a year ago.

Another reason he was upset was that Harvey Haddix thought Peterson was tipping off his pitches.

"Harvey thinks it's the way I hold my glove before I go into my windup," said Peterson. "I don't know if I do or not, but the next time I face those guys, I'm going to decoy them. If they're trying to call my pitches, somebody is going to get hurt."

In the fourth inning Robinson signaled for Ken Berry to steal second base. It was unorthodox strategy because the Indians had runners on first and third with two out, John Ellis at bat, and the Yankees ahead by five runs. Not only did the steal fail, Berry was spiked in the ensuing rundown.

"We played the game as well as we can play; we just lost,"

was Robinson's crisp appraisal. "I don't get upset when we lose, I get upset when we lose and play bad baseball."

When asked about the attempted stolen base, Robinson shrugged. "Sure, some people say you shouldn't do it in that situation, but the way we're not hitting, I thought the element of surprise might get us an extra run. What we really tried to do was steal a couple of runs, but it didn't work."

APR. 29—Frank Robinson was honored before tonight's game and "fined" after it, a 3–1 victory over the Yankees on a four-hitter by Don Hood in his first start.

The honor, bestowed by the Edwin Gould Services for Children, a nonprofit child care agency, was the first Image Award to recognize "outstanding individuals who, through their public images, can motivate youngsters to positive achievements." Roy Campanella, the paraplegic former catcher of the Brooklyn Dodgers and a member of the Hall of Fame, was chairman of the committee that selected Robinson. He said, "I wish Frank had 25 good players so that his job would be easier." Monte Irvin, an aide to Bowie Kuhn and also a Hall of Famer, expanded upon Campanella's remarks. "I wish Frank had nine good players," he said. Rachel [Mrs. Jackie] Robinson said as she presented the award, "I just hope everybody sticks with Frank when things start going bad."

In the face of three consecutive defeats and the Indians' last-place lodging, Robinson proved capable of retaining a sense of humor. "As far as I'm concerned, things are going bad enough right now to hope everybody sticks with me . . . and all I'd really like to have are three or four good players, never mind 25 or even nine."

Robinson added, "I'm proud to be an American and black," a remark that pleased Bob Fishel, an executive of the American League. "I liked it because not many people nowadays say they are proud to be an American—or do you suppose he meant he is proud to be an American Leaguer?"

After the game Robinson was fined one dollar in the Indians' Kangaroo Court. Oscar Gamble plays the role of judge because, "I've had the most court experience." Robinson's penalty was levied because "he took up valuable time in batting practice and then didn't play."

It was Robinson's intention to be in the lineup because of injuries that have sidelined two left fielders, Gamble and Ken Berry, but even before taking batting practice he was skeptical. "I haven't caught a fly or thrown a ball from the outfield all spring." Then, jokingly, "Holy smokes, when Hood finds out I'm going to play, he might refuse to pitch."

However, after practice Robinson decided he was unable to throw well enough and erased his name from the lineup. "I tried some easy tosses and I could feel my arm hurt. If I had had to cut loose with a throw, I would have torn everything in my arm. I wouldn't have been able to help the club doing that to myself, and it wouldn't have been fair to the rest of the guys."

BOSTON, MASSACHUSETTS, APR. 30— Gaylord Perry beat the Red Sox, 8-1, on a five-hitter. It was his thirteenth consecutive complete game victory over Boston; his lifetime record against the Red Sox in 3½ years is now 14-1, another reason they'd like to trade for Gaylord.

Does he bear down harder against the Red Sox because of their interest? Gaylord grinned and replied, "I'm happy here," but he winked as he made the statement.

Boog Powell really is happy with the Indians, primarily because he was very *un*happy with the Orioles last year. Boog whacked his fourth homer tonight, then talked about how much he enjoys his new team and new manager. "Frank Robinson is tough but fair. He chewed our butts off a few nights ago, but we had it coming and the atmosphere is really good. Everybody is putting out, and everybody is happy."

MAY 1—This being a "getaway" day—that is, the Indians return to Cleveland after the game—everyone was well-dressed and bright-eyed after a good night's sleep. It didn't, however, help much on the field.

Jim Perry failed again, yielding five runs in less than two innings. Frank Robinson singled in three at bats, but was picked off first base by Bill Lee in the second inning, moments before John Ellis doubled for what would have been a big run. In diving back to the base, Robinson wrenched his left shoulder, suffering an injury that is destined to become increasingly significant. Of being picked off, Robinson sneered, "Lee committed a balk but the umpire [Nestor Chylak] wouldn't call it."

In the ninth inning, with the potential tying run at third and the go-ahead run at first with two out, Robinson was to bat against reliever Diego Segui. He took himself out for pinch hitter Leron Lee, who promptly struck out.

The move was second-guessed until Robinson revealed his injured shoulder prevented him from swinging normally. "I couldn't hold the bat up the way I like to, although if Bill Lee had still been in the game [instead of the right-handed Segui], I would've tried to hit anyway."

Some Boston writers were unconvinced. "A one-armed Frank Robinson is still twice as good as a Leron Lee in this park, unless the guy has lost his guts," one of them charged.

The Cleveland writers were more interested in what Jim Perry had to say.

"I can't believe the good stuff I had in the bullpen, and then how bad it was in the game," Perry spoke of his fourth straight unimpressive performance. "I think the mounds made the difference. The one in the bullpen is steep; the one on the field is flat. I think that's what caused me to be wild high, but I'm not concerned."

Harvey Haddix *is* concerned. "He threw terrible in the bullpen, and he threw terrible in the game," said the pitching coach. "That stuff about the mounds is an alibi. I'm very worried about Jim and so is Robby. We can't keep sending him out there the way he's pitching."

Robinson admitted, "I'm not satisfied with either Jim Perry or Fritz Peterson, but that doesn't mean I'm giving up on them. Not yet. It's early, although we do have to think about who stays in the rotation and who doesn't. It's good to know we have some kids to move in if necessary."

Other things were bothering Robinson, too. Four bunt signs were missed. "I'm giving everybody the benefit of the doubt because it's a new set of signals we're using, but I don't want this to happen again," he said sternly. On two occasions Charlie Spikes missed the cutoff man on throws from right field, allowing runners to take extra bases and causing Robinson to frown.

After this initial shakedown cruise through the Eastern Division the Indians headed home with a 7-9 record. They won four and lost five on this trip, which disappointed Robinson. "To be honest with you, I had hoped for 7-2," he said. "I thought we were ready to do at least that well."

5. *"An Amazing Person"*

CLEVELAND, OHIO, MAY 2—Frank Robinson's shoulder was sore, but there was nothing wrong with his mind as the Indians beat the Baltimore Orioles, 4-3, in another confrontation with Earl Weaver. Robinson made all the right moves and reliever Dennis Eckersley gained his first major league victory.

Robinson talked about the upcoming 10-game home stand. "It's important because we've got to be more consistent. If we keep fooling around, we'll find ourselves needing to catch four or five clubs. I think we're ready, based on the things I saw the last couple of games. We're all swinging the bat better, and our injuries are much improved."

What about Robinson's sore shoulder? "I'll be okay when I get a shot of cortisone. I've had this before and once I get the shot, I'll be okay."

Robinson talked also about Jim Perry and Fritz Peterson. "We've got to get them straightened out. They're not doing anything specifically wrong; they're just making mistakes."

Rico Carty homered in the second inning and his single in the eighth broke a 3-3 tie. But Eckersley, or somebody, had to stop the Orioles in the ninth.

That somebody was Robinson. The crowd booed the manager when he changed pitchers in the ninth after Eckersley retired the first batter. Elrod Hendricks, a left-handed hitter who crashed a homer in the third inning, was at the plate. Robinson signaled for Dave LaRoche.

"I knew Weaver would make a change if I switched pitchers," said Robinson. "That's what I wanted. I didn't want Eckersley pitching to Hendricks. I wanted someone to come off the bench cold, and I knew it would be Dave Duncan [a righthanded batter] if I brought in LaRoche."

Which is what happened. Duncan flied out. Quickly, Robinson called for Tom Buskey to face Doug DeCinces, also right-handed. Weaver could have substituted left-handed Al Bumbry or Tom Shopay for DeCinces, but he didn't. "I knew Weaver would leave DeCinces in the game," he said. "I knew it because DeCinces was his last infielder. Weaver had to let DeCinces bat, or use an outfielder or pitcher at shortstop if he tied the game."

Buskey retiring DeCinces would have made a better story, but DeCinces walked. Buskey made switch-hitting Ken Singleton ground out, however, getting the home stand off to a good start.

Later, Weaver grudgingly admitted Robinson backed him into a corner. "But you tell Frank," he added, smiling in his feisty manner, "that tomorrow we both should just play our best nine men, my nine against his nine, and we'll see who comes out on top."

MAY 3—Earl Weaver played his best nine today, but Frank Robinson used three extras, including himself. The Indians scored six runs in the eighth to beat the Orioles, 6–1. Afterward, third baseman Buddy Bell spoke in awe of Robinson. "He's an amazing person, but I knew that when he played against us. Anytime you played against him you knew, somehow, he was going to do something to beat you."

With the Indians trailing 1–0 in the eighth, after Bell opened

with a double, Jack Brohamer was to bat against Ross Grimsley. Robinson wasn't expected to play because his shoulder
was too sore. "Usually a shot of cortisone is all I need," he said,
his left hand supported in his jacket pocket. "It didn't work
this time because the doctor put the needle in the wrong place.
I knew it because when they hit the right spot, it hurts. This
one didn't. I kept hoping it'd be okay by morning, but it
wasn't."

With Bell on second representing the tying run, Robinson
limped out of the dugout as he always does, dragging a bat behind him. The 17,714 fans roared.

"I wouldn't have wanted to be in Frank's shoes," Bell admitted. "I didn't think he would bunt, but the way he plays the
game, I knew he'd do something to get me to third base. It
takes a certain kind of individual to play the game the way he
does."

Bell should know. The son of All-Star outfielder Gus Bell,
when he was five years old, Buddy used to hang around the
Cincinnati Reds' clubhouse when Robinson was winning the
National League's Rookie of the Year Award in 1956.

Robinson not only got Bell to third base, he got him home
with a single to center. A few moments later Frank Duffy also
singled, scoring Robinson to give the Indians a 2–1 lead. Before Weaver could do something to quell the uprising, the Indians totaled six runs.

Robinson, who preferred to talk about winning pitcher Fritz
Peterson, Bell, Duffy, and almost everybody else, reluctantly
discussed his rally-igniting hit. "It gave me a better feeling
than my homer on Opening Day because this was more important."

MAY 4—Frank Robinson levied his first fine—a stiff one, as
promised. Charlie Spikes paid $100 because of a bad throw in
the first game, an 11–1 loss to the Orioles. The Indians won the
nightcap, 4–3, in 11 innings. "It meant the difference between
a good weekend and a bad one," said Robinson. "If we had lost
the second game, it would have been terrible." The Indians
didn't lose because in the eleventh inning Frank Duffy led
with a double and scored on George Hendrick's fourth single.

Despite his feeling that it was a good weekend, Robinson wasn't overjoyed. Several things besides Spikes's bad play upset him. Spikes and Hendrick allowed a routine fly to fall between them for a single that led to the Orioles' first run in the first game. Also, three times the Indians were unable to lay down sacrifice bunts when the signal was given.

Spikes took the blame for the ball that fell between him and Hendrick. "I just screwed up, that's all. I should have called for it, but I didn't. If George said anything, I didn't hear him." George wouldn't say anything after the game, but another player did. "He's driving me crazy," he said of Robinson. "And he's got Spikes all screwed up, too. He's second-guessing us for everything. I know we're not hitting, but he's not helping by getting on us all the time."

Of the fine, Spikes said, "I'm not mad. Frank had his reasons. After he warned me in Boston last week, I knew right away when I threw the ball over the cutoff man, it was going to cost me $100."

MAY 5—Jim Perry lost tonight to the Boston Red Sox, 7–5. Now, in his last three starts, Jim has been knocked out in the fifth, second, and fifth innings.

Jim was mad at the writers for stories suggesting his age, 38, is his problem. "I've been pitching 16 years and I know myself and how I pitch," he snapped. What's really bothering Perry is speculation that he'll be taken out of the starting rotation and replaced by one of the young pitchers, Jim Kern or Dennis Eckersley. Eckersley pitched effectively again out of the bullpen, but by the time he got into the game, the loss was a foregone conclusion.

Jim and several other fringe players are afraid they will be released in the next couple of days. If they are released by May 8, the Indians need pay the players only two months' salary.

Charlie Spikes remained on the bench. "The only reason he's not playing is because he's not hitting," said Robinson. "It's not for any other reason, so don't read anything into it. [Spikes' average is .143 with no homers and only three RBI.] He's not in my doghouse. I don't even have a doghouse!"

John Ellis isn't sure. He has been brooding for several

weeks, partly because of a .200 batting average, and also because of what he considers "constant second-guessing" of his catching by Robinson. But Ellis won't discuss his relationship—really his problems—with Robinson. Not yet.

"Oh, the hell with it," Ellis said of the situation. "Just quote me as saying I'm a happy guy; happy, happy, happy."

Gaylord Perry, seated nearby, admonished the catcher. "Johnny," he said, in mock seriousness, "you know you'll never sleep nights telling lies like that."

Ellis laughed. And yawned.

MAY 6—"This is like watching reruns on television," declared Frank Robinson after the Indians lost again to the Red Sox, 4–1. The Indians' starting pitcher, Dick Bosman, was kayoed early and the Indians couldn't overcome Boston's lead.

"Naturally, I'm concerned with our starting pitching," said Robinson. "We're practically out of the game before the fifth inning. But what can we do about it? Do we tear apart our bullpen and start the kids? It's a shame to waste the good relief pitching we've been getting, but we can't continue to lose games in the first three or four innings. I don't want to panic, but I won't go too far. This is getting old."

MAY 7—The reruns continued. Fritz Peterson was kayoed in the sixth inning; Tom Buskey then blanked the Red Sox on one hit the last four innings. The Indians lost, 4–2, again unable to overcome Boston's early lead. Frank Robinson lamented, "Everybody looks like Cy Young against us. With our lineup we should score five or six runs a game, and if we hold the other club to three or four runs, we should win. But we're not scoring five or six runs a game. Everybody pitching against us can't be that good. The few guys who are swinging the bat well are trying too hard, and the guys who aren't swinging the bat well are pressing too much."

Before the game, Don Hood injured his pitching thumb as he and Dave LaRoche fielded grounders during batting practice. On one, they collided, jamming Hood's thumb. Though no bones were broken, his thumb is painful, which might cause him to miss his next start. Robinson was annoyed because he believes pitchers should not chance injury taking infield practice. "A pitcher's job is not to field ground balls. If they get hurt, they can't do the job they are paid to do. In spring training I talked to them about staying out of the infield, but they wanted to continue to take grounders. I let them go ahead against my better judgment. Now if they want to continue, it will be at their own risk."

After the game, Bob Quinn, the Indians' farm director, talked to one of the Boston writers. Speaking of the Indians' pitching problems, Quinn said, "It's a cinch Phil Seghi will make a trade by June 15: there's no way he and Robby will let this go on and on without making a move."

MAY 8—One of the players was strangely aloof again today, during an open-date workout. When he was asked what was wrong, he looked around to see who might be watching. "I've been warned about being too friendly, about talking too much to the writers. We'd better be careful who's around."

This is another example of the grim, tight-lipped, security-conscious character of the Indians' organization, despite Phil Seghi's usually cheerful facade. Once in 1973 Seghi called a meeting of the coaches in the office of Ken Aspromonte. Making sure the door was tightly closed, Seghi put his forefinger to his lips and whispered, "I think one of the writers has hidden a microphone in here."

MAY 9—Frank Robinson announced that Jim Perry has been dropped from the starting rotation. He also took measures to prevent the pitchers from working out in the infield and risking injury. Both actions created negative responses. Gaylord Perry was further dismayed by a 2–0 loss to the Chicago White Sox. He had a no-hitter for five innings and finished with a four-hitter.

Prior to the game and Robinson's official announcement, Gaylord was asked about the pitchers' meeting with Robinson. His reply was uncharacteristically guarded. "I've got nothing to say about it except that I'm not going to work out in the infield anymore. It wouldn't be worth it."

Robinson didn't mind talking. "If the pitchers want to take

grounders, they're doing it on their own from now on. If they get hurt and can't pitch, they'll be docked a day's pay for every start they miss.

"If Hood is okay, he'll pitch tomorrow night and Jim Kern will pitch Sunday. Jim Perry goes to the bullpen." Jim Perry is unhappy but won't talk.

MAY 10—Jim Perry warmed up as a starting pitcher, but so did Don Hood, who got the assignment. The game turned out to be a one-sided, 8–3 loss to the White Sox.

Jim Perry was very upset. "I had to read in the papers that I'm going to the bullpen. Harvey Haddix talked to me, not Robinson, but all he said was that I'm missing this turn. I haven't pitched well, but there are other things, like bad support. It wasn't always my fault. It makes me mad, too, the way you guys harp about my age. Sure, I'm 38, but I've just made some bad pitches. What do you expect? All the days off and the open dates we had in spring training, a guy can't get the work he needs. But I'd better not say any more. I can't afford to get into any more trouble."

In the clubhouse, following this fifth straight defeat, Robinson maintained his cool. "We've got to keep plugging away and try to keep everybody from getting uptight. The main thing is that the guys don't get down. I'm not losing confidence in them, so they shouldn't lose confidence in themselves. We're just not hitting; that's the big thing. We'll come out of this together."

MAY 11—The Indians did come out of it together. They won, 4–3, scoring two runs in the eleventh inning when Tom McCraw hit a 20-foot single and two Chicago players threw the ball a collective 500 feet, committing two errors on one play, wiping out a 3–2 White Sox victory.

"Holy cow! Our guys acted like they'd just won the World Series," said Frank Robinson. "I'm glad we won, but I'm not happy the way the game was played. We are still failing to execute and think."

Robinson was particularly displeased with Ed Crosby, who missed a bunt signal in the ninth inning, and because he did, a double play ensued.

What of the White Sox? "They stole their three runs by doing the little things we let them do, the little things we couldn't do ourselves."

Robinson was asked if Crosby would be fined. "No, but it's the last free mistake I'm letting anybody make."

Chuck Tanner of the White Sox, one of the acknowledged better strategists in baseball, violated the book on managing and the maneuver turned against his team. In the eleventh inning, after Chicago had gone ahead by one run, Rico Carty drew a lead walk. He was sacrificed to second and took third on a long fly-out. Tanner ordered Terry Forster to walk John Ellis intentionally, though he represented the winning run. Three pitches later McCraw nubbed his single between home and third base, scoring Carty. When Forster threw to first base, but actually down the right-field line, Ellis ran to third. Bob Coluccio threw the ball to the plate where it bounced past catcher Brian Downing, enabling Ellis to score.

When the Indians tied the score at 2–2 in the seventh, Robinson made another successful pinch-hitting appearance, earning a standing ovation from the 37,228 fans. Carty started the uprising with a homer. One out later, Buddy Bell and Ellis singled back to back. Robinson trudged out of the dugout as a pinch hitter. "I didn't ask Robinson the player if he was ready," said Robinson the manager. "If I had, he probably would have told me no. I put him up there because we didn't have anybody left." Robinson delivered a rifle-shot single to center, scoring the tying run.

Because the rally ended, Jim Kern, pitching for the first time in the starting rotation—in Jim Perry's place—was unable to gain credit for his first major league victory, though he deserved it. Kern is now solidly in the starting rotation, and Jim Perry will remain in the bullpen.

After Phil Seghi visited the manager's office, Robinson said, "Oh, Phil was just taking a Sunday stroll and stopped in to do some slumming, I guess," brushing off speculation that changes might be in store.

When Seghi left, Robinson called catchers John Ellis and Alan Ashby, and coach Jeff Torborg, a former catcher, into his office. "We just talked, that's all. I told John and Alan I'm not putting the blame on anybody, that I'm happy with the catching. It's just that I want them to be more in charge. It wasn't criticism," Robinson emphasized.

This home stand, the one Robinson said at the onset would be "very important because we've got to get going," produced only four victories in ten games. The Indians remain in fifth place but fell from 2½ games behind Milwaukee to five, which is not progress.

6. "I Should Have Worn My Jacket"

CLEVELAND, OHIO, MAY 12—"It's times like this that a manager is important, when he really needs to be a good manager," said Frank Robinson on today's open date, prior to a six-game trip. "When things are going well, a manager isn't necessary except to write the names on the lineup card. When things are not going well, as they are not with us, a manager must have understanding, compassion, and most of all, patience.

"The big thing is to keep everybody from getting down. Basically, we're playing the game okay, we're in a hitting and pitching slump. Everybody is trying hard and hustling. How can I chew out a guy for not getting a hit, or a pitcher for giving up a hit? I've been down this road before and all we can do is stay together. I know it sounds like a stuck recording, but it's the truth. It's all a manager can do at a time like this."

Robinson and Phil Seghi talked about the situation. "Yes, getting some help was discussed, but only very casually. Pitching is my first thought. I'd like to have a tenth man on the staff."

Robinson revealed that Dennis Eckersley, quickly becoming a key man in the bullpen, is suffering tightness in his shoulder. "It's nothing serious, but we've got to watch how we use the kid," which explains why Eckersley has not pitched in a week despite a nearly perfect record.

Seghi's comments were guarded. "We've had some well-pitched games and some badly pitched games, but I don't think what we're going through is that serious. We don't contemplate doing anything."

But something was done. Angel Hermoso was taken off the disabled list where he'd been hidden since April 5, and demoted to Oklahoma City. When Hermoso balked, his contract was sold to a team in Mexico.

MINNEAPOLIS, MINNESOTA, MAY 13—Frank Robinson's avowed patience wore thin tonight. In a meeting before the Indians beat the Minnesota Twins, 3–2, he announced the implementation of a system of fines. After the game, in which Dennis Eckersley recorded his first major league save, Robinson fined John Ellis $100.

Robinson told the players, "When Ed Crosby missed a bunt signal, when he didn't even look for one last Sunday, I made up my mind it would be the last free mistake. From now on, every missed sign will cost $100. We can't afford to make mistakes. There are enough other things that can beat us without our helping to beat ourselves."

Ellis missed Robinson's hit-and-run signal in the second inning, and Rico Carty was an easy out at second. "I missed it, it was my fault," confessed Ellis. "I looked for a sign, but I didn't see one. Rico saw it so I guess it was there. I have no excuse, but I'm not going to let Frank let anybody else get away without a fine when it happens again."

Cocaptain Frank Duffy appealed to Robinson on behalf of his teammates that $100 is too high. "Hell, skipper, that's the price of two meals in New York." Robinson wouldn't back down. "If you're going to fine a guy, you might as well make it enough so he feels it. A $25 fine is a minor league fine. So is a $50 fine."

MAY 14—For the fourth time the Indians were unable to win

three games in a row, losing to the Twins, 3–0. Rod Carew stole home against Gaylord Perry, then threw his bat at Gaylord when the pitcher brushed him back in a subsequent appearance at the plate. Perry, who now has lost three in a row, refused to talk to writers after the game, but Carew didn't. "I've got to protect myself," he said of the bat-throwing incident.

Robinson said, "What Carew did is weak, and beyond that it doesn't deserve a comment." Of the Indians' performance, Robinson snapped, "It's getting to be ridiculous. Gaylord wasn't sharp, but nobody can win without runs. I would've bet this team wouldn't be shut out five times all year. How many times have we been shut out already?" Three. "It's ridiculous."

Today Phil Seghi met with Bob Short, who owns stock in the Texas Rangers. He also owns the Hotel Leamington where the Indians stay in Minneapolis. Short, charmingly unpretentious, doesn't consider the game a life-or-death struggle.

According to Short, "Seghi is trying to get the Rangers to take Jim Perry. I don't blame Seghi, but I don't know if the Rangers want Perry and his $68,000 salary. If Perry could still pitch, why wouldn't the Indians want to keep him? I asked Phil, but he didn't exactly answer. But then, Perry and Billy Martin [the Rangers' manager] always got along well and Jim pitched well for Billy at Minnesota and Detroit. I told Billy and Danny O'Brien [the Rangers' general manager] it might be worth a gamble, but I also told Danny if he waits a little while, he probably can get Seghi to pick up part of Jim's salary."

Short also talked about Seghi's interest in Rangers' outfielder Tom Grieve. "We're not giving up Grieve for Jim Perry. We're not giving up *anybody* for Jim Perry, except maybe a token $10,000. We offered Grieve and [pitcher] Jim Bibby for Gaylord Perry last winter. That would have been a helluva deal for the Indians. Seghi wanted more, even though he's been ready to trade Gaylord for a couple of years, but that other guy, what's-his-name [Ted Bonda], wouldn't let him."

MAY 15—Gaylord Perry lounged in the lobby of the Hotel Leamington and talked. "I'll remember that SOB [Rod Carew]. If he'd thrown the bat *at* me, I'd have gone in and got him, but it wasn't even close." Then Gaylord changed subjects. "The biggest thing we're lacking is motivation. Frank [Robinson] has got to start patting guys on the back, especially Charlie Spikes. Charlie is really down. A big part of the manager's job is to motivate, and Frank isn't doing it."

After the game, another loss, 7–6, to the Twins, in which Carew singled home the winning run against Dave LaRoche with two out in the ninth, Robinson sat for a long time and talked.

"What's happening is like the kid who stuck his finger in the dike to plug one hole, and two others spring leaks. Sure, I'm disappointed. I don't understand. We're making the same mistakes time after time, game after game, and when you're in a slump, every little mistake is magnified. It wouldn't be so bad except we worked on these things so much."

Is Robinson confused, as so many superstars-turned-managers have been, because they cannot comprehend why everybody cannot play the game the way they did? "No, I don't think that's it. I don't think I expect too much. I believe I have the right to expect them to play the game the way it should be played. I can truthfully say I have never been on a team that has made so many mental mistakes as this one."

. Is that an indictment of the Indians' farm system for not teaching fundamentals in the minor leagues? "I don't think it's that, either, but I don't know. We've worked so much on those things, and still work on them, but the mistakes still happen."

Perhaps Robinson overestimated the abilities of the Indians in spring training. "I don't think that's it. The ability is there, I'm sure. If we continue to play this way, well, maybe I was wrong about their ability. We can't afford to go on this way. I *won't* go on and on, waiting and hoping and all the while falling farther back. You reach a point where something has got to be done. We're not there yet, but it's time to show improvement. I think we can play better, but will we?" The question went unanswered.

CHICAGO, ILLINOIS, MAY 16—Who said things couldn't get worse? The Indians lost to the Chicago White Sox, 3–2, because the bullpen couldn't protect a 2–0 lead. Jim Kern, working on a three-hitter toward his first major league victory, walked Bill Melton to start the ninth and was immediately replaced by Tom Buskey. Three hits followed, scoring one run and leaving the bases loaded. Dave LaRoche was summoned and struck out the only batter he faced. Then Dennis Eckersley hit Buddy Bradford with his first pitch, sending the tying run home, and walked Jorge Orta, forcing in the winning run.

"I'm open to suggestions," shrugged Frank Robinson as reporters converged in his office. "We get some good starting pitching for a change, and the bullpen goes." Ordinarily Robinson is communicative when the Indians are losing, as if striving to understand *why* by discussing it. Not this time.

Earlier today he had read a story by Ed Fowler in the *Chicago Daily News.* Under the headline "Sox players have little love for F. Robinson" was written:

. . . Some of the White Sox have already formed an opinion |of Robinson| and they didn't need that series in Cleveland last weekend to do it . . .

"Remember that game last year in California [Robinson was playing for the Angels] when Jack Kucek drilled him?" asked one, grinning from behind his beer.

He went on to explain for the benefit of those who hadn't been there that Kucek, the young pitcher now with the Sox' Class AAA Denver club, had tickled Robby's ribs with a fast ball.

"Kucek blew him back with the first pitch," he said. "Robinson's bat went one way and his helmet went another. He just turned him inside out. Then on the next pitch Kucek hit him in the ribs. Robinson started toward the mound, but stopped and just went to first. You gotta say he had grounds to go to the mound. If Kucek had just hit him it would have been different, but he blew him back first."

The reason some of those present were reliving this episode with such relish was a disaffection for Robinson they picked up in Puerto Rico, where they had played against teams he has managed there for the past several years.

"He's really big down there," said one, "and he likes to lord it over everybody. He has all the umpires intimidated. One time he was kicking at a catcher's mask and he missed and kicked the umpire. Nothing happened.

"One night I was in a bar where all the players hang out. My wife was with me. Robinson walked right past me and wouldn't even acknowledge my existence. He never has."

Of one thing this guy was certain: "Robinson may have been big down there," he said, "but it won't be like that here."

Robinson studied the White Sox roster as the Cleveland writers found places to sit in the manager's office. A clipping of Fowler's story lay on his desk.

"Yes, I saw it, but it doesn't bother me because it isn't true," Robinson said. "When did you ever see a manager kick an umpire and not get thrown out of a game? What I did was take off his mask three times, and then I stepped on his toes. We were arguing face-to-face, and he kept bumping me in the nose with his mask. So I'd take it off, he'd put it back on, and I'd take it off again. When I stepped on his toes, he threw me out of the game, but I only did that because he stepped on my toes first.

"I know the guy he [Fowler] was quoting, too. The guy who didn't have guts enough to let him use his name. It was Rich Gossage. I'm not surprised. Gossage and I never hit it off down there."

Gossage, incidentally, was the winning pitcher tonight.

MAY 17—The less said about tonight's fourth straight loss, 10-1, to the White Sox, the better.

Prior to the game, one of the pitchers spoke privately about two aspects of the Indians' losing streak, indicating a breach in team morale. "Several of us have gone to Harvey Haddix because we prefer to pitch to Alan Ashby. I don't think it's any secret that John Ellis wants to play first base, not catch. Not only does that affect his catching, it affects our pitching. He's blaming his batting slump on having to catch, and it's not fair to the rest of us.

"Something else that bothers me is the attitude around here. Most of these guys are getting used to losing. It doesn't bother them anymore. If it goes on much longer, it'll be too late to turn things around. It's good to be relaxed, which we are, but it's bad when getting beat doesn't really eat at you."

Robinson said he knew what the player meant, but insisted that getting "used to" losing isn't a problem. "I don't think that's the case yet, but the point is well taken because most of the guys have never been with a winner and the natural tendency is to say, 'Oh, oh, here we go again, the hell with it.' I don't believe in tearing up the clubhouse, or cursing and screaming after we lose. That doesn't do any good either. I'd rather that energy be exerted on the field. We're trying hard and we're hustling. Maybe the problem is that we're trying too hard.

"If I thought it were a bad situation, I'd get tough and all that. As it is, I've been talking to some of the guys individually, but it's also possible to talk too much. I've been on teams that got used to losing, so I think I know the signs. The Orioles in 1967 got that way. By the middle of May they were accepting defeat without doing anything about it. As I said, I don't think that's the case with us yet. You're right about one thing. We are at the point where we've got to get going, or do something to get us going."

Maybe that's what Robinson had in mind in the sixth inning. With a runner on third and two out, Jorge Orta lined a Jim Perry pitch to right field. Several fans leaned out of the stands trying to catch a souvenir. The ball caromed off the wall—or the fans—away from Charlie Spikes, and Orta raced to third.

Before the dust settled, Robinson was on the field, behind first base where Jerry Neudecker was umpiring. Robinson argued heatedly that, because the ball had been touched by the fans, Orta's hit should be a ground-rule double. As they screamed at each other, Neudecker bumped Robinson with his chest. Robinson shoved Neudecker with both hands. The umpire lurched backward several steps. Robinson had to be physically restrained by three or four of his players. The altercation continued several minutes before order could be restored. Robinson was ejected.

Later, Robinson said he was provoked by Neudecker. "I just asked him if he saw the fans touch the ball. Everyone in the park saw it but not Neudecker. He didn't because he didn't go out to look. He was out of position. He kept insisting the ball wasn't touched, so I asked him why it deflected as it did. He stuck his face next to mine and said, 'I don't know and I don't care!' I asked him to check with the second-base umpire, Art Frantz, and he yelled at me, 'I don't have to ask anyone!' Then off comes his cap and he bumped into me. Not once but twice. The reason I pushed him was because he charged into me."

Neudecker denied he had provoked Robinson.

"Sure, there were some fans reaching out of the stands for the ball, but it hit below their hands. Nobody touched the ball. That's what I told Robinson, but he kept screaming, 'You've got to ask Frantz.' I told him I didn't have to ask anybody. I probably was as much to blame as he was for what happened next, but I didn't really bump him. Then he used abusive language. He called me 'horse----,' and I don't take that from anybody. That's when I ejected him, and it was *after* I ejected him that he pushed me. After he pushed me, he said, 'The next time I'll knock you on your ass.' "

As for bumping Robinson, Neudecker said, "Aw, we just came together when we were face-to-face, that's all. It was only a light brushing of our bodies. If the same thing had been done to me by a player, I wouldn't have called it a bump, although contact was made."

Robinson: "If Neudecker said he threw me out before I pushed him, he's a liar; he's wrong again."

Neudecker: "I don't have anything against Robinson and I don't think he has anything against me. The altercations we've had [twice previously this season] were coincidental."

Robinson: "I always had trouble with him because he's the kind of guy you can't talk to.

"I guess I am guilty of one thing. I should have worn my jacket like I usually do so I could have kept my hands in the pockets."

That night Neudecker telephoned league president Lee Mac-Phail. Robinson took part in a meeting with his coaches and Phil Seghi to discuss his ejection and what happened prior to the argument—and what might happen next.

MAY 18—The telephone in Frank Robinson's suite in the Executive House jarred him into consciousness early for what was to be the start of a long and eventful day. Lee MacPhail wanted the manager's version of the argument with Jerry Neudecker.

"I told MacPhail, and he said, 'That's basically the way Neudecker reported it. It sounds to me like he was partly at fault, too,' " related Robinson. "Then he told me, 'Under the circumstances, I suspend you for three days and fine you $250, but you can appeal if you want.' I said, 'What happens if I win the appeal?' He said, 'You'll get back your $250.' I said, 'The money isn't important, but you can't give me the three days back, can you?' It was then Mr. MacPhail suspended the suspension pending the hearing on my appeal."

The official release read: "Manager Frank Robinson of the Cleveland Indians has been suspended for three days and fined an unannounced sum for bumping and shoving Umpire Jerry Neudecker in the sixth inning of last night's game at White Sox Park.

"But Manager Robinson has appealed the suspension and therefore it will not be invoked until after an appropriate hearing before Mr. MacPhail. It is hoped that Mr. MacPhail will have been able to review the film and videotape of the incident before the hearing, which will be held in a convenient location at the earliest possible date, probably in New York."

Robinson was elated. "I appreciate what Mr. MacPhail is doing, and I know I'll win the case when he sees the evidence. I've been told the tape shows Neudecker bumping into me twice before I got mad and shoved back. I'm being penalized for something Neudecker provoked."

Neudecker was asked his opinion. "I have no reaction. It's none of my business," snapped the umpire.

If Neudecker didn't have any reaction, White Sox manager Chuck Tanner did. "I've never heard of such a thing. Does that mean if one of my players is suspended, all I have to do is appeal and he can continue playing?"

Subsequently, Robinson told the coaches to inform the players that all pregame practice would be canceled. He ordered nonteam members out of the clubhouse and locked the doors at 11:30 A.M. For the next hour and 33 minutes, until 12 minutes before game time, the Indians, their coaches, and Robinson rapped.

When it was over, Robinson reported, "It was a very open and very good session. It was the most involvement we've had. I told the guys when we started I wanted them to speak out and speak up, which they did. Nobody's feelings were spared. I told them if they had anything on their minds, let's hear it. Everybody didn't talk, but most of the guys did. Sure there was criticism of each other, that's what it was all about. It's a hell of a lot better to sit around together and criticize than it is for guys to go off in little groups griping about each other behind their backs."

Robinson himself was criticized. "They told me they think my $100 fines are too stiff, but I'm sticking to my guns."

Some of the criticism was directed toward George Hendrick. "You've got to be more aggressive or we're dead," one of the players told the center fielder. Was John Ellis a target? "No, not really," confided one of the pitchers. "John really was tougher on himself than anyone else. Nobody got burned. It wasn't bad, but how much good it'll do, I don't know."

Another one of the players, when questioned about the rap session and remarks directed toward Ellis said, "I like John. He's a helluva competitor and a good guy, but between you and me, he won't finish the season as the regular catcher."

Before the meeting, Robinson had told the writers, "It has come to the point where I must take a firmer hold on the club. We don't resemble the team that came out of spring training. We're not executing even the simple things." Later he elaborated. "When I say I'll take a firmer hold, I mean I will be more in control of what happens. I'll take some of their freedom away, pull in the reins."

Neudecker did not fail to notice that, because of the rap session, the Indians violated an obscure rule. "I'm going to call Mr. MacPhail again tonight," said the umpire, "and report that the Indians broke the rule that says there must be some action on the field from the moment the gates open. The visiting players are allowed to skip hitting or fielding practice, but if they do, they've got to tell the home team at least three hours in advance. The Indians didn't tell anybody."

When Neudecker's remarks were relayed to Robinson, the manager shrugged. "That's okay, what we did in the clubhouse was a helluva lot more important than what we could have done on the field, or what might come out of the league office."

After the game started, the Indians vented their frustration on the White Sox, building up a 7–2 lead in five innings behind Gaylord Perry. Then Gaylord lost his mastery. He was driven to the showers in the sixth by five consecutive hits that cost him four runs and cut the Indians' margin to one. "I got so many runs," said Perry, who had been shut out in his two previous starts, "I didn't know what to do with them." He could chuckle because the relievers preserved the victory. Chicago got the potential tying run to second base with two out in the ninth, but Dennis Eckersley came on to strike out Bill Melton on three pitches.

Eckersley's excellent performance recalled a remark by Phil Seghi over the breakfast table, possibly at the very time Mac-Phail was speaking to Robinson. Seghi was asked what progress he was making in talks with other general managers, particularly in his efforts to trade Jim Perry and Dick Bosman. He shrugged. "What I'd really like to do is force the kid into the starting rotation," he said. The kid? "Yeah, the kid Eckersley."

On the flight home, Mudcat Grant, one of the television voices of the Indians, sat next to Robinson. Suddenly Mudcat looked up from his newspaper and laughed. "Hey, lookee, it says Fred Stanley pinch-ran for Chris Chambliss in New York yesterday. It must have been the first time a white guy ran for a black guy in 20 years!" The writers chuckled with Grant. Robinson joined in, laughing perhaps for the first time since the beginning of this trip.

7. "We've Got to Do Something"

CLEVELAND, OHIO, MAY 19—While everyone talked about Frank Robinson's appeal of his $250 fine and three-day suspension, the Indians played their worst game of the season tonight. They were beaten, 12–5, by the California Angels. Don Hood was knocked out early and Jim Perry was no improvement. Perry was booed when he was removed under duress— probably the first time either Perry brother was booed in Cleveland.

"We've got to do something, we cannot continue to go the way we are," said Robinson. "We have to get somebody, other than Gaylord Perry and Jim Kern, who can start and give us six or seven good innings. I'm going to see Phil Seghi in the morning."

Not only did the Indians lose, they gave up three home runs to the Angels, who stress pitching and speed rather than slugging. Dave LaRoche pitched well as the second reliever, and when Robinson was asked if he'd consider starting LaRoche, he replied, "Right now I'd consider starting anybody."

California Manager Dick Williams said he didn't mind that Robinson is being allowed to play while he's appealing his suspension. "More power to Frank. He's justified in requesting a hearing, and as far as I'm concerned, it's okay for Mr. Mac-Phail to allow one."

It was pointed out that, had Robinson accepted the penalty, he would have missed only two games in three days. If the appeal is rejected and the suspension invoked next weekend, Robinson could miss as many as four games in three days. "That might be a break for your club," sarcastically suggested a member of the Angels. Why? "Because then Dave Garcia would do the managing."

Later, someone else commented, "So the suspension is being suspended! I wonder, if Mr. Robinson were not black or if he were not the first black manager, if the appeal would have been granted."

MAY 20—The Indians traded veterans Dick Bosman and Jim Perry to the Oakland A's for reliever John (Blue Moon) Odom and about $15,000 today. To fill the vacancy on the roster, minor league pitcher Eric Raich was recalled from Oklahoma City.

Phil Seghi preached patience when the Indians were losing 10 of their last 13 games, hoping to enhance the trading value of Bosman and Perry, but A's owner Charlie Finley didn't want to wait. Neither did Frank Robinson. "We had to do something," said the manager.

When the Indians were in Chicago last weekend, Finley called Seghi, trying to trade Odom for Bosman. Seghi offered Jim Perry for Odom. Finley rejected it. Seghi made a counter-proposal. "If you want Bosman, you must take Perry, and you've got to give me some money to make it look better."

Seghi justified the deal: "What I really did was trade Bosman and Jim Perry, two old guys who weren't in our plans any longer, for three young starting pitchers, Dennis Eckersley, Jim Kern, and Eric Raich. They will go into the rotation, but wouldn't if we had the other guys around." The trade also relegated Don Hood to the bullpen, leaving the Indians with a "Big Five" of Gaylord Perry, Eckersley, Kern, Raich, and Fritz Peterson.

After Odom arrived in Cleveland, he initially expressed happiness in leaving the A's. "In Oakland everybody got down on me and I got down on them. Besides, I've always wanted to play for a black manager. Now I will."

Raich was delighted with his first opportunity in the big leagues. When a photographer asked him to pose between Robinson and Odom, Raich quipped, "Hey, I feel like an Oreo cookie!"

In New York, Seghi's old pal Gabe Paul offered his insight. "They were trying to get rid of the guy," said Paul. Who? "It was a three-way tie."

MAY 21—Jim Kern won his first major league game tonight, beating the Angels, 3–2, and Frank Robinson cracked his second and third homers of the season—and 576th and 577th of his career—off former teammate Frank Tanana.

Following the game, Robinson bantered words with writers who travel with the Angels. They were sure Tanana had tipped his pitches to Robinson, who denied it, but not convincingly. After about 10 minutes Robinson grew impatient. "Sure, I resented it," said the manager later. "To me, they were implying my reflexes are gone, that I'm not good enough anymore to hit home runs unless I know what's coming. I can read the pitches of about one-fourth the pitchers in the league. I mean, I know when a fast ball or breaking pitch is going to be thrown. Some guys I can read every pitch, but you've still got to have good reflexes and I don't like anyone questioning mine. Heck, I hit 575 homers before tonight. It's a matter of timing, of playing, and I'm playing more now."

When Dick Williams was asked if Robinson was reading Tanana's pitches, the Angels' manager replied, "I don't know. All I can tell you is that, if Robinson had batted again in the eighth inning, he wouldn't have faced Tanana."

Before the game it was announced that Lee MacPhail would hear Robinson's appeal three days hence, which did nothing to raise Phil Seghi's hopes that his manager will be exonerated. "In all the years I've known Frank," said Seghi, "I've never seen him so mad as when he pushed that umpire. Maybe you'd better not write that yet. Wait until after MacPhail turns down Frank's appeal."

Paul Tepley, Cleveland *Press*

Frank Robinson.

William A. Wynne, Cleveland *Plain Dealer*

Left to right: Blue Moon Odom, Eric Raich and Frank Robinson.
"Hey, I feel like an Oreo cookie!"—see page 114.

"I don't know why everyone is so sure it will be turned down," Robinson wondered. "I don't understand why Phil thinks it will, and why you guys [the writers] also think I'll lose. I wasn't in the wrong as much as he [Jerry Neudecker] was."

Also before the game Seghi reacted sharply to criticism of the trade for Blue Moon Odom. At a Wahoo Club luncheon a show-of-hands vote indicated the fans were opposed about four to one to the deal. Seghi took the podium and said, "There have been insinuations that the Indians are surrendering, that we're going with kids because we don't think we have a chance to win this season. I want to stress that nothing could be further from the truth. We're not giving up. As a matter of fact, we think we're getting fortified to take a run at the whole thing. I was criticized heavily for the Ray Fosse deal, too [in which the Indians got George Hendrick and Dave Duncan in 1973, and Duncan subsequently was swapped for Boog Powell and Don Hood]. A man in my position must do what he thinks best. That's what I am doing now. I think you'll find our pitching will be stronger. Just look at the combined record of the guys we gave up. It's 1-8. I shouldn't have to say more."

From there Seghi went to a meeting of the partners who own the Indians, to discuss the reasons for the team's lack of success. "They didn't really give me any trouble," reported the general manager. "They're grumbling a little because all they look at are the people in the park, but they're all right. Hell, if they give me problems, I'll just go somewhere else."

MAY 22 Phil Seghi and Frank Robinson want to call up Rick Manning from Oklahoma City. Manning is a 20-year-old, freshly scrubbed-looking outfielder who plays the game with the enthusiasm of Pete Rose. He's sure to be a crowd pleaser and Seghi knows it. First, however, Seghi must create room on the roster by disposing of a player.

But that was not the general manager's primary problem when he reached the office this morning.

Seghi's day began with a telephone call from Charlie Finley.

"What kind of a ------- guy did you trade me?" Finley demanded.

"Who do you mean?" asked Seghi.

"That Perry guy."

"Oh. I'll bet you're calling to tell me Jim Perry wants to ne-gotiate a contract for 1976, at a raise, naturally."

"How did you know?"

"I'll bet he asked for something else, too. I'll bet he told you, because of all his business interests in the Cleveland area, he feels he should be compensated to move to Oakland."

"Yes, dammit. How do you know that?"

"I know it because that's what he did to me when he came to us a year ago."

"You want Perry back?"

"No," said Seghi. "Do you want Blue Moon Odom back?"

"No," said Finley. They both hung up.

Seghi's last question was not without good reason. When he reported to the Indians, Odom requested an appointment with Seghi "because I want more money. I'm leaving a team that won the World Series three years in a row and probably will win again this year. Look at all the money I'm losing. I should be reimbursed. If I'm not, I don't want to stay here. When we get to Oakland next week, if I don't get a raise, or if I'm not traded, I'm going to pick up my wife and drive home [to Ma-con, Georgia]."

Robinson told Odom, "It's not my business. You can talk to Mr. Seghi if you insist, but I don't think you'll get more money. If you jump the club, not only won't you get a raise, you won't get *any* money and you'll probably be fined, too. Think it over, Moon." Odom did and went to Seghi.

"They [the Indians] traded two players to get me, and they also got money in the deal," Odom told writers. "I want some of that money. A player has got to be happy, and I'm not. I know there's nothing in the contract that says the Indians must give me a raise, but when a guy is traded to a new club, he usu-ally does get a raise. We're all in this game to make money and a few more dollars from the Indians won't hurt them, and it'll make me a happy player. Seghi must think something of me; he traded for me."

Seghi told Odom bluntly, "There's no way we'll pay you more than your contract says we must. If you don't want to pitch for us under the terms of your contract, then do whatever you want. If you go home, if you jump the club, I'll fine you like nobody has ever been fined, so help me."

"Then trade me to somebody else."

"If you think somebody wants you, call them up and have them call me," responded Seghi.

"I will," Odom assured him.

Seghi called the St. Louis Cardinals and Philadelphia Phillies, but not on behalf of Odom. He contacted the Cardinals and Phillies because both had previously expressed interest in buying the contract of seldom-used outfielder Leron Lee. Now they declined, citing roster problems of their own.

Seghi went to the field where the Indians were practicing. He summoned Lee and asked if he would consent to return to the minor leagues to make room for Manning. Lee said no. "It's past time to go back to the minors," Lee told Seghi. "I know I can hit in the big leagues. I only need a chance. I never got one here, but I'm the only guy in your outfield who ever hit .300."

Seghi was unconvinced. "All right, then. We will release you. Good luck."

MAY 23—Rick Manning was exuberant. "It's too hard to believe! This is something I've been working toward since I was a kid. Am I scared? I'm too excited to feel anything." Playing in his first major league game Rick singled in his third at bat, receiving a standing ovation from 15,608 fans.

There was little else to cheer about as the Oakland A's beat the Indians and Gaylord Perry, 3–0. Gaylord has now yielded 12 homers in 88 innings.

"Yes, I'm concerned about the home runs," acknowledged Robinson. "Gaylord has been giving up a lot of them. I'm not sure what's wrong unless it's that he's not challenging the hitters the way he used to."

Manning said, "the fans were great. A standing ovation for a single and a ball I *almost* caught! I guess the first hit is the hardest to get, but I didn't see anything special. It was just regular pitching, nothing I haven't seen before."

Farm director Bob Quinn was pleased, too, and offered another prediction. "Rick is a better center fielder than George Hendrick, even though Robinson and Phil Seghi won't admit it yet," he said. "Watch, you'll see Manning playing center before this season is over."

While Manning and Quinn grinned, Robinson scowled. The

usually placid Boog Powell was ejected by umpire Joe Brinkman for kicking dirt in the seventh inning. Robinson argued a
call at first base by Terry Cooney that deprived Frank Duffy of
a hit. Through it all he kept his hands firmly in the back pockets of his uniform pants.

Asked to relate what transpired in his argument with
Cooney, Robinson said, "I told him that was one of the worst
calls I've ever seen by an umpire. He said, 'I saw the play and I
called it right.' I said, 'You were the only guy to see it that way.'
He said, 'I call them the way I see them, Mike.' I said, 'Mike!
My name is Frank, not Mike.' He said, 'Uh, oh, yeah, Frank.'"

MAY 24—Frank Robinson's heralded hearing with Lee Mac-
Phail finally took place this morning. After an hour and a half
of discussion and four videotape viewings, MacPhail was unable to reach a decision. "I'll decide within 24 hours," promised MacPhail. The postponement will permit Robinson to
play in Sunday's doubleheader against the A's, which might be
the reason MacPhail couldn't decide today.

Robinson remained optimistic, at least on the surface. "I was
provoked by [Jerry] Neudecker, and because we're both
wrong, it's unfair to penalize me."

The Indians lost today's game despite a 5-0 lead after three
innings. Eric Raich made his major league debut but ran into
trouble in the fourth. Raich hit Sal Bando with a pitch, then Joe
Rudi lined a fast ball for a single. "I don't understand it," said
Raich. "That was a good pitch Rudi hit." As the ball whistled
past Raich's ear, the pitcher confided later, "I thought to myself, Gee, what's a guy got to do to get 'em out up here?"

Billy Williams promptly slugged "another good pitch" into
the right-field seats. "I got a little nervous then," confessed
Raich. Robinson quickly summoned relief, which turned out
to be no relief.

"I didn't want the kid to struggle. I didn't want him to lose
his first time out," said Robinson, again revealing a compas-
sionate side not always seen.

However, he was much more critical of Don Hood and Blue
Moon Odom, the two relievers who allowed the game to become a 10-5 rout in favor of the A's. "You wouldn't be able to
write what I thought of their performances," he snapped.

Frank Robinson, supported by (left to right) Dave Garcia, Boog Powell—vs. Umpire Joe Brinkman.

Robinson's summary of the long day: "Anytime you've got a team down by five runs and you lose by five, it's a bad day."

MAY 25—The Indians will be without the services of Frank Robinson for the next three days. Lee MacPhail rejected the manager's appeal and the suspension will begin tomorrow. However, in his ruling, MacPhail might have promoted the togetherness Robinson has tried to develop, without success, since spring training.

The action on the field featured Dennis Eckersley's three-hitter which beat the A's and Jim Perry, 6–0, in the openeɪ of the doubleheader. Perry, to the delight of some and the dismay of others, was kayoed in the third inning. In the nightcap, Dick Bosman beat his former teammates, 6–3.

Robinson blamed part of Jim Kern's problem (he was routed in the sixth) on what he called "a cheap shot" by Oakland's captain and third baseman Sal Bando. According to Robinson, Bando elbowed Kern as the pitcher stood close to the base line after Bando popped up in the first inning.

"He's got to be kidding," Bando retorted. "It's ridiculous and I'm surprised at Frank. It's a bush remark. I tried to avoid Kern. I angled out of my way so I wouldn't run into him, and we just brushed together. I can't believe Kern got hurt because he threw harder afterward than before."

Robinson received word of the rejection of his appeal during the second game. In a prepared statement, MacPhail said, ". . . it is very clear that Robinson deliberately and forcefully shoved Neudecker with both hands in the course of their argument. Intentional physical contact against an umpire's person cannot be condoned."

Robinson's response was simply, "I accept it. What else can I do?"

His players, in a show of unity, tried something else. On the flight to Los Angeles after the doubleheader, Tom Buskey and Dave LaRoche borrowed a typewriter from this reporter, drafted a petition, and circulated it for their teammates to sign. All did. Then Buskey and LaRoche presented the petition to Robinson.

The petition read: "We, the undersigned, in unanimous accord, hereby announce our disapproval of Mr. MacPhail's decision concerning the suspension of Frank Robinson. We believe it was an unjust and unfair decision and, to show our disapproval, have agreed to sit out the suspension with him."

Robinson was stunned, but wouldn't permit the players to follow through. "It makes me feel very good," Robinson told the Indians in a meeting 35,000 feet over the Rocky Mountains, "but I can't let you do this. The best way to support me is to play hard and win the three games I'll miss."

Later he told the writers, "The repercussions would not be worth it because we'd automatically lose [by forfeit] three games."

LaRoche spoke for his teammates. "We need Frank and it's unfair for him to be suspended. What he did was a natural instinct. It shouldn't be a one-sided decision in favor of the umpire. We also feel Frank is on trial as a player-manager and because of that we hate to see him get a bad rap. Most of all we're trying to prove our overall support of Frank, and to prove our team unity."

It was not a grandstand play and the offer to strike on behalf of their manager revealed the deep respect the Indians have developed for Robinson.

After the meeting with his players, Robinson returned to his seat and smiled, knowing he finally had achieved a significant goal: unity, togetherness. It was a long time coming.

8. "I Think We've Finally Turned the Corner"

ANAHEIM, CALIFORNIA, MAY 26—Dave Garcia's ambition, as with most men who have spent their lives in baseball, has been to manage in the big leagues. Although the next three days are not what Garcia had in mind, he is acting manager of the Indians during Frank Robinson's suspension. Today he arrived at Anaheim Stadium only two hours early instead of his usual six or eight. Mrs. Dave Garcia was the reason. She's here visiting her husband from their home near San Diego.

"You know me," Garcia lamented as he waited restlessly in the lobby of the Grand Hotel. "I always feel good when I'm in uniform and doing something at the park, even if doing something is doing nothing. But my wife doesn't understand, so I've got to wait awhile.

"Jeez, what time is it, anyway?"

It was 10:00 A.M. An hour later Dave, smiling again, shuffled around the clubhouse in his red uniform, tobacco stuffed in his cheek, using a fungo bat as a walking stick. When Robinson arrived, they disappeared into the manager's office.

Under the rules of Robinson's suspension, he may take pre-game practice with the team, make out the starting lineup, and outline the relief pitching to Garcia. Once the game begins, he must dress and vacate the clubhouse. He may sit in the stands, but not anywhere near the Cleveland dugout.

The Indians won, 9–3, behind the seven-hit pitching of Fritz Peterson and despite Rico Carty's pulled right hamstring muscle. Carty, the team's hottest hitter, retired to the sidelines in the seventh inning, joining three other key teammates who are unable to play: Boog Powell has a sore neck and shoulders, Jack Brohamer has a badly bruised left hip, and John Ellis is nursing a pulled hamstring muscle in his left leg.

Robinson watched the game from the booth of radio station WWWE. "I just want to make sure the announcers [Joe Tait and Herb Score] don't second-guess Garcia too much," he quipped.

Early in the game a friend telephoned Robinson. The operator switched the call to the WWWE radio booth. In the seventh inning, Indians' trainer Jim Warfield called Robinson to report Carty's injury. Harry Dalton, general manager of the Angels, seated in his nearby executive booth, noted both calls.

Robinson and Garcia were pleased after the victory. "Don't give me any credit," pleaded Garcia. "Peterson threw the ball well, and the guys hit it and picked it up for him, which is the way Frank wants us to play the game. I just followed Robby's orders. It's better that you talk to him because he commands the show, whether he's on the field or not."

Despite winning, Robinson admitted being let down. "Yeah, it's kind of an empty feeling, not having anything to do with it. I'm glad we won, but it was tough not being able to do anything except root, and bite my fingernails." Talking about the game, Robinson said, "It's presumptious to say, 'At last we're moving,' but this could be the start of something. What I'm looking for is a winning streak of about five straight."

Blue Moon Odom is still looking for something else. Now resigned that Phil Seghi will not enrich his contract by the $8000 he was seeking, Odom has been calling other clubs, trying to find one willing to make a deal with Seghi.

"I wish Odom would expend that kind of energy to improve

his pitching," grumbled Seghi. "What I really hope is that Blue Moon goes through with his threat to quit and Charlie Finley calls me to get him back. Charlie always liked Odom, and he loves to reacquire players he's traded." Finley is not interested this time.

Nor was Seghi much interested in Odom even before he finalized the trade with the A's. Seghi's primary goal was to get rid of Dick Bosman and Jim Perry, to get as much for them as possible. Odom—and $15,000—were the most the market would bear. He reluctantly took Blue Moon, thinking he could get some service out of the pitcher, but that was before Odom demanded more money, infuriating Seghi and clouding the situation.

If Odom deserts the Indians as he has threatened, it would solve another problem, however. That is, how to find room on the roster for Fred Beene, the pitcher who has remained "hidden" on the disabled list with a torn muscle in his back incurred in spring training, but now healed. When asked if he'd like to replace Odom with Beene, Seghi snapped, "Yes, even if I have to shoot that --- -- - ----- Odom."

MAY 27—Dave Garcia led the Indians to another victory over the Angels, 6–3, as Gaylord Perry evened his record at 6–6. However, off-the-field action was more heated than what transpired between the white lines. Frank Robinson found himself in the center of another controversy. He was prohibited from sitting in the WWWE radio booth, though Lee MacPhail said it was not an edict, merely a "suggestion." It resulted from the Angels' complaint that yesterday Robinson talked to the Indians' dugout "four" times by telephone to discuss strategy.

"I wouldn't be that stupid, not with Harry Dalton sitting in the booth next to us," insisted Robinson. According to Dalton, the operator at Anaheim Stadium said she had switched two calls for Robinson to the phone in the WWWE booth and that on two other occasions Robinson had called the Cleveland dugout.

MacPhail took action following a call from Dalton. "It wasn't a protest, it wasn't even a complaint," claimed the Angels' general manager. "All I did was call for clarification of what Robinson is allowed to do while he's serving a suspension."

"The rules aren't that clearly defined," said MacPhail. "The rules only stipulate that a suspended manager cannot sit in the press box. Technically, the press box includes the radio booths, but it's certainly not grounds for a protest. All I did was suggest to Phil Seghi that he get a booth where he and Robinson can sit and watch the game in privacy." A booth without a telephone? "That would be best."

Dick Williams was ejected during the first inning of the game by umpire Larry Barnett. An argument developed when Rick Manning was ruled safe at the plate as he scored the Indians' second run. After the ejection Williams remained in the runway between the Angels' dugout and clubhouse, directing the team with signals to coach Whitey Herzog, according to the Indians.

"I could complain about that, but I wouldn't stoop to Williams' level," sneered Robinson.

MAY 28—Dave Garcia ended his career as acting manager of the Indians with a third victory over the Angels, 9–2. It was the team's longest winning streak of the season.

Eric Raich won his first major league game, besting Nolan Ryan. "This is the biggest thrill of my life," he said, "and beating a guy like Nolan Ryan makes it even greater."

Robinson watched the game from a private booth with Phil Seghi, while the Angels watched *them* very closely. "Maybe they watched me so close they forgot what to look for on the field," said Robinson, relishing the triumph. "I think we've finally turned the corner, and I think the guys know it, too. The big thing is that we're winning with 25 players, despite injuries. You have to wait for something like this. It can't be forced. This is a young club; it was a young club when we started and it has gotten younger as we went along."

After the game the lighthearted banter in the clubhouse was interrupted by an argument between two of the players. "If you don't want me on this team, why don't you say so?" one demanded. The other angrily issued a threat before Tom McCraw moved between them. Don Hood pleaded to a writer who had witnessed the incident, an indication of disharmony, "We've finally got something going, don't ruin it for us." The writer didn't.

Anyway, it was past his deadline.

OAKLAND, CALIFORNIA, MAY 29—The Indians are now 41 games and 53 days into the 1975 season. They have compiled an 18-23 record for fifth place, five games behind the division-leading Boston Red Sox. What has transpired thus far? Charlie Spikes, counted upon to deliver at least 20 homers and drive in close to 100 runs, is hitting .175 with one homer and five RBI. Oscar Gamble, expected to duplicate last year's 19 homers and 59 RBI with a .291 average, is hitting .230 with one homer and four RBI. John Ellis, another major producer in 1974 (10 homers, 64 RBI, .285 average), is hitting .229 with three homers and 12 RBI. Gaylord Perry, whose statistics a year ago this date showed an 8-1 record, is struggling with a 6-6 mark and an uncharacteristic 3.14 earned run average. Jim Perry, supposed to be "just as good" as he was in 1974 when he won 17 and lost 12, is no longer with the club after winning one game and losing six with an earned run average of 6.69.

Shouldering most of the load have been Rico Carty (.297), George Hendrick (.280, six homers, 24 RBI), Boog Powell (.278, six homers, 16 RBI), Buddy Bell (.259), Jack Brohamer (.277), and Frank Duffy (.234, 13 RBI). Robinson, seeing action in only 21 games, is hitting .220 with four homers and nine RBI. Though he doesn't complain, Robinson's left shoulder continues to hamper his swing since it was injured more than four weeks ago.

The Indians have not done well but neither has any other team in the Eastern Division. Boston is ahead of Cleveland by five games, Milwaukee is ahead by three, New York and Detroit are ahead by one, and Baltimore, the defending champion, is 2½ behind.

MAY 30—The corner the Indians so recently turned led straight to a solid wall tonight: Dick Bosman, the Oakland A's pitcher, beat his former teammates, 6-2. His record since leaving Cleveland is 2–0, both victories against the Indians.

"It doesn't give me any special feeling, I like to beat anybody," said Bosman. "But it's great to be here, it's a dream come true: a shot at the World Series. These guys believe they will win it all again. They give me more confidence because they have pride and a reputation, and they know how to win. They told me to keep the score close and we'd beat the Indians."

Jim Kern, one of the three rookies who went into the starting rotation when Bosman and Jim Perry were traded, was Bosman's victim. Kern walked seven in less than six innings. Robinson was displeased.

"You keep giving them opportunities to score and they're going to score," bristled the manager. "It was walk, walk, walk, asking for trouble. At first Kern was being too careful, then he began overthrowing the ball. When he rears back and throws naturally, over the plate, nobody hits him."

Boog Powell and John Ellis tried to play, but neither did well because of their injuries. Powell left the game in the sixth inning when his back stiffened in the cold night air. Ellis was little help despite two hits. After his first single in the second inning, he hobbled badly.

Later Ellis admitted he reinjured his leg by playing without a protective wrap "because it bothered me too much." Rather than being sympathetic, Robinson was incredulous. "I can't believe a man who has been in the game as long as Ellis doing something like that!"

MAY 31—As a boy in Fremont, California, Dennis Eckersley was a fan of the San Francisco Giants and then the Oakland A's. Today he beat the A's again, 4–1, on a six-hitter. Only Eckersley was unimpressed. "Aw, I wasn't throwing the ball all that good. The only good thing I did was throw strikes." The Bay Area reporters enjoyed Eckersley's talking about his disappointment when he was drafted by the Indians in 1972. "When their scout called me and told me, I said, 'Oh, no! Not Cleveland!' I was hoping the Giants would pick me." Eckersley was asked how much bonus he received. "I'm not supposed to say, but it was $32,500. I spent most of the money on cars. I've bought a Challenger, a Vette, and a van." Of his success: "The hitters up here aren't that much better. In fact, in many ways it's easier to pitch in the big leagues than in the minors."

The run Eckersley allowed in the sixth ended his consecutive scoreless inning streak at 28⅔. Frank Robinson cited Eckersley: "That's what pitching is all about. That's what I've been trying to tell the others. You've got to go at them with something on the ball, throw strikes, and you'll win."

Eckersley's sidearm delivery has worried some Indians' minor league coaches. "They told me, because I throw sidearm, not to turn the ball over, that if I continue to pitch that way I'll hurt my arm. But they don't know what they're talking about," said the brash rookie.

Eckersley wasn't the only member of the Indians in the news today. Speculation is rampant again that Gaylord Perry will be traded to the A's before the June 15 deadline.

Charlie Finley admitted he is trying to get Perry. "Yes, we are interested, but you'll have to talk to Phil Seghi about it."

"Charlie thinks he made an offer, but I don't consider it one," said Seghi without emotion.

JUNE 1—"Did you see what happened in the fifth inning?" asked one Indians' staff member after Gaylord Perry was beaten by Oakland, absorbing his seventh defeat. "I've never seen Perry do that before. It was as though he lost everything, just like that," and the man snapped his fingers. "It makes you wonder, doesn't it? I mean, the man *is* 36 going on 37."

Perry, trying to keep the score (3–2) close, had a 1-and-2 count on Gene Tenace. His fourth pitch went behind Tenace's head and thudded against the screen. His next pitch was nearly as bad, ball three. Ball four was over Tenace's head again. One pitch later Claudell Washington hit a home run, putting the A's ahead, 5–2. The next batter popped up Perry's first offering, ending the inning, but Phil Garner started the sixth with a double. Finally, Perry was replaced by Tom Buskey. The Indians lost, 6–3.

Frank Robinson said only, "Gaylord didn't have much." Alan Ashby expressed puzzlement. "The first and last of those pitches to Tenace were hard sliders, but they didn't do a thing. The middle pitch was a fork ball that stayed up. I don't know why, or what happened. After the first one, Tenace looked down at me. He didn't say anything, but I'm sure he wondered, too." Perry said, "I felt good. Those pitches to Tenace just got away from me."

The defeat ended a six-game trip with a 4–2 record. "It wasn't bad, but it could have been great if we'd won just one more game here," said Robinson.

This was the last trip Blue Moon Odom will make with the Indians. "Charlie Finley will take him back, but only to send him to their Tucson farm club," said Phil Seghi. "Before Odom can be sent to the minors, we've got to get waivers on him. I'll do that this week; they should clear by next Friday."

CLEVELAND, OHIO, JUNE 2—For Frank Robinson this was a day to summarize, to reflect, to evaluate.

"I thought our offense would be more explosive, but it turns out we have to hit-and-run and bunt more, sacrifice even with one out at times. The pitching shows signs of being much better than we expected. The lack of consistent hitting by the guys we felt would hit is my biggest disappointment. So many times we've gotten a pitcher in trouble but can't finish him off. I think we'll improve, but we've got to get Charlie Spikes going and we need Boog Powell healthy. John Ellis and Oscar Gamble have to do more, too. I'm also disappointed in our base stealing. It seems that everything we were taught by Maury Wills we've forgotten. We've reverted to old, cautious ways."

Is the manager disappointed in Robinson the player?

"Yes," he replied without hesitation, "mostly because I haven't been more consistent. I've found I do not have the time to devote to my playing that I should. There always are so many things to do, so many interviews and meetings. But I will devote more time to my hitting from now on."

What about the numerous controversies? "I don't enjoy it, but I can't change. I've always spoken up for myself, and now I'm speaking up for myself and my team. Now the things I say get more attention because I am a manager. I guess it'll always be this way as long as I am a manager."

Most satisfying to Robinson have been the emergence of Dennis Eckersley and the steady play of George Hendrick. "I felt Eckersley could do this kind of a job when I saw him in spring training, and Hendrick was supposed to be my big problem. That hasn't been the case, and I'm not surprised."

Robinson still believes there'll be a five-team race for the division championship, including the Indians but not the Detroit Tigers. He bases his hopes for improvement on the three young pitchers now starting regularly—Eckersley, Jim Kern, and Eric Raich. "We're better off now than when we ended spring training. The other teams had their chances to put us away early, but they didn't, and we'll be on their backs before it's over."

JUNE 3—"We're at a point where we can't even pinch-hit for anybody," lamented Frank Robinson, referring to the injuries keeping John Ellis, Rico Carty, and Jack Brohamer on the bench. "All we can do is keep showing up until we get some of the guys healthy again."

The 5–2 loss to the Kansas City Royals began as a close game until the sixth inning. Fritz Peterson went to the showers early, beaten by rookie Dennis Leonard. Is Leonard that good? "You can't judge what kind of a pitcher he is by our attack," Robinson brushed off the question.

Eric Raich was supposed to pitch tomorrow night but came down with the flu. In Raich's place Robinson plans to start Blue Moon· Odom. Why? "Well, who else? Let's see what Moon can do." Perhaps let *everyone* see what Odom can do. In the lexicon of baseball, that's known as "showcasing."

JUNE 4—Blue Moon Odom pitched a two-hitter and the Indians beat the Royals, 4–0. Before the game Odom admitted, "I feel like I'm over a barrel; I don't know what to do. If I pitch good, the Indians might want to keep me and I don't want to stay. If I pitch bad, maybe nobody will want me and I'll have to stay."

Odom pitched "good" anyway. He didn't allow a hit until the sixth inning when Hal McRae singled with one out. Three pitches later John Mayberry did the same, but that was all.

When he walked into the clubhouse—ignored by many teammates who would have been happy for different circumstances—Blue Moon said with sarcasm, "There, that ought to teach anybody who wonders if I can still pitch. I feel the same way I did before. I want to go somewhere else, unless Seghi wants to give me the money I've been asking for." Seghi doesn't.

Robinson was asked if Odom's performance complicates the Indians' pitching plans. "No, not as far as I'm concerned. My plans for Odom are the same as before, to use him in long relief and as a spot starter." The manager insisted he started Odom because "I thought he was the best man I had available to do the job."

Before the game Robinson met with the coaches and Seghi. The players speculated that either another deal was in the making or that somebody else would be shipped off to the minors.

"I wonder who's going to die this time?" Fritz Peterson asked. Gaylord Perry was sure the meeting concerned a trade for him. Several borderline players sweated privately, especially Ken Berry.

Asked about the meeting, Robinson said, "I just called the coaches in for a chat and, as we were sitting down, Phil dropped by for a chat, too." Seghi was equally noncommittal. "We just talked." Does he have an offer for Gaylord Perry? "Yes, a lot of them, but none I'll consider."

JUNE 5—The friendly chat Frank Robinson had with his coaches and Phil Seghi resulted in the call-up of second baseman Duane Kuiper from Oklahoma City. He'll replace Jack Brohamer whose left hip, injured May 25, has become worse because of nerve damage.

While Blue Moon Odom grows more impatient, Seghi plays a waiting game. "I've asked waivers on Odom to see who's interested," said the general manager. "The deadline for claiming Odom is 2:00 P.M. tomorrow." What about Blue Moon's two-hitter yesterday? "He only did what he's paid to do," snapped Seghi.

If Odom is claimed, the Indians can sell him for $20,000 or make a deal for another waivered player. If he is not claimed, the Indians can sell or trade Odom to any team in baseball, including the Oakland A's whose owner, Charlie Finley, is interested but only to send Blue Moon to the minors.

Jim Kern pitched tonight but did not do well, though the Indians came back to win for Dave LaRoche, 8–7, on Buddy Bell's eleventh-inning homer. An eighth-inning rally, triggered by Rick Manning, produced three runs, and Manning's triple in the ninth scored the tying run. Rick is rapidly becoming the darling of the Cleveland fans.

"They call me a Pete Rose type of player," acknowledged Manning, "but I don't want to be him. I want to be Rick Manning, to help the club win with my arm or my legs or my bat, anything. I don't think the excitement of being here will ever leave me."

Robinson, while unhappy with Kern's performance, was pleased by the comeback. "This club has proved it has heart. It won't quit. If it didn't have heart, it would have given up." He smiled.

JUNE 6—Blue Moon Odom angrily flung a shoe across the clubhouse. "Those dirty, lying-------," bellowed Odom, loudly enough for Frank Robinson and Phil Seghi to hear as they conferred in the manager's office. "They're no good. They're liars. They're ------ ------. If you want to know what's going on, go and ask them yourself. They'll probably lie to you just as they lied to me. The Braves claimed me but now Seghi won't let me go. He says they won't give me away. The -------- backed out of the deal with Charlie Finley, too." Odom stalked off to the trainer's room, off limits to all but the players and management. Seghi left Robinson's office through the outer door rather than through the clubhouse, avoiding a confrontation with Odom.

"Blue Moon is right; we are not going to give him away," said Robinson. "But we did not back out of a deal with Finley. The truth is, Finley told us earlier this week, before Odom pitched, that he had to go back and talk to his people. Since the Braves claimed him on waivers, we can't deal Odom to Oakland anyway. As for Odom going to the Braves, we told him at the beginning we want something more than the waiver price for him. That's the way things stand right now.

"It's my recommendation that we move Odom along because of his attitude. It's so bad, it might infect the rest of the guys, though I don't think it will. They know he's wrong and they're ignoring him. He's just with the club, that's all. I have no plans to use him as a starter or a reliever. We'll wait and see. If we let him force us into giving him a raise or giving him away, half the guys on the team would do the same.

"Odom is trying to make the club look like the goat. He sat in this office with Phil and me and made the statement that he could not pitch here and did not want to pitch here. So he won't. But we still won't give him away. We'll only make a deal that will help the club."

If nothing develops, will Odom be suspended? "That's one avenue to go. It won't help the club, but it won't hurt it either."

Robinson was particularly disappointed because he recommended last winter that, if Odom became available, Seghi should try to get him. "It disappoints me personally, as a manager and as a player. The fact that both of us are black has nothing to do with it. I'd feel the same if I were white or if he were white. I'm especially sorry because things seemed to be going so well. This could get nasty and disrupt the team, but I won't let it."

Robinson personally led the Indians to another comeback victory, 7–5, over the Texas Rangers with Dave LaRoche winning in relief of Dennis Eckersley. Robinson smashed a three-run homer in the first inning and another three-run homer in the eighth. This raises his season total to six and his career total to 580; it's also the fifty-fourth time in his career Robinson delivered two homers in one game.

Later Robinson spoke in his usual calm manner. "Both times I was just looking for the ball, to hit it hard somewhere. Against a pitcher like Ferguson Jenkins you've got to discipline yourself. You've got to know what you want to do, and how to go about doing it. When I go to the plate, I'm able to lock everything out of my mind except what I'm trying to do. When I hit a ball like I did tonight, I see it going but I never hear the crowd. I don't snap out of it until I get to second base. By the time I got to the dugout tonight, I was thinking about how to get them out in the ninth inning. I get more excited watching the kids produce, the Dennis Eckersleys and the Rick Mannings, and seeing George Hendrick lay down a sacrifice bunt like he did in the eighth inning. I guess you might say opposites attract; I excite them and they excite me."

✿ ✿ ✿

JUNE 7—Blue Moon Odom got his wish, the Indians got a new pitcher, and harmony returned to the Wigwam. Odom was traded to the Atlanta Braves for Roric Harrison in a waiver deal.

In today's game, Gaylord Perry was unable to prolong the Indians' three-game winning streak. He lost for the sixth time in his last eight starts, 5–4, to the Rangers in 12 innings after the game went into overtime on the fourteenth homer relinquished by Perry this season.

"Yes, I am still concerned with Gaylord," acknowledged Frank Robinson, growing impatient with the same questions.

Among the long faces in the clubhouse, Odom's smiling countenance stood out. "I'm not just happy, I'm very happy. I knew I'd be going somewhere, either to the Braves or the Rangers. I like going to Atlanta best because it's close to my home." Odom also believes the Braves will give him the $8000 raise the Indians wouldn't. "I don't think I'll even have to ask for it; they know the reason I wasn't satisfied here." Phil Seghi thinks Blue Moon is in for a rude surprise. "Eddie Robinson [the Braves' general manager] told me, 'Hell will freeze over before I'll give Odom any more money than his contract calls for,'" said Seghi.

Harrison was happy to leave Atlanta. He doesn't plan to ask for a raise, which pleases Seghi. "I'm not in the position to ask for anything but the opportunity to pitch," said the 28-year-old right-hander whose Braves' record was 3-4. "I am anxious to play for a good organization and I'm told Cleveland is one. I don't think the Braves can be a contender until they get a catalyst to pull the different factions together. I was brought up in a winning organization, the Baltimore Orioles, but then I ran into some guys who were going the other way. Normally, I'm a happy guy, but as soon as I'd get to the park in Atlanta, I'd get unhappy. I think the good Lord must have heard me and got me here."

Fred Beene and Ken Berry worried about their futures. "I don't know what to think," lamented Beene, "disabled" since April 5 but able to pitch for at least three weeks. "I thought when Odom left I'd be added to the roster, but now we've got another pitcher. Where does that leave me? I'm not the kind of guy to make waves, but I'm going to have to do something pretty soon. What kind of an argument will I have next winter, when it's time to negotiate a contract?"

Berry was signed last winter after being released by the Milwaukee Brewers. He has not played at all since Rick Manning's arrival. "What do you hear?" he asked this writer. "They've got to find a way to activate Beene, and I figure I'll be the one to go. See what you can find out."

In the loss to the Rangers, Oscar Gamble was picked off third base in the seventh inning, aborting a rally that might have won the game. He insisted, "I started to go home because the coach [Dave Garcia] told me to go. I was only following orders."

Garcia maintained privately that Gamble was at fault, and Robinson supported his coach. "For the record," said Garcia, "just quote me as saying, 'Yes, it was my fault.' I don't want to say anything that will split this team, but if you want to know what happened, it was that Oscar got fooled."

"If Gamble had thought in advance," said Robinson, "and noticed the infield playing in, he would have known there was no way he should try to score."

Gaylord Perry backed Gamble. "I don't care what they told you, I know Garcia told Oscar to try to score. It wasn't Gamble's fault; it was Garcia's."

JUNE 8—Before the Indians reported to the Stadium for a seven-hour doubleheader with the Rangers, Ken Berry was released and Fred Beene was returned to the active list.

The Indians won the opener, 3–2, but lost the 17-inning nightcap, 7–6. Rick Manning rapped five hits, giving him nine in his last 15 times at bat. Eric Raich got relief help from Tom Buskey and Dave LaRoche to win the opener, but Buskey was charged with the loss in the second game, sent into extra innings by John Ellis' ninth-inning homer. The Rangers won it on a hit by Lenny Randle that would have been a double play except the ball grazed off Buskey's foot and deflected away from shortstop Frank Duffy.

Once again, what happened off the field commanded equal space in the newspapers.

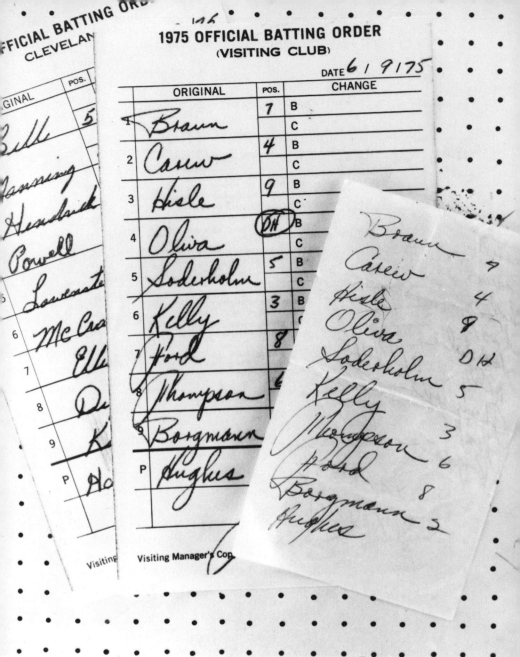

Richard J. Misch, Cleveland *Plain Dealer*

Minnesota Twins' incorrect lineup cards, June 9—see page 139.

Marvin J. Miller, executive director of the Players Association, sent a confidential memo to the members of the Cleveland team. Miller commended the Indians for their recent show of unity and support of Frank Robinson with their offer to sit out the manager's three-day suspension. Miller also denounced Lee MacPhail's handling of the case.

Miller wrote, "Unjust decisions should be criticized and the unity of the players in opposition to such a decision was most appropriate. Perhaps the worst part of the entire procedure is . . . that a player, or a manager, who is disciplined for some action on the field, is deprived of due process. The league president determines the discipline in the first instance and then, when an appeal is made, the same man who invoked the discipline is the one who decides if he was right in the first place! The entire procedure is a farce. No one can be a prosecutor, a judge and an appeal judge all wrapped in one."

Undoubtedly Miller wanted Robinson to file a grievance, forcing a formal reivew of the procedure as part of Miller's crusade for more "equality" on behalf of the players. Robinson could not chance such a move though he was inclined to agree with Miller.

In ceremonies between games Earl Averill, a former Indians' great recently elected to the Hall of Fame, was honored and his uniform, number 3, formally retired. That number is being worn by Dave Garcia. "Earl told me it would be okay to wear number 3 for the rest of this season," said Garcia, "but I wouldn't care if they gave me number 199 and it had polka dots, as long as it's a major league uniform."

JUNE 9—Until today Frank Robinson has maintained, "I haven't made a mistake yet because I never second-guess any of my decisions." Tonight, in an extra-inning loss to the Minnesota Twins, 11–10, Robinson admitted committing a costly blunder.

"It was all my fault," said the manager after he discovered, too late, that the Twins had batted out of order four times prior to the ninth inning when they scored four runs to tie. They won the game two innings later against Tom Buskey, after Roric Harrison made a so-so debut as a starting pitcher. "It would have been something to laugh about if we'd won like we should have," said Robinson, not laughing. "It doesn't embarrass me, but I know I made a mistake, that's all there is to it. But it won't happen again."

The erroneous batting order came from Minnesota manager Frank Quilici. Two hours before the game when field announcer Bob Keefer asked Quilici for his lineup, Quilici said, "I'm not sure what it'll be. I've got a few guys hurt, and I don't know yet if they can play."

"Well, give me what you think it'll be," said Keefer, "and I'll check with you later." Quilici did. He thought the lineup would have Dan Ford batting seventh and Danny Thompson eighth. Quilici scribbled the batting order on a slip of paper for Keefer, who telephoned press box attendant John Krepop. It was then printed on the chalkboard and relayed to the scoreboard where it was posted for the fans.

Later Keefer asked Quilici to confirm the lineup. "It'll be the way I gave it to you." "Do you want to see the way you gave it to me?" asked Keefer. "No," said Quilici. "I've got it here," and he pointed to his head. In making out the official lineup card, however, Quilici penciled Thompson in the seventh spot and Ford in the eighth. It was handed that way to the umpires and a copy given to Indians' cocaptain George Hendrick, who represented Robinson at the pregame meeting at the plate. When Hendrick returned to the dugout, instead of handing the lineup to Robinson, he laid the card on the bench and it remained there.

In the first inning Thompson lined to left field, ending a two-run rally for the Twins. In the fourth, Thompson singled but was stranded. In the fifth, Thompson fouled out, ending the inning. Ford tripled leading the sixth and scored a run that would have been nullified had the Indians realized the two players were batting out of turn. In the seventh, Thompson again batted ahead of Ford, but both were retired.

In the ninth, with the Twins rallying for three runs to tie, Thompson knelt at the on-deck circle. One run was in and the potential tying runs were on second and third bases. "I was looking at my lineup card because I had a couple of changes in mind," testified Quilici. "I realized Thompson was going to bat ahead of Ford. I called him back and said, 'What the hell are you doing? You follow Ford.' He said, 'Well, I've been batting ahead of him all night just as the lineup on the scoreboard has us listed.' I told him, 'Not anymore, you're not. Get out of there and let Ford bat.'"

Keefer, seated nearby, overheard the conversation and checked the official card: Ford was in the seventh spot, Thompson in the eighth. "I had to announce Ford as the batter, but I tried to do it very softly," he said.

The Indians initially thought Ford was batting out of turn. "Hey, this isn't the way they have been batting," said John Ellis to umpire Lou DiMuro. "I know it," said DiMuro, who is not allowed to call the other team's attention to such an offense. Robinson suddenly realized a mistake had been made but knew it was too late to protest.

Even stranger was the fact that Dennis Eckersley, as the pitcher for tomorrow night's game, sat in the dugout charting pitches. He had the correct Twins' lineup, but each time Ford and Thompson batted out of turn, Eckersley put their performances in the right place. Eckersley didn't point out the Twins' mistake to Robinson. "I just thought it was something *I* was doing wrong," said the embarrassed pitcher.

When the disappointment of defeat had worn off somewhat, Robinson made light of the blunder. "See what the first black manager has achieved? He has made everybody color blind. You guys can't even tell a white guy from a black guy." Ford is black and Thompson white. But then, neither could Robinson tell the difference.

Privately, several players thought it poetic justice that Robinson should be caught in an embarrassing situation. "Just the other day I read where he said he hadn't made a mistake," said one. "I thought to myself, 'Isn't that something! It must mean everything that's going wrong is our fault, the players.' Last year when we were playing so bad, everybody blamed the manager [Ken Aspromonte], *not* the players."

One reason Robinson may have been errant is the anonymous telephone call to the Indians' switchboard this morning. "If that nigger shows up tonight we're going to kill him," threatened a voice. The operator relayed the message to Phil

Seghi, who did not tell Robinson. The manager heard about it from another source.

"Sure, I thought about it," he conceded, "although I didn't take it too seriously. I was more worried about my wife and children being upset."

That telephone threat was similar to the hate mail sent to Robinson, though his (and Seghi's) secretary, Trudy Hargis, screens most of it and keeps it away from the manager. "Most of the letters are unsigned, which tells you something about those kind of people," she said.

(During the World Series, when Robinson was in Boston for the first two games, another threat on his life was telephoned to the Indians' offices in Cleveland. On that occasion the caller talked to Ted Bonda, saying, "If you don't fire that nigger, I'm going to shoot him." The commissioner's office was notified and Henry Fitzgibbon, a former FBI agent now on Bowie Kuhn's staff, organized a special security force to protect Robinson, though he disdained the offer of a personal bodyguard.)

JUNE 10—Frank Robinson finally blew his cool as the Indians sinned mightily in losing, 5–3, in 12 innings to the Twins. It was a third straight setback, fourth in the last five games, and ended what could have been a productive home stand with a disappointing 4-6 record. The Indians are now in fifth place, 6½ lengths behind Boston, 5½ behind New York, 2½ behind Milwaukee, 1½ behind Detroit, and ½ ahead of Baltimore.

"If we'd just had four hits on four different occasions, we would have won the last four games. If we had, our record would be 27-26 (instead of 23-30) and we'd be in third place," lamented Robinson. "I think it's time for me to get tough. I don't like to hold meetings after losing a bad game because I might say something I'd regret later, but I will have a meeting tomorrow night in Kansas City. Part of it is that we're tired. We've played an awful lot of innings the last few days [five extra-inning games of the last seven, over six days, a total of 81 innings]. What makes it worse is that we have so little to show for it, mainly because we're not doing the little things a team has to do to win."

Among those "little things" tonight were five instances of

players being unable to lay down sacrifice bunts in key situations. Robinson also was miffed at George Hendrick, who ran at less than full speed after bunting in the first inning.

"I will talk to George about it tomorrow night," promised Robinson, "but I'm not going to fine him. George isn't the only offender, but you guys [the writers] don't seem to notice the others, only Hendrick."

After the first inning Hendrick played well, hitting his eleventh homer in the eighth inning to send the game into overtime. Earlier, Dan Ford and Rod Carew homered off Dennis Eckersley, who was removed after nine innings. The loss was charged to Dave LaRoche, who walked four batters around a broken bat single in the twelfth.

What turned out to be the winning run scored because Frank Duffy failed to make a routine tag at second base. Publicly, Robinson defended Duffy in his argument with umpire Jim Evans. Privately, the manager lamented the lack of aggressiveness on the part of his cocaptain and shortstop.

Will a change of scenery (Kansas City and Texas) help?

"A change of scenery won't help us bunt," Robinson replied. "It won't help us execute. It won't help us get a sacrifice fly when we need one. I guess we'll just have to go back to the fundamentals." To nobody in particular he muttered, "Where does it all end?"

Another problem is that, after a promising start, the turnstiles have stopped clicking at their previously merry rate. If the losses continue to mount, attendance will suffer. Perhaps that's why Phil Seghi was willing to discuss Gaylord Perry with this reporter. The trading deadline is only six days away.

"Oh, you guys would crucify me if I traded Gaylord, wouldn't you?" he asked. Assured he wouldn't be "crucified," Seghi spoke candidly. "I am concerned with Gaylord's pitching. So is Robby, and so are the coaches. He's not the same pitcher he was and if I don't move him now, his value will go 'way down by September. If we're ever going to get anything good for him, we've got to trade him now." He revealed that three clubs are interested: Texas, Kansas City, and Oakland, all vying for the Western Division championship. Two others, Boston and Baltimore, have a passing interest.

Ted Bonda and several of the partners are very concerned

about finances, including Gaylord's salary. The financial problem is directly related to a $6 million loan negotiated by Bonda in August 1973. None of the principal has been repaid, only the interest, about $600,000 annually. It has been suggested that Perry be traded for players and as much cash as Seghi can get. Seghi is trying to resist the hierarchy's request that money be included in any deal for Perry. Seghi would prefer to trade Perry for two established pitchers, plus two minor league prospects.

The urgent need for money is what's bothering Seghi the most, which is why he is concerned about being "crucified" if he trades Perry.

9. Good-bye, Gaylord

KANSAS CITY, MISSOURI, JUNE 11—"Are you still here?" Jim Kern asked Gaylord Perry as the Indians deplaned in Kansas City to begin a five-game trip against the Royals and then the Texas Rangers in Dallas.

"Are *you* still here, Rook?" Perry replied to Kern.

"What'd he mean by that?" Kern wondered.

Sitting in the Sheraton Royal Hotel lobby before tonight's game, Gaylord seemed depressed.

"Nobody's happy around here," he complained. "There's no communication. Sure, losing has a lot to do with it, but so does the man. We've got to do something soon, or the whole season will be down the drain."

If nobody is happy, why not talk to Robinson about it?

"Are you kidding? He never makes a mistake. That's what he keeps saying in the newspapers."

Is Robinson making mistakes?

Perry snorted. "Look what he's doing to Johnny." He gestured toward John Ellis seated across the lobby. "He's playing him every day, even doubleheaders, and it's killing him physically. At the same time, he's killing the other guy [Alan Ashby] mentally."

Perry left for the park early, to go through his ritual of preparing to pitch. It includes about an hour in the trainer's room, which has not escaped Robinson's notice. "I don't know if Gaylord is hurting, but I have to wonder about the heavy [tape] wrap he wears on his ankle and the other one he puts on his thigh," said the manager.

During the game Robinson became even more puzzled. "Between the fifth and the sixth innings I saw Jimmy [Warfield, the trainer] rub a whole tube of Capsulin on Gaylord's shoulder and upper arm. They were in the runway to the clubhouse. Capsulin is the hottest ointment you can use. Some guys can't even bear a little of it. I found out Gaylord uses it during every game, and he also has a full tube of it rubbed into his shoulder *before* every game. When I've seen other guys use Capsulin like that, it's so they don't feel pain. I've asked Gaylord if he's hurting and he says no, but I wonder."

Robinson was in the runway to observe Gaylord and Warfield because the manager was ejected in the fourth inning by umpire Ron Luciano. It was Robinson's second ejection of the season.

An argument developed after Luciano called George Hendrick out on a checked-swing, third strike. Initially, coach Tom McCraw got into it with Luciano. The umpire insisted McCraw had no right to argue, and that's when Robinson joined in. Luciano said, "I told Robby, 'Please don't make me run you. This is going on too long.' He didn't curse, but he wouldn't leave. I had to throw him out."

As for his promised "chewing out" session with the Indians, Robinson had another change of heart and spoke instead with understanding. "I was mad last night, but I calmed down the more I thought about it. I believe the best way to handle this club is to not get tough. I think I'll get the best out of the guys with an easy, soft approach."

Did he talk privately to Hendrick as he said he would? "No, but I still plan to. It'll not be a big thing. I'm satisfied the way he's playing even if some of you guys aren't."

On the field Gaylord was no better than he's been—not very

good—and the Indians lost, 7–1. "I can't understand. I feel super, great," said the pitcher, who gave up two more homers for 16 in 15 games. "We're not this bad, and neither am I."

Robinson suggested, "Perry's main problem is that his velocity is not the same as before. Another thing is his location. He's not throwing the ball where he wants to. It also bothers me that he doesn't seem to have the same bulldog spirit, the same determination to win."

Is Perry experiencing a slump? "Pitchers don't go into slumps like hitters," said Robinson. "Every time he goes to the mound I expect to see him pitch like he did last year, but I've only seen him do it a couple of times. I don't buy the bad-luck theory either. He just isn't throwing like I've known Gaylord to throw."

Trade rumors now have Perry going to either the Texas Rangers for pitchers Jim Bibby and Jackie Brown, a minor league player or two, and as much money as the Indians can get; or to the Kansas City Royals for pitchers Paul Splittorff and Doug Bird. The money is a major factor as Ted Bonda has made clear to Phil Seghi. Unloading Gaylord's $160,000 salary, guaranteed through 1976, also is important, though Bonda and Seghi deny it.

Will Gaylord be surprised if he's traded?

"No, sir," he replied. "I'll be surprised only if I'm *not* traded."

JUNE 12—Now there is no doubt. Gaylord Perry will be traded before the deadline in three days. The only question is whether he'll go to the Rangers or the Royals.

"We've talked to both clubs and, yes, we're close," conceded Frank Robinson before the Indians lost, 2–1, to Kansas City in another extra-inning game. "If we get any closer, we'll have a deal. I think something will happen soon, if not today or tomorrow, then by Sunday for sure."

Joe Burke, general manager of the Royals, indicates the Indians will trade Perry to the Rangers; Danny O'Brien, Texas general manager, seems less positive.

"I learned my lesson in the Catfish Hunter bidding contest," said Burke. "We stayed in that one and kept increasing our offer every time they got a better one from somebody else.

That's not the way I do business anymore, and I'm not going to let Phil Seghi drive up the price on Perry. I've told him how high I'll go and that will be it. We'd like to have Gaylord, but I'm not going to let Seghi rape this club. I hear the franchise [Cleveland] is in trouble again. Well, I told Phil Tuesday what we'll do to get Gaylord. The rest is up to him. He said he'd get back to me before he does business with anyone else."

O'Brien didn't seem much more hopeful and also pointed out the Indians' obvious need for money. In fact, that need for money was one of the big reasons O'Brien wasn't sure his club could make a deal for Perry.

"We're talking to several clubs, including the Indians," said O'Brien. "We might do something with one of them that could help us deal with Cleveland. But that's all I can say about it now. Are we close to getting Gaylord? How close is close, really? It all depends upon your interpretation."

Gaylord is convinced he is, as he says, "gone." After Eric Raich was beaten tonight on Harmon Killebrew's homer and John Ellis' passed ball, Perry told writers, "I feel like an outcast, and I have for a week or so; like I'm not part of things anymore. I expect to go, but I'm not sure where. I called my wife and told her not to go to Cleveland next week, but to wait and see where I wind up. I think it will be good for me to start new again somewhere else. I thought we had a chance to be a contender, but a few of us are having bad years and they gave up on us. They gave up on Dick Bosman and my brother Jim too soon. I am trying as hard as I ever have. I'm just making too many bad pitches, and when I have pitched well, I got no runs and lost.

"More than anything the team has lost confidence in itself, and that's as much the fault of the people running it as it is the players. Better communications would help, but that's not my problem. I only work here—for now, anyway."

ARLINGTON, TEXAS, JUNE 13—Gaylord Perry was personally delivered to the Texas Rangers today—in a baggage truck. Before the Indians left Kansas City this morning, two announcements all but confirmed the deal exchanging Perry for pitchers Jim Bibby and Jackie Brown, plus minor league southpaw Rick Waits and $150,000 cash.

As the Indians waited for their bus to leave the hotel in Kansas City, news came that the Rangers had sold shortstop Eddie Brinkman to the New York Yankees for an estimated $100,000. "That's how they're getting the money to give the Indians for me," said Gaylord. Then came the report that the Rangers would hold a 4:00 P.M. news conference at Arlington Stadium. The Indians were to arrive at 1:55. "There's no doubt now, is there?" Gaylord asked. He was right, even if Frank Robinson wouldn't immediately confirm it.

Finally Perry was told he was, indeed, traded to the Rangers and that he should go directly to Arlington Stadium upon the Indians' arrival at the Dallas-Forth Worth airport, while the rest of the team went to the hotel.

Gaylord rode to the stadium in the baggage truck carrying the Indians' equipment to the park. "It seemed appropriate for me to do that," he said. At four the formal announcement was made and Gaylord Perry, carrying a Texas Rangers' cap, was introduced to the media. Danny O'Brien turned the microphone over to Brad Corbett, chairman of the board of the Rangers. Corbett said, "Gaylord always was one of my favorites. We consider him to be a superstar. We know he'll be a credit to our organization on and off the field."

Rangers' manager Billy Martin, who had often protested what he thought were Perry's illegal spitballs, was penitent. "I realize now how wrong I was in accusing Gaylord of cheating."

In Cleveland, Phil Seghi reacted as expected to criticism of the deal. "The reason I traded Gaylord lies in simple mathematics. In getting Bibby and Brown we are getting 32 victories and giving up Perry's 21 [of 1974]." However, Seghi conveniently failed to point out that with Bibby and Brown the Indians also were getting 31 losses, while giving up Perry's 1974 total of 13.

Seghi also claimed, "I still think we are a contender. We added two arms that should stabilize us." As for the accompanying $150,000, Seghi said, "It had no real bearing on the deal, but no one will scoff at cash." Observers scoffed at Seghi's statement.

Asked if the Indians are in a financial bind, Seghi said the answer would have to come from Ted Bonda, "but I haven't heard of any problem," he added. Observers scoffed again. In Kansas City, Joe Burke scoffed, too. "First, let me say I was surprised because I expected to hear from Phil before he made any deal for Gaylord. He gave me his word that he'd get back to me, but I'm still waiting. I think the players I offered are better than the players he got from the Rangers, but I told him right from the start I wasn't going to go through another Catfish Hunter bidding contest with anybody, for anybody. I told him what we could do and that was it."

The Royals' last offer: Doug Bird, a relief pitcher, and either a starting pitcher from among Paul Splittorff, Bruce Dal Canton, Marty Pattin, or Nelson Briles, or an outfielder from among Jim Wohlford, Al Cowens, or Vada Pinson.

Seghi reacted predictably again. "That's not true," he said of Burke's remarks. "I told Joe the only way I'd trade him Perry was if he'd include Al Fitzmorris in the deal. He wouldn't, so we didn't have a deal."

Though Gaylord talked pleasantly about his 3½ years in Cleveland, he pointed out, "I'm sure the trouble Robinson and I had in spring training was the thing that started all this. If I had won every game I pitched it might have been different. But the deal probably is for the best. My being gone should help Frank relax. It should help me relax, too. I also know a big factor was that the Indians needed money, and also wanted to get rid of my high salary. That's the reason they got rid of my brother earlier."

Did Robinson and Gaylord part on friendly terms? "As far as I'm concerned, we did," Robinson replied. In trading Gaylord, do the Indians concede they can't win the pennant? "Not at all. If we were conceding, we would have insisted upon getting all prospects instead of proven pitchers like Bibby and Brown. We think we have strengthened our team. We think we're better with Bibby and Brown than we were with Gaylord."

Through it all O'Brien smiled contentedly. He had thought Gaylord would wind up with the Royals. "I was scared the Indians would take the Kansas City offer, and if I were in their shoes, if I could have gotten Bird in a deal for Perry, I might have gone that way. I guess it was the money that made the difference."

Seghi continued to lament the deal Bonda did not permit

him to make in 1973 with Boston. It would have left the Indians in much better shape today, a fact Seghi seldom fails to point out.

A postscript: The Indians said Kern was being demoted to Oklahoma City with Seghi's promise he'll be recalled after 10 days. Now Kern understands what Perry meant when he asked, "Are *you* still here, Rook?"

Finally, after all the traded players moved into their new clubhouses and were issued uniforms, the two teams took the field for an anticlimactic game. The Indians lost, 2–1, despite fine pitching by Fritz Peterson; it was their sixth straight setback.

When it was suggested to Robinson that perhaps he should consider shaking up the lineup, he replied, "You know what they say about horse manure: no matter how you stir it up, if it smells, it's going to keep on smelling."

JUNE 14—Boog Powell a lead-off batter? "Well, we've got to do something. Can you think of anything better to try?" Frank Robinson, despite his remark about horse manure smelling, selected his batting order for tonight's game by lottery. He put slips of paper numbered one through nine in a cap, then shuffled around the clubhouse, inviting each of the starting players to draw. The number each picked would be his place in the order, which is how Powell became a lead-off batter for the first time in his career.

"I think it's great," chortled the 265-pound, 6-4 first baseman. "I've always wanted to lead off. It just goes to prove, once you think you've seen everything, you find out you're wrong." Duane Kuiper, the 175-pound second baseman, drew number four and became the Indians' clean-up batter. "I've never batted fourth anywhere, not even in the Little Leagues, and I was a star then," said the pleased rookie.

Before Kuiper drew, Robinson held the cap out to shortstop Frank Duffy, who is in a wretched 2-for-35 slump. "Pick one, but please, Duff, don't pick number four," said Robinson. Duffy grinned weakly, dipped into the cap, privately peeked at the slip of paper, and quickly put it back. "Oh, no! Was it number four?" asked Robinson. "That's one secret I'm going to keep," replied Duffy, who then drew number seven.

In the end, Robinson's batting-order-by-lottery was: Powell first, George Hendrick second, Rick Manning third, Kuiper fourth, Robinson fifth (as the designated hitter), Buddy Bell sixth, Duffy seventh, Charlie Spikes eighth, and John Ellis ninth.

"Wait'll Phil Seghi hears the game on the radio tonight," this reporter suggested to Robinson. "He'll think you've flipped. Maybe somebody should call him and explain." Replied Robinson, "That might be a good idea."

Seghi was called, not to explain Robinson's lineup but to check a report that Jim Kern was refusing to go to Oklahoma City unless he obtained written assurance he'd be called back in 10 days, as the general manager had promised. "If I know Seghi, he'll never put it in writing," speculated one of the players. "But if I were Kern, I'd demand the same thing. Too many promises are broken around here."

Seghi surprised everybody by complying with Kern's demand. "It's no big thing. I told him we'll bring him back in 10 days and we will. The only reason we're sending him down is because he's having a little trouble with his elbow, nothing serious, but enough to affect his pitching. But I want to make it clear I wasn't forced into signing the statement. I did it of my own free will," said Seghi.

Kern was satisfied. "It's not that I don't trust the Indians, it's just that I wanted to make sure they weren't sending me down and forgetting about me. If they don't call me back as they promised, I'll take the letter to Marvin Miller and the Players Association. Miller will force them to keep their promise and bring me back."

The fact is, the Indians have a history of making promises when it is expedient to do so, and then "forgetting" when the promise comes due. In 1974, for instance, Steve Blateric, a journeyman relief pitcher, was left behind in spring training though he compiled the best record of all pitchers in the exhibition games. Blateric was promised he'd be recalled by May 15. When the date came and went, Blateric made waves and the Indians sold him to a minor league team belonging to the Chicago White Sox.

Robinson's lineup-by-lottery didn't work and the Indians lost, 2–1, despite a good pitching performance by Roric Harri-

Nancy Engebretson

First baseman Boog Powell (left) and Frank Robinson.

son. John Ellis hit a home run but it was the only run allowed by Ferguson Jenkins. The Indians' losing streak climbed to seven.

Afterward Robinson imposed a curfew. He ordered all players to be in their rooms 2½ hours after the bus returned to the Sheraton-Dallas Hotel. Why? "Maybe it'll help," shrugged the manager. "At this stage, anything is worth a try." Does it mean Robinson detected some abuses of his no-curfew policy? "No. It's just something I think might help," he repeated impatiently.

Before retiring to his room, one of the players yawned and said, "You know, it seems more like the middle of September than the middle of June. It seems like it's all over and we're just playing out the schedule, doesn't it?" Yes.

JUNE 15—Before tonight's game Dennis Eckersley talked about facing his former teammate, Gaylord Perry, who would pitch for the first time for the Texas Rangers. "I'm really looking forward to it; I really want to beat him bad," said Eckersley. "I think everybody is dying to beat him. It's nothing personal, I just think it would be good for our club to beat Gaylord. He was nice to me, but we weren't real close. He never told me a lot. I had to ask him things, like how to pitch to certain guys, just to get him talking. He used to kid me a lot about being a rookie and things like that. So did Jim Kern. That's funny now. They're both gone but I'm still here."

Gaylord wouldn't admit any anxiety about facing his former team. "I want to beat them just like any other team, but no more, no less. Sure, there might be some things about them I know that could help me, but they also know some things about me that could help them."

Frank Robinson now admits Perry has been throwing, on occasion, his illegal greaseball. "If he throws one tonight, I'll be out there to call him on it," threatened the manager.

The Indians scored two runs in the first inning and con structed a 5–1 lead in the fifth, so Robinson wasn't interested in accusing Gaylord of anything illegal. "We were winning and I didn't want to start something that might make our guys think about the greaser. I figured Gaylord wanted me to start fussing about it, so I didn't. Sure, he threw some, but his other stuff wasn't good. Like I said before, Gaylord isn't throwing hard like he used to."

Eckersley made the four-run lead stand up and did indeed beat Gaylord "bad." Perry yielded 10 hits in only six innings, and when the seventh began, he was gone. In one respect it was a successful night for the Rangers. Perry's presence on the mound against his former team attracted 27,171 fans, providing some of the $150,000 the Rangers gave the Indians in the deal. The crowd might have been larger if either Jim Bibby or Jackie Brown had pitched against Perry, but Rangers' manager Billy Martin made that impossible. He pitched Bibby and Brown the night before the trade was finalized, making it impossible for them to be used before Monday, the day after the Indians leave town.

"Me do something like that?" Martin asked in mock innocence.

Added suspense to the game would have been Robinson in the lineup as the Indians' designated hitter against Perry. The manager declined. "No way I was going to give Gaylord the satisfaction of knocking me down," he said, uncharacteristically.

Perry tried to mask his disappointment. "It would have been nice to win," he admitted, "but I felt good, that's the important thing. I was getting my pitches up again. That's been my trouble most of the season. I'll be all right. Give the kid [Eckersley] credit. He pitched a super game."

Disappointed, too, was Jim Warfield. The conscientious trainer said, "Gaylord was like a father to me. I felt bad looking out there and seeing him in a different uniform. I kept hoping Gaylord would pitch a good game, but that we'd win, 1–0."

Before and after the game Robinson was busy in his office conferring with Del Rice, scout for the California Angels. This being the last day for making trades until the end of the season, the Angels were trying hard to deal for Charlie Spikes and John Ellis. The Indians resisted. "Just because we're going bad everybody thinks we'll jump at anything that's offered," said Robinson. "We especially won't consider trading Spikes."

Robinson and Rice continued to talk and eventually proposed sending pitcher Andy Hassler and catcher Ellie Rodriguez to Cleveland for Ellis and outfielder John Lowenstein.

The Angels liked it and Robinson reportedly did, too. Seghi didn't. He wanted either pitcher Ed Figueroa or Frank Tanana in place of Hassler, or minor league first baseman Dan Briggs in addition to Hassler and Rodriguez. Harry Dalton wouldn't go along with the counterproposal, and it died when the trading deadline passed at 3:00 A.M. Cleveland time.

Dalton and Seghi were still talking, however, when the Indians boarded their plane to return to Cleveland. Ellis, aware of the negotiations, was convinced he would be traded. He was pleased. On the flight home Ellis walked up and down the aisle shaking hands and saying good-bye. When the plane landed in Cleveland, he was still a member of the Indians, a disappointed member.

Seghi rejected several other offers before the deadline passed, emphasizing, "Just because we're not playing well, we're not going to do anything impulsively. I never have and I never will."

Seghi's old pal in New York, Gabe Paul, made a pitch for Lowenstein, but offered pitcher Mike Wallace while the Indians insisted upon Rudy May. No deal. Charlie Finley tried to reacquire George Hendrick, but Seghi said no again. The Rangers attempted to get Jackie Brown back, the same Jackie Brown they dealt to the Indians with Jim Bibby in the Gaylord Perry trade of four days ago, but Seghi laughed.

Indeed, baseball people are funny.

10. "I'm Disillusioned by Some Things"

CLEVELAND, OHIO, JUNE 16—Jim Bibby debuted unimpressively for the Indians tonight, knocked out in the sixth inning of an 8–3 loss to the Baltimore Orioles. The fans booed everybody wearing a Cleveland uniform, especially Buddy Bell and Frank Robinson.

On two occasions the Indians were unable to execute what Robinson calls "little things"—sacrifice bunts—large factors in the team's lack of success. "I don't know if discouraged is the right word to describe my feelings," said Robinson. "Disappointed is better. We aren't putting anything together. We're better than we've played, I'm sure of it, but when we get good pitching, we don't get any hitting. When we're hitting, we don't get decent pitching."

JUNE 17—Is it possible the Indians are not in a slump, that they're playing as well as they're capable of playing? "No," declared Phil Seghi emphatically. "No," echoed Bob Quinn. "I can't believe guys like John Ellis, Oscar Gamble, and Charlie

Spikes are not better hitters than they've shown," said Frank Robinson.

"All you can base your judgment on is a guy's track record and what interest other clubs show in him," said Seghi. "By every yardstick our players are better than they've shown. We're in a slump, that's all."

Robinson added, "Every team goes through streaks, a couple of hot ones and a couple of cold ones, but all we've been is cold. Even if we were to admit we're not as good as we thought when spring training ended, can you honestly say we're as bad as we've looked?"

Apparently, Robinson doesn't believe the Indians are too far behind (they're last in the American League East, 10 games behind Boston) to get back into the race.

"We can still get into it," he asserted, "but we can't afford to fall much farther back. We've got 13 games the rest of this month. If we win 10 of them, we could pick up, say, six games on the leader. We'll need help from some of the clubs ahead of us, but neither Boston nor New York has had a cold streak yet."

Robinson closed the door to the clubhouse and held a meeting with the players. "I was a little stronger than I've been, though I don't think I came down hard," he said. "I don't know if I did any good or not. It sure didn't make us play any better."

Indeed not. The Indians lost to the Orioles, 5–3, their ninth defeat in 10 games.

"I don't know what else to try," confessed Robinson. "Last Thursday in Kansas City I told them all to go out and get drunk. They did, but it didn't help either."

JUNE 18—Something changed tonight. Frank Robinson lost his cool in a 13–6 loss to the Orioles. In the eighth inning, after Boog Powell's homer kayoed Baltimore starter Ross Grimsley, Robinson, from his place in the on-deck circle, began shouting insults at Grimsley in the Orioles' dugout and then to catcher Dave Duncan at home plate. Grimsley and Duncan shouted back. Robinson had yelled to Grimsley, "You're really horse----, you can't even hold a nine-run lead!" Grimsley countered, "If they'd let me stay in for one more batter, I sure as hell would've gotten you out." Then, "Why don't you give up, old man, and give a younger guy a chance?" When Duncan joined in, Robinson rushed to the plate and challenged the catcher, saying, "If you want some of me, come and get it." Duncan didn't. "Why should I break my ass against you?" he said to Robinson. "We've got a chance to win a pennant, but you guys aren't going anywhere."

Quickly umpire Bill Haller interceded as players from both teams swarmed onto the field. They milled around, but order was restored without any punches being thrown.

The near-scuffle didn't arouse the Indians, maybe the real reason for Robinson's aggressive actions. Later, all he'd say was, "We played ourselves out of the game in the first couple of innings." A factual report. When the writers persisted, Robinson commented calmly, "If I didn't think we were a better team than this, I wouldn't be here now."

Has he ever experienced a season as disappointing as this? "Yes, in 1968." That was the year the Orioles failed to repeat as pennant winners partly because Robinson hit only .268, playing despite injuries most of the season. "This is worse. Now it's an entire team. In 1968 it was just me."

How does Robinson try to cope? "Each day I go to the park I try to put things in perspective, try to figure out what I can do to get things going." Robinson said the booing by the fans didn't bother him. "The fans should be frustrated. This game ranks right up there with the worst we've played."

Angry about reports that the Indians are financially unstable and that money was a major reason for trading Gaylord Perry, Phil Seghi continues to issue the party line: "We are not in any kind of a cash bind. I traded Perry because I believe the players we got for him will help us more." Arguing that contention with this writer tonight, Seghi snapped, "I wish you could be the general manager for three or four years and see what some of our problems are like." The reply: "I do, too, Phil," making Seghi even angrier.

JUNE 19—Fritz Peterson, who asks almost daily, "Did anybody die?" found himself on the disabled list. He sliced open two fingers on his pitching hand in an accident with his riding mower; three stitches were taken in each finger. The incident is significant because it means that nobody, including Fred

Beene, need be disposed of when Jim Kern rejoins the team in four days. Peterson must remain disabled for at least 21 days, until July 11, and on July 6, Beene will complete four full seasons in the major leagues, the minimum requirement for a baseball pension.

Away from the field, Phil Seghi and Ted Bonda appeared on television to dismiss speculation that the club is in a financial bind and that Frank Robinson is under fire from the front office. "Frank is doing everything he's supposed to do," said Seghi. "He's playing a sound game and has control of the club. I'm well satisfied."

Bonda strongly insinuated that writers have lied in their reporting of the Indians' financial affairs. "Newspaper people have a reluctance to tell the truth," is the way Bonda put it.

"We are not desperate for money. We are not having trouble with banks. We are not in a cash bind. Maybe at the end of the season it will be different because we need an attendance of 1.3 million to break even, but we can handle a cash loss of $500,000. If we were as desperate as some people say, we could have sold Gaylord Perry for $500,000. It was offered and we turned it down."

When moderator Herb Kamm, an associate editor of *The Press,* asked Bonda, "Did you ever tell Phil Seghi to get $100,000 or $125,000 in a deal for Gaylord Perry?" Seghi interrupted. "The only reason we took money in the trade for Perry is because the Rangers couldn't give us enough players who, in my opinion, equaled Perry's value," said Seghi.

Then Bonda claimed, "At no time did I tell Phil to get money in the deal." Seghi's face paled before the camera turned away. Bonda added, "I still have some of the optimism I had at the beginning of the season. We are not short of funds. We are meeting payrolls and paying our bills promptly."

The latter remark, when published, raised one more question, however, in the mind of Dick Svoboda, a reporter for United Press International. Svoboda also serves as secretary-treasurer of the Cleveland Chapter of the Baseball Writers' Association. In that position Svoboda was responsible for selling tickets—at $20 apiece—for the writers' Ribs and Roasts dinner show of last January 20. Svoboda asked, "If the Indians are so well fixed financially, why haven't they paid us the $1720 they've owed us for more than six months?" When the question was relayed to Bonda, he blanched but promised payment would be forthcoming. It arrived three days later accompanied by a scathing latter from Dudley S. Blossom III, the treasurer, who accused the writers of ingratitude and called them free-loaders.

JUNE 20—Frank Robinson slumped in his chair and shook his head slowly. "I don't believe it, even when I see it. No way I'd have thought last March, last April, even in May this would be happening to us. It's amazing. It's unbelievable." The Indians lost tonight, 6–0, to Milwaukee.

"I really expected this would be the game we'd come out of it. The attitude in the dugout was good and I think the guys thought the same thing I did."

Another reason for Robinson's frustration was that John Ellis missed two take signs, swinging and making outs in consecutive key situations. Robinson fined Ellis $100 for the first offense and $200 for the second. Ellis had no rebuttal—then.

"What will I do now?" Robinson repeated a question. "I'll go home, watch television, and come up with something else to try tomorrow. I know I've got to keep a clear head, retain a sense of humor, and try anything to snap us out of this. Every day I feel like we're going to get started, but we don't. I can't understand it."

JUNE 21   Frank Robinson tried a new lineup with John Lowenstein at third base and Ed Crosby at shortstop, but the result was the same: the Indians lost to the Brewers, 11–9. Now the losing streak is five and includes 12 out of 13 games since June 8.

There were some encouraging signs. The Indians collected 13 hits, keeping the game in doubt until the final inning. Dennis Eckersley, quickly establishing himself as the best rookie pitcher in the American League, was knocked out in the seventh inning and gave up two homers, though "the kid," as Robinson calls him, struck out 10.

"I don't know if we should be encouraged or not," said Robinson. "We got some hits, a lot of them, but not the big ones. They tried to give us the game, but we wouldn't take it."

George Scott, the Brewers' first baseman, an avowed admirer of Robinson, had some advice. "Tell Robby he's got to keep a positive attitude. Tell him the Indians will come out of this, but nobody knows when except the Man upstairs, and He won't tell anybody."

JUNE 22—"Yes, before you ask, I'm telling you we'll take it," quipped Frank Robinson in a rare display of good humor following today's 3–2 victory. "I just hope we don't have to go another week before we win again." Rico Carty was hit on the left arm by a pitch from the Brewers' Ed Rodriguez with the bases loaded in the tenth inning; the Indians were forced to score a run and win. "I think if I really wanted to, I could have gotten out of the way," said Carty. "When I saw it coming close to me, I just said to myself, Oh, heck, and I closed my eyes. But I didn't think it would hurt so much."

Robinson was pleased. "Overall it was one of the best games we've played in a long time. We played them tight. We got steady pitching and the defense was good. We're still not hitting the way I think we can, but the other things were encouraging."

Today first-base coach Tom McCraw switched positions with third-base coach Dave Garcia. "I thought it might change our luck," explained Robinson. "I hope they stay where they are until September." McCraw thus became the first black man to coach third base for a major league team.

BOSTON, MASSACHUSETTS, JUNE 23—Frank Robinson should have been wearing a broad smile after an 11–3 victory over the Red Sox tonight. The Indians slugged 14 hits, including homers by Robinson and Frank Duffy, and Eric Raich won his third major league game. Instead, Robinson was grim after he kept reporters waiting for nearly 10 minutes while he met with his coaches.

When his office finally opened, Robinson was asked if he were upset. "Just say I'm disillusioned by some things," he replied curtly.

One player wanted to know, "What's wrong with Robby? There seems to be a change in his personality. Is someone in trouble? He put in a curfew, almost as punishment."

Robinson's disillusionment stemmed from a complaint by

John Ellis, whose body and ego are bruised. Ellis has a sore left elbow and a sick bat that has produced only a .221 average, five homers, and 20 RBI in 50 games.

Ellis also is angry about the $300 Robinson fined him three days ago. The two men exchanged heated words, but Robinson refused to relent. The fines will stand.

Then the catcher told Robinson he didn't think he should play again until he is 100 percent healthy. Robinson, who often "played hurt" during his career and even now is an occasional designated hitter despite a sore left shoulder, finds it difficult to comprehend Ellis' attitude.

Robinson met with the coaches to tell them of his argument with Ellis, and his decision to rest Ellis. Did he and Ellis resolve their differences? "That's up to John," snapped Robinson. Is there a rift between the player and the manager? "Not as far as I'm concerned."

Ellis tried to make light of the meeting. "It was nothing. I was telling him about my sore elbow. I'm not frustrated about my hitting. I'm hitting as well as most catchers. I know this looks like something big, but it isn't." Ellis initially denied his discussion with Robinson also concerned the $300 fine. After Robinson confirmed the subject matter, Ellis rejoined with, "I just didn't want to comment, and I still don't."

This is not the end of the matter, however. More problems will arise between the two men.

As for the curfew, one team member remarked, "I think it is being put into effect because Frank discovered a couple of guys abusing the privilege of no curfew. I think he knows now he was wrong when he said in spring training that no curfew would be necessary."

Robinson disagreed, "The curfew is not a penalty. It's not that I caught anybody out late. I can tell if a fellow is abusing not having a curfew just by looking at him in the clubhouse the next day, by watching what he does. I'm not admitting I was wrong about not having a curfew at the beginning. It's just that, well, I want to know where the guys are when they're supposed to be getting their rest."

The manager promises a heavy penalty for anybody caught breaking curfew. "It'll be between $100 and $500, depending upon how I feel and the extent of the violation."

Robinson considered the victory over the Red Sox "a fine all-around game, good offense and good pitching. If we can keep it up this way, we'll be all right." Does he have a goal for this seven-game trip? "Winning four would be good, but winning five would be exceptional." If the Indians should win the first five, then what? "Then I'll want more. I am never satisfied when it comes to winning."

JUNE 24—The Indians won a game, Frank Robinson lost a bet.

After George Hendrick's ninth-inning, three-run homer off Boston reliever Dick Drago gave the Indians a come-from-behind, 8–6 verdict, Robinson declared, "That's what I've been looking for. Even if we had lost, I would've liked what I saw. I've been waiting a long time to see somebody pick up somebody else all through the lineup, and that's what we did tonight for the first time. We continued to make mistakes and we didn't do some of the little things again. But we overcame those mistakes. All games are good to win, but this was great."

Hendrick's homer was his second of the game. When asked about them, Robinson replied, "Why don't you ask George?" Reminded that Hendrick declines to talk to reporters about his performances, Robinson said, "I'll bet you a drink he will talk. Go ahead, give him a chance." Hendrick, however, was firm. "Fellows, I have nothing to say. Describe it the way you saw it."

Later, Robinson admitted, "That disappoints me. I thought now he would talk, and I'm surprised he wouldn't. It takes something away from him as a player. If he'd talk about his game, it would add to his popularity and let the fans know him better. It'd be good for him in terms of publicity and endorsements. By not talking, George is hurting himself."

Robinson is not disappointed the way Hendrick is playing. "George's mind is free to concentrate on baseball. He is more talented than I ever was. He can hit the outside pitch as good as any hitter I've ever seen. His presence on this club has been a pleasure. He gives nobody any trouble and, look it up, he has played in every game."

Jim Kern, demoted to Oklahoma City when Gaylord Perry was traded, returned and started today's game, though the victory was credited to Tom Buskey.

The happiness of the comeback victory also got to Charlie Spikes and Rico Carty. Spikes was grinning about a second-inning homer, his second of the season. Carty enthusiastically bellowed in his booming bass voice, "Now we're looking like a ball club, a real ball club. And that's no bull ----, no sir!"

JUNE 25—Before today's game Frank Robinson talked about managing. "The toughest part is coping with all the problems that come up involving the players, their injuries, personal matters, things like that. There are times you think you have everything figured out, but all of a sudden here comes another problem. It seems a day never goes by without something."

Of his treatment by the press, Robinson said, "By and large I've found the media to be open and honest with me. Oh, there have been some incidents of unfairness, but only in the form of a few editorials and columns by guys who are not around enough to see and know what's going on." He referred specifically to a *Plain Dealer* editorial criticizing him for arguing too vehemently with umpires, and also for drawing his batting order out of a hat in Texas on June 14.

"It's easier to concentrate if I'm managing and not playing, but I don't know if I'd be a better manager if I weren't also a player. I was disappointed the way we performed until this trip. Mainly I was disappointed with our hitting and some execution of fundamentals. I cracked down a little and perhaps it has helped."

The Indians knocked the Red Sox out of first place by sweeping this series with an 8–5 victory today. "Everybody came through, especially the little guys—Duane Kuiper, Frank Duffy, and Alan Ashby," commented Robinson. "We played well in the field, too. This is the type of team play I expected but hadn't seen much until now."

The little guys' contributions: Duffy, 3 for 3; Kuiper, a key single and a spectacular catch; and Ashby, a home run (he's catching while John Ellis is on the bench).

The victory delighted Roric Harrison. It was his first in a Cleveland uniform. After his previous three starts, all nonvictories, Harrison insisted, "I can pitch better than that." After today's game he explained, "that's what I meant. I finally threw the ball like I knew I could. I had some fun again.

"The most important thing is that we are beginning to be-lieve in ourselves. Losing 12 out of 13 cost us our confidence. Now we've got it back and it might be all we need."

MILWAUKEE, WISCONSIN, JUNE 26—After the Indians beat the Milwaukee Brewers, 9–2, Frank Robinson had a message for Cleveland fans. "Tell 'em," he chortled, "we're alive and breathing and we're a long way from dead, even though a lot of people have buried us. I don't look at how many games we're behind the first-place team [they're 10 behind New York], I only look at the team that's directly ahead of us. The thing we've got to do is catch one at a time, the team that's directly ahead of us, and when we catch that one, then we've got to go out and catch the next one."

Four players in the Indians' starting lineup—Dennis Eckers-ley, Rick Manning, Duane Kuiper, and Alan Ashby, none of whom figured prominently in the team's plans as recently as 2½ months ago—were singled out for praise by Robinson, par-ticularly Manning and Eckersley, whose record climbed to 5-1. "I hate to keep repeating myself," said Robinson, "but Man-ning has such great baseball instincts it's hard to believe. He's the kind of a kid you just let go, just let play."

Eckersley, however, was unhappy about being taken out of the game after he'd blanked the Brewers on five hits through the first eight innings. Reliever Jackie Brown pitched the ninth and yielded a two-run homer.

"I took Eckersley out when I did because he'd made 122 pitches and that's about all I ever want him to throw," said the manager. "He's got a long career ahead of him and I'm not go-ing to do anything to endanger it. He wanted to stay in the game today and I like that. But the important thing is to protect his longevity. I'm not going to rush him to get a shutout."

Eckersley wasn't placated. "Sure, I wanted to finish the game. I had them easy. I wanted the shutout. What's going to happen next winter at contract time when the general manager says to me, 'Well, you didn't pitch many complete games.' I don't want to get screwed again like I did last winter. I was dumb before, but not anymore."

Eckersley shook his head. "This game is unreal. My fast ball wasn't sharp after the first couple of innings, and my slider was spotty. When I faced the Brewers six days ago, I had great stuff and they killed me. Today I didn't have good stuff and I killed them. This game is unreal, I'm telling you."

JUNE 27—Two weeks and three starts since coming from the Texas Rangers, Jim Bibby won his first game for Cleveland. He scattered five hits to beat the Brewers, 6–1. It was the Indians' sixth straight victory. Frank Robinson is getting greedy. "Now we're shooting for a sweep of this trip, a grand slam. Why not?"

Robinson was being interviewed by reporters when he overheard from the Kangaroo Court in the main clubhouse some testimony that mentioned "last year." Since becoming manager of the Indians Robinson has made an effort to avoid any reference to the 1974 season, emphasizing, "What happened last year is done and gone. Forget it! Don't even think about it!" Now, quickly, he shouted to the players, "That's an automatic fine! You know we don't talk about 'last year.'" Quickly the offender was fined one dollar and Robinson was satisfied.

Robinson's smile was immediately replaced by a frown when he returned to the writers. He was asked about the umpiring competency of Jerry Neudecker, Art Frantz, Jim McKean, and Nick Bremigan, who are working this series. Frantz had ejected Alan Ashby in the seventh inning, so John Ellis played for the first time in a week. "That crew is a bad one. You know Ashby never swears, but Frantz had him so worked up, Alan couldn't help himself. He called Frantz a name, not a bad one, but it's the one umpires resent the most. Ashby called Frantz horse----, and he's right." Ashby was too embarrassed to comment. When Ellis went into the game, he said to Frantz, "Art, you've got to be wrong when Ashby says something like that." Even Frantz had to chuckle.

JUNE 28—All that good pitching the Indians had been getting ended tonight and so did their winning streak in a 10–6 loss to the Brewers. To complicate matters, it was disclosed that Jim Kern has a problem with his shoulder that will prevent him from pitching tomorrow.

Frank Robinson was undismayed. "I wish we had won, of course, but there were some encouraging signs. We kept battling back, which is good. I'm not unhappy. You didn't really think we'd never lose again, did you?"

A splendid catch by George Hendrick deprived Sixto Lezcano of a grand slam homer but injured the center fielder's shoulder. George hooked his arm over the top of the fence in leaping for the ball and wrenched his shoulder when he fell to the ground.

Usually unwilling to talk, Hendrick discussed the catch. "I was afraid I broke my arm. Everything was numb from my shoulder to my hand. I thought to myself, Oh, no, not now! But I was lucky. My shoulder and arm are sore but not real bad. I can play."

JUNE 29—Frank Robinson accepted today's 4–3 defeat by the Brewers philosophically. "Losing the last two games after starting the trip so well leaves a bitter taste in my mouth, but I'm still encouraged. I still believe we're going in the right direction. We just have to keep plugging away, one step at a time. I told you at the beginning of this trip I'd consider a 5-2 record exceptional, and I do."

The Indians are now in fifth place with a 30-41 record, 10½ games behind Boston, 10 behind New York, eight behind Milwaukee, three behind Baltimore, and 2½ ahead of Detroit. When the Indians left Cleveland a week ago, they were in last place, 12½ games behind the Red Sox, so progress has been made.

Don Hood's splendid pitching performance was wasted as two errors gave the Brewers three unearned runs, enough for them to win. "I just hope the man [Robinson] doesn't forget about me," said Hood. "I go crazy in the bullpen. If they're not going to use me, I hope they'll get rid of me."

Robinson called Hood's performance "a good effort, he deserved something better," and didn't blame the loss on the errors. Instead, he was critical of John Lowenstein, who surprised everybody, especially Robinson, by bunting in the seventh inning when the Indians trailed, 3–2, and had runners on first and third with nobody out. Lowenstein's bunt scored Frank Duffy from third, but the next two batters made outs. The Indians failed to score again, and the Brewers got the winning run in the ninth.

"That was a foolish thing for Lowenstein to do," said Robinson. "He bunted on his own. I would have told him not to do it. I've learned it's better not to let some guys think too much. In a situation like that, Lowenstein had to swing away. There were so many better ways to score the man from third."

Lowenstein justified his bunt as an "element of surprise." "I don't like surprises like that," grumbled Robinson.

Larry Doby, formerly one of the Indians' all-time great players, was in Milwaukee. Doby was a coach for the Indians last year and was expected to become major league baseball's first black manager, until Robinson was acquired. By then, Doby had fallen from favor. Doby said he is no longer bitter toward the Cleveland organization but has no respect for Phil Seghi. "Seghi does not deal with men as men, he deals with men as kids. He's a liar, too, and if I ever see him again, I'll tell him to his face."

Early in 1974, Ted Bonda led Doby to believe he would replace Aspromonte. "He told me in May, 'You're getting close,'" said Doby. But by September, with Robinson aboard, Doby knew he would not become manager.

"I have nothing against Frank Robinson," said Doby. "He should do a good job because this is a good team, if Seghi doesn't screw it up. I learned a lot last year in Cleveland. The most important thing I learned was that not all baseball people are straight shooters. I didn't know how to cope because I always had dealt with honest men. Some people told me I didn't get the job with the Indians because I don't 'cooperate' enough. If cooperate means let the man upstairs [general manager] tell you what to do on the field, that's right."

Before returning to his job as minor league batting coach for the Montreal Expos, Doby visited with George Hendrick, Charlie Spikes, and Oscar Gamble, but not Robinson. "I expected Larry to come up and say hello, but he didn't. I didn't go to him because I didn't think it was my place to do so. He went out of his way to talk to the other guys, but not me." Did that bother Robinson? "I never thought about it until you asked," he replied.

11. *"Punch a Hole in Your Mask!"*

CLEVELAND, OHIO, JUNE 30—It was a night for standing ovations, generosity by the visitors, and progress by the Indians. They opened a nine-game home stand against the Detroit Tigers, sweeping a doubleheader, 4–1 and 3–2.

"Now we're moving in the right direction; we're going to be okay," said Frank Robinson in the Indians' happy clubhouse. "I realize we're still 9½ games out of first place and there are four teams ahead of us, but there's time. These two games were very important. We were coming off two straight losses."

Robinson was delighted with Rick Manning and Duane Kuiper, as were 26,114 fans who roared their approval.

"The fans give me the greatest feeling of my life," said Manning, who drove in the tying and winning runs in the nightcap. "They make me want to play the hell out of myself for them. I don't know if they can feel me, but I sure can feel them. They make me want to do crazy things, though I realize I've got to keep my poise."

Kuiper got three hits in the first game and two in the second.

There is no doubt he will remain the Indians' second baseman when Jack Brohamer comes off the disabled list. "Sometimes I'm not sure all this is happening to me," said Kuiper. "But if I'm only dreaming, I don't ever want to wake up."

Robinson wasn't completely happy. As he sat in his office two hours before game time, he noticed a player report late. The manager shook his head and said quietly, "You know, one thing I'm learning is that the more you give these guys, the more they want and will try to take."

Tom McCraw was taken off the roster to make room for Bill Sudakis, a journeyman infielder-outfielder-catcher released a week ago by the California Angels. "Phil [Seghi] and I have been looking for a third catcher for some time," admitted Robinson, "but there were no clubs that would give us the kind of guy we felt we needed, and I didn't want to trade anyone. We really wanted a guy who could do more than catch. When Sudakis was released, he was just what we needed."

Were Robinson and Seghi looking for a third catcher because of problems with John Ellis? "There is no rift between us, as some of you guys are reporting," insisted Robinson. "John was unhappy about the money I fined him, but there are no hard feelings on my part. I don't think there are on John's part either."

McCraw now will be strictly the Indians' first-base coach; he cannot be reactivated as a player before next spring. Although he does not want to remain retired, McCraw accepted the decision like the good team man he is. McCraw will someday make an excellent manager.

JULY 1—"The best thing to do is file it and forget it," somebody suggested to Frank Robinson after a lackluster, 6–2, loss to Mickey Lolich and the Tigers. "Yeah," he agreed, "and that's probably what [Lee] MacPhail will do with our protest, too."

Robinson lodged a protest in the seventh inning after Aurelio Rodriguez bunted. In John Ellis' rush to get to the ball, he collided with Rodriguez and Rodriguez was safe at first base. A few minutes later, Buddy Bell committed an error, the Tigers scored to break a 2–2 tie, and Lolich made it stand up. The fans booed. Robinson complained bitterly to umpire Jim Evans that Rodriguez interferred with Ellis, but to no avail.

"In my judgment it was a natural collision," said Evans. "There was contact, but in my judgment Ellis initiated it." Snorted Robinson, "There it is again, 'in my judgment.' That ends every argument."

JULY 2—"Beautiful, beautiful," intoned Frank Robinson, after the Indians rallied in the ninth inning to beat the New York Yankees, 3–2. "Those kids make things happen with their speed and baseball instincts." He was speaking of Rick Manning and Duane Kuiper, both of whom played key roles, giving rise to great optimism inside the Wigwam.

Dave LaRoche trotted in from the bullpen in the seventh inning to quell a rally against Dennis Eckersley. Manning got three hits; two were instrumental in the Indians' first two runs in the third and fifth innings. Kuiper got three hits, including a single in the ninth that launched the winning uprising with two out. Ed Crosby followed with a single, and when Kuiper boldly continued to third, outfielder Bobby Bonds threw wildly to that base, allowing the rookie to come home and climax the comeback.

"The kids [Manning, Kuiper, Eckersley, Raich] have turned it around for us," continued Robinson. "I believe we can get back to respectability by the All-Star Game break. We can get to within five or six games of first place by then, and we don't need a long winning streak to do it."

JULY 3—Frank Robinson learned from orthopedic specialist Dr. Earl Brightman, one of the Indians' team physicians, that the ache in his shoulder is caused by a torn tendon. Only an operation will correct the problem, and surgery will require three to five months' recuperation and rehabilitation. "I'm certainly not going to have the operation now, and I probably won't next winter," said the manager. "For now, I'm going to do what I can the way it is." The injury dates to 1970, when Frank played in Baltimore, and has been aggravated many times since then, including last May in Boston when he dived back to first base on a pick-off attempt.

"It aches all the time," said Robinson. "It throbs like a toothache. There are nights it keeps me awake, especially if I roll over and try to sleep on my left side. It really hurts when I

swing a bat and miss." Is Robinson depressed by Dr. Brightman's report? "It's a disappointment, but I'm kind of relieved.
Now at least I know how to cope with it, and I know that cortisone won't do any good. I thought the cortisone helped, but Dr.
Brightman told me it was only because they gave me novocaine
with it, which dulled the pain for a while."

Don Hood was excellent in the 3–2 victory over the Yankees,
allowing only two hits—both homers by Bobby Bonds—until
he tired with one out in the ninth. Dave LaRoche, quickly becoming the best relief pitcher in the American League, came in
to retire the last two batters.

Said Robinson, "It's great to win like this. The pitching has
been excellent, the defense good, and the hitting timely. It's
the way you've got to do it. One guy tonight, another guy tomorrow night. Now we have to follow through, keep it going."

JULY 4—Pennant fever raged in the Cleveland Stadium as
36,124 screaming fans endorsed the Indians' 3–2 success over
the Boston Red Sox. The Indians are now only seven games out
of first place. The margin was Oscar Gamble's third homer of
the season and second in two days, a two-run shot off Luis Ti-
ant in the seventh inning. Eric Raich received credit for the triumph.

"If you're not going to hit in bunches, you've got to hit when
it counts, and Oscar did again," grinned Frank Robinson.

Robinson's face had shown only anger earlier. In the sixth
inning a fight between Buddy Bell and Boston's Bernie Carbo
erupted, threatening to become a full-scale brawl involving all
50 players and the coaches and managers. Carbo tripled and
barged into third base standing up, an instant before Bell
caught Gamble's throw. In grasping for the ball, Bell lunged
into Carbo. Carbo pushed back. Quickly the players were bear
hugging and Don Zimmer, Red Sox third-base coach, was
knocked down in the ensuing wrestling match. "I jumped into
it instinctively, just to break them up," Zimmer said later. "All
I could think to do was protect my head, but I wasn't really
hurt." Zimmer was concerned about his head because he has a
metal plate on the left side, the result of a severe beaning that
ended his playing career several years ago.

The players' fear for Zimmer's safety ended the fight. "Zimmer got smothered. He was in a daze, out of breath, almost un-conscious," said Robinson.

Once the fight ended, Robinson quarreled with umpire Bill Haller. "I thought he should have ejected Carbo because he's the one who started the fight," complained Robinson. Haller disagreed. "Both teams are involved in a pennant race and I didn't want to hurt either one of them," said Haller.

On another occasion, Robinson found fault with Ron Lucia-no, the umpire he's called a "showboat" because of his flam-boyant calls. "It's no longer amusing. Luciano is getting to be a bad umpire. He has no pride, that's obvious."

More and more Robinson is outspoken in his criticism of umpires, contrary to his spring training vow not to be an um-pire-baiter. Then he said, "I don't want my team to be known as a bunch of crybabies because it will come back to haunt us. Don't let umpires tell you they don't talk to each other about teams and players. They do. It gets around the league and pret-ty soon you don't get the close calls." Umpire-baiting is one of the few faults Robinson found with Earl Weaver.

Robinson's enthusiasm for his team continues to grow. "I can't say enough about our pitching, and we keep getting the hits when we need them, which is great. It was a tremendous effort by Raich; he bowed his neck every time he got into a tough situation and kept us in the game [saved by Dave LaRoche]."

Raich praised John Ellis, who is catching regularly again—but not for long. "Ellis handled me super. He always seems to fall for the right thing. Give him a lot of credit," said Raich.

Ellis, still depressed, shrugged off the remarks. "Yeah, that's nice," he said without emotion.

JULY 5—When Buddy Bell was introduced in the Indians' starting lineup today, 22,361 fans in the Stadium cheered rath-er than booed as they have done lately. "I guess it takes a fight to get the fans on your side," he said half seriously. "I'd rather do something else to win them over." Then he did. Bell blasted two home runs, one with the bases loaded, and a double. The Indians fed the fans' pennant fever with their fourth straight victory, 12–2, over the Red Sox, credited to Roric Harrison, his third in a row.

The victory, the Indians' fourth straight and thirteenth in the last 16 games, wasn't the only news today. Frank Robinson reported he was placing himself on the 15-day disabled list and Jack Brohamer, who injured his left hip on May 25, was being activated. "My shoulder is no worse, but it's no better either. I could play if I had to, but I want Brohamer on the eligibility list." Does it mean the end of Robinson's career as a player? "I hope not," he said.

Brohamer, who has lost his regular job to Duane Kuiper, was happy to be reinstated, but reserved. "Sitting around is the worst part of this game. There's no way I could win back my job while I'm on the disabled list." How does he *really* feel? "Ask me next week in Anaheim." He resents Phil Seghi's keeping him on inactive status.

With the Indians only six games behind the Red Sox and Milwaukee Brewers, who are tied for first place, Robinson said, "These are the real Indians. The whole team seems to be reborn. I see four teams going right down to the wire." The Indians are one of them.

Boston manager Darrell Johnson wasn't sure; the anxiety of two straight defeats has begun to show. Johnson was asked if he watches the scores of other games involving the contenders. "No, just the game we're playing," he said. But when the reporters started to leave, he asked, "You didn't hear the finals on the other games, did you?"

JULY 6—It could have been a disaster in front of the largest crowd in the major leagues this season—59,161 fans. Instead, the Indians split a doubleheader with the Red Sox. The Tribe lost the opener, 5–3, as Bill Lee beat Jim Bibby, but battled back from a five-run deficit to win the wild nightcap, 11–10.

"As it turned out, it was a good day and a great home stand," said Robinson after nearly seven hours of activity. "It was important for us to win the second game. If we had lost, everything we've done this week would have been lost, too. This team has heart. It could have quit after the Red Sox took a 5–0 lead in the second game. Before, when we were losing, we'd fight back, but it seemed the best we would do was tie, not get the winning run across.

"This is the highest point for me since I took over the club.

I'm not concerned about getting out of fifth place. What I'd like to see is for us to be only three or four games behind the leader by the All-Star break."

Fred Beene, the winner in relief, completed his fourth full season in the major leagues today, the minimum time needed to qualify for a pension at 45. "I never thought I'd get it. I've had to do an awful lot of clawing and scratching," he said. The 32-year-old reliever arrived in the big leagues with Baltimore in 1968 but has been up and down ever since.

Despite Robinson's pleasure with winning for the thirteenth time in 17 games, he grumbled about arguments with umpires Armando Rodriguez and Bill Haller. The latter quarrel particularly upset Robinson.

"I don't remember who was batting, but once he checked his swing and Haller signaled strike. He did it without being asked by the plate umpire. So I yelled to him, 'Let the plate ump make the decision, and if he needs help, he'll ask you.' Haller yelled back, 'What ------- difference does it make?' I told him, 'It makes a lot of ------- difference.' Then he got mad. He came over to the dugout and asked me, 'What did you say?' I said, 'I said the same thing you said to me.' He said, 'Oh, I thought you called me a ---- ------.' I said to him, 'Well, are you?' He just gave me a dirty look."

Robinson said something else to Haller that didn't get an answer either. He pointed to his left wrist, actually the *color* of the skin, and asked Haller, "'Does this bother you?' Haller knew what I meant." It was further manifestation of Robinson's growing antagonism toward umpires.

OAKLAND, CALIFORNIA, JULY 7—Before tonight's game Jack Brohamer voiced his complaints against Phil Seghi. He accused Seghi of double-talk, if not outright lying, and revealed he has asked the Indians to trade him to another organization. "For 3½ years in Cleveland I stayed in line. I said things that weren't always completely true because that's what the organization, what Seghi, wanted me to say. But I'm finished lying. It's time for me to think about me and my family. I had to force Seghi to take me off the disabled list. I've been ready to play for more than a week, but it was more convenient for the organization to use me as an insurance policy. If the Indians hadn't activated me, I would've gone to Marvin Miller and filed a grievance. I'm tired of Seghi breaking his promises. He always backed off by saying, 'Well, things have a way of changing.' Things had a way of changing with me, too, and I'm not lying for Seghi anymore. I know other organizations are not like this one, and I know all general managers are not double-talkers. I have no resentment toward Robinson, or toward Duane Kuiper. I realize Frank has got to keep Kuiper in the lineup. Kuiper did what I would have tried to do if the situation were reversed. But whatever respect I felt for Seghi is gone."

Seghi later called Robinson about Brohamer's outburst. Was he angry? "Yeah," reported Robinson. "The thing he was maddest about was that Jack gave me some good ink and blamed him for everything."

During the game that followed, controversy erupted in the second inning when Jim Perry, pitching for the A's, struck out George Hendrick. "He's throwing spitballs, greasers just like his brother Gaylord," charged Robinson. "He'll do anything to beat you," added the manager, who has that reputation himself. "I didn't see any illegal pitches," countered umpire Larry Barnett.

The next inning, after the Oakland A's took a 4–0 lead, Robinson grew angrier. Dennis Eckersley was pitching to Reggie Jackson and fired a pitch "right down the pipe," according to the outspoken rookie. When Barnett called it ball three instead of strike three, Eckersley threw up his arms in dismay, John Ellis muttered a complaint, and Robinson shouted from the dugout, "Why don't you punch a hole in your mask?"

Barnett whirled toward the Cleveland dugout and quickly ejected Robinson. It was Robinson's third ejection this season. He finally left the field, but only after a violent argument.

"I've heard that remark before, but I don't hear it for long," said Barnett. "Robinson has the misconception that he can say anything he wants from the dugout. After he asked me to punch a hole in my mask, I asked him to vacate the premises. It was a gentleman's ejection," chuckled Barnett. The other members of the umpiring crew—Marty Springstead, Don Denkinger, and Hank Morgenweck—also chuckled.

Robinson found nothing funny. "They are out there hurting my team, and they think it's all a joke. When you're incompetent, you'll do anything to cover up. There's no way he'd run any other manager for saying the same thing." It was a serious charge with doubtful validity.

Robinson was asked if he meant what he said. "What do you think I said?" he replied. Did he mean Barnett ejected him because he is *black*, that he would not have ejected a white manager for making the same remark?

Robinson replied without equivocation, "Yes, that's right." He elaborated, accusing "certain" umpires of prejudice against the Indians.

"I am not saying I think they're prejudiced because I am black," he stressed. "I am saying they are so aware of my situation [as baseball's first black manager], they are determined to keep me in my place, not let me get away with anything." Some players agreed but most did not. All declined to comment publicly.

"I've kept quiet long enough. Certain umpires are getting back at me through my club. Every close call goes against us, and I think they are taking out on the club the way they feel about me. I think they don't like me because of the type of competitor I am. When I see something wrong, I let them know, and they don't like to be reminded of those things. They [American League officials] know who they are. If they want me to name names, I will. I don't want them bending over backwards for me. All I want is to be treated like any other manager."

Reminded that he is sure to be reprimanded by Lee Mac-Phail, Robinson shrugged, "Let them do something to me, and not to my team. Sure, this will get me into trouble, but things can't get any worse."

When apprised of Robinson's charges, Barnett expressed amazement. "Robinson's remarks are totally ridiculous. I feel sorry for him because he feels the way he does. He makes me sound like a racist, and I'm not. If he means what he says, we're in a helluva state."

The Indians lost to the Oakland A's, 7–3.

JULY 8—"I don't know what has happened, why we suddenly have gone so flat," said Frank Robinson. The Indians lost to the A's, 15–5, but Robinson wasn't uncertain about the um-

Nancy Engebretson

Frank Robinson and the 1975 Cleveland coaching staff. Left to right: Harvey Haddix, Jeff Torborg, Robinson, Dave Garcia, Tom McCraw.

Russ Schneider, Jr.

Frank Robinson vs. umpire Bill Deegan.

pires. In the second inning, he strolled out of the dugout and
spoke briefly with Hank Morgenweck. "I talked to him about
the weather," Robinson reported. "I complained about the way
Morgenweck was *predicting* the weather."

Morgenweck's version: "Robinson came out and said to me,
'If you guys have something against me, don't take it out on my
players.' I told him nobody has anything against him."

A few moments after Robinson returned to the dugout, Marty Springstead, chief of the umpiring crew, began shouting at
the manager. "I told him to quit his damned begging," related
Springstead. "If anything is close, he's yelling and never stops.
You'd think he was at a damned revival meeting. Hell, we're
not perfect, but neither is he. I told him, 'As crew chief, I don't
want you yelling at my umpires.' That's what I said to him."

Countered Robinson, "I don't beg anybody, and I never
have. Springstead just stuck his nose where it doesn't belong.
It's all right for them to yell at me, but not for me to yell at
them."

Later, Robinson resumed criticizing the umpires, rating
them in ability. Reading from the roster, Robinson named 10 as
"creditable." "Nestor Chylak is okay; Larry Barnett, Bill Deegan, Don Denkinger, Jim Evans, Richard Garcia, and Bill Kunkel are not bad; Jim McKean and Dave Phillips are good but
they're in with bad crews; and Marty Springstead can be good
but his temper gets the best of him."

That left 14 umpires less than creditable in Robinson's un-
spoken opinion. They are: Merle Anthony, Nick Bremigan, Joe
Brinkman, Terry Cooney, Lou DiMuro, Art Frantz, Russ
Goetz, Bill Haller, Ron Luciano, George Maloney, Larry
McCoy, Hank Morgenweck, Jerry Neudecker, and Armando
Rodriguez. Robinson said he hadn't seen enough of Cooney (a
rookie) to be sure about him. "There are some who could be
good but are in the category of being around for a while and
saying to themselves, 'Oh, the hell with it.' There are others
who are just not good umpires, period. This is my opinion, and
I'm entitled to it. I don't care if they don't like it. If they want
to come out and say I'm a lousy manager, that's their opinion,
and they're entitled to it, too," snapped Robinson.

Is Robinson worried that the umpires might be even more
difficult to work with, or that Lee MacPhail will take punitive

action against him? "I don't see how the umpires could get any worse than they have been. It wouldn't surprise me if Mac-Phail comes down on me, but I don't care. What I said had to be said, I believe."

MacPhail promised he would "come down" on Robinson. "I was surprised and disappointed at Robinson's statement concerning American League umpires, implying the possibility of bias. It was irresponsible, unfair, and, of course, totally incorrect. I plan to discuss this matter with Frank privately."

Phil Seghi rushed to support his manager. "Frank is on the field so he knows the full extent of it. From my box during the last series in Cleveland, I saw four half-swing decisions go against us. I saw two terrible calls on the bases go against us. Dennis Eckersley lost five perfect strikes at the knees. We have rookie pitchers and often they don't get the breaks a veteran does. I've seen umpires who should be good umpires. Instead I see complacency setting in. They have the idea they can do nothing wrong. Besides, why can't umpires be criticized? Managers and general managers are," said Seghi.

When asked about the racial aspects of Robinson's complaint, Seghi hedged. "I think it's more that the umpires don't understand Frank's personality. He was a fighter as a player, and he's a fighter as a manager. We have coaches who do not protest often, so Frank has to do it more than most managers. The umpires misinterpret Frank. They seem to think he is belligerent. I don't think they are overreacting because of the color of his skin, but they are listening and looking into the dugout, just waiting, and I think overall the calls are going against us."

JULY 9—Frank Robinson forgot his criticism of umpires and became angry with the Indians, who lost for the third straight day in Oakland to former teammate Dick Bosman, 3–1. "Bosman wasn't that good," complained Robinson. "We gave the A's two runs and they shouldn't have had any." The Indians scored once in the ninth; the game ended with the tying runs on second and third as Bill Sudakis took three pitches, all called strikes. "We shouldn't have had to wait until the ninth to lose it. We gave them six outs in the first inning. First, Sudakis dropped a pitchout when the runner should have been thrown out at second. Then Buddy Bell lost the pop-up in the sun. The fly ball should have been caught."

Whose ball was it? "It was nobody's fault," the manager snapped. Not whose fault was it, whose ball was it? "It's anybody's ball. I didn't like the way nobody went after it."

Later, Robinson apologized. "I didn't mean to get mad at you," he said. "It's just that I was mad at myself because we lost."

ANAHEIM, CALIFORNIA, JULY 10—Buddy Bell made what he called "the biggest decision of my baseball career" and withdrew from the All-Star team because "I don't deserve to be on it. For two weeks now, this has been eating my insides." On the final day of the voting, Bell was overtaken by Graig Nettles of the New York Yankees and Sal Bando of the Oakland A's. Alvin Dark, who'll manage the American League, planned to choose Bell as an alternate.

Bell convinced his father, a member of several past All-Star teams, he was doing the right thing. "He kept insisting I was wrong until I said to him, 'Dad, the way I feel really is your fault. Yours and Mom's. You brought me up to feel the way I do.' After I told him that, he couldn't argue anymore."

George Hendrick was selected in Bell's place, the Indians' only representative. Hendrick belongs on the team: he has played in 82 of the Indians' 83 games this season, more than anybody else, and is hitting .281 with 16 homers and 52 runs batted in.

JULY 11—The Indians broke a three-game losing streak tonight with a 5–3 victory over the California Angels, but Frank Robinson was still smarting from the defeats in Oakland. The manager spoke to the players in a five-minute meeting after the game. "We are just not communicating on the field, and I won't have it. I didn't say anything in Oakland because, after a loss, you might say some things you will regret later. I am unhappy the way we are playing. It's not the attitude, it's mainly a lack of communication, one guy letting another know what he's going to do. It happened again tonight, and it cost us three runs because nobody covered first base on a grounder. A word yelled here and there can prevent that sort of thing. I just told them what I want and walked off. We can't go on giving three or four runs, or four or five outs an inning."

Boog Powell hit his fifteenth homer, and Rick Manning's first major league homer in the seventh inning broke a 3–3 tie. Manning hit a line drive to left that either outfielder Dave Collins or Mickey Rivers should have caught but didn't. They collided and the ball went to the fence while Manning scampered around the bases.

"I knew it was gone right after the collision, and I saw the ball rolling toward the fence," chortled Manning, acting the part of a powerful home run hitter while his teammates laughed.

JULY 12—Whatever the reason, Anaheim has a good influence on the Indians. They won today as Dennis Eckersley beat Nolan Ryan, 9–1, and Oscar Gamble whacked his fourth homer in the last 10 games.

"The thing I like so much about the kid [Eckersley] is that even when he doesn't have good stuff, as he didn't tonight, he's still around the plate," said Frank Robinson.

"I haven't had my good slider for the last three games," said Eckersley. "If I'd had my slider, I wouldn't have had any trouble. What got me by was that I had good defense."

By Eckersley's own admission, he also got a break from umpire Jim Evans. "I couldn't believe a call he gave me in the first inning." It came with the bases loaded, two out and Dave Chalk at bat. Eckersley's first three pitches were balls. "Then I threw one low and outside, and he called it a strike. I couldn't believe it! It should have been ball four." After another strike, this one legitimate, Chalk popped out. Eckersley went on to blank the Angels until the eighth, when the Indians were coasting on a 5–0 lead.

In the midst of his first-inning troubles, Eckersley was visited by Harvey Haddix. What did Haddix say? "I don't know," replied the pitcher. "I never pay any attention. I just took a breather, and then the umpire gave me that call."

JULY 13—Rick Manning went 0 for 5 and grounded into two double plays. However, Rick was one of the Indians' heroes in an 8–7 victory over the Angels on the eve of the All-Star Game break that traditionally signals the halfway point in the season.

In winning their thirteenth game in a row in Anaheim Stadium, the Indians tied an American League record for consecutive victories on an opposing team's field.

Manning, though hitless, contributed two sensational catches, saving at least three runs and making it possible for Jim Bibby to win in relief of Don Hood. Dave LaRoche came out of the bullpen to earn another save, and his acquisition is becoming one of Phil Seghi's best deals.

Frank Robinson's praise was primarily for Manning and Duane Kuiper. "They have given us a new dimension. They put pressure on the defense, and their aggressiveness has rubbed off on the other guys. It's very unusual to have two young kids influence a club like this."

Then Robinson looked at the overall situation. The Indians are in fifth place, 9½ games behind the division-leading Boston Red Sox, five behind the Milwaukee Brewers and New York Yankees, 1½ behind the Baltimore Orioles, and one ahead of the Detroit Tigers. The Indians' record is 40-46, as close to .500 as they've been since June 18, when they had won 23 and lost 28, but then were fifth, only 6½ games behind Boston.

"The only thing that's disappointing is that it took us two weeks to make up 3½ games, and we lost them in four days when the A's beat us three straight," said the manager. "But I think we're in the right groove again, and if we can play the rest of the season the way we have the last three weeks, we'll be okay." The Indians have won 15 of 22 games since June 22.

"Yes, I think we can keep up the pace. I think we can do even better, and I'm sure the Red Sox will come back to the pack. We can go as far as we want if we keep this tough, hustling attitude. We can fight and claw back into contention before the first of September. Our record could be better with just a few little things having gone differently. A month ago I'd have settled for what we've got."

At the halfway point, what have the Indians accomplished?

With an almost completely revamped staff, the pitching is satisfactory. Only one man remains who was considered a starter when the season began—Don Hood. In place of Gaylord and Jim Perry and Dick Bosman are Jim Bibby, Eric Raich, Roric Harrison, and Dennis Eckersley. Eckersley, the

big winner with a 6-2 record, was promoted from the bullpen.
Raich, recalled from the minors on May 20, is 5-3. Harrison,
who came from the Atlanta Braves on June 7, is 4-2. Bibby, acquired in the June 13 trade with Texas for Gaylord Perry, is
2-3. Hood is 2-5. Fritz Peterson, 4-7, remains on the disabled
list, and Jim Kern, 1-2, has been sidelined with first elbow and
then shoulder troubles. Dave LaRoche, who began the season
as a spot reliever, has joined Tom Buskey as a bullpen stopper.
Fred Beene and Jackie Brown, two long relievers, are sweating
out their major league futures.

Though inexperienced, the pitching shows signs of develop-
ing into an excellent staff. How soon it develops could well de-
termine how soon the Indians become a bona fide contender
for the division championship.

The offense, expected to be productive, has been disappointing until recently. Only Boog Powell (.284, 15 homers, 47 RBI)
and George Hendrick (.282, 16, 53) have delivered with the expected consistency. Kuiper and Manning, not deemed ready
for the big leagues when the season began, also are hitting well
(.335 and .275, respectively). Oscar Gamble (.227, 5, 17) is beginning to show signs of living up to expectations, but greatly
disappointing have been Charlie Spikes (.196, 4, 13), John Ellis, (.218, 5, 24), Buddy Bell (.238, 8, 33), and Frank Duffy
(.226, 1, 27).

Robinson the player has delivered many key hits but has
been unable to play often because of injuries. Currently disabled, he has a .233 average, eight homers, and 27 RBI. Despite
those subpar (for him) figures, Robinson's return to active duty
is vital to continuing success.

Robinson the manager has been embroiled in one controversy after another and ejected from three games, all testifying to
his fierce competitive spirit. There was the squabble with Gaylord Perry, the pushing incident with umpire Jerry Neudecker,
the Angels' complaint that Robinson actively managed the Indians by telephone during his suspension, his determination to
"do something" that led to the trading of Gaylord Perry, his argument and resulting disillusionment with John Ellis, and
most recently his criticism of American League umpires, challenging their integrity and charging them with discrimination.

Otherwise, Robinson has established himself as a shrewd

tactician, capable of matching moves with the best. By and large, Robinson's relationship with the players has been good. More than anything, he has demonstrated remarkable patience in the face of adversity, a trait essential in handling a young team. He has restrained himself when other managers, even those considerably more experienced, would have exploded in anger and frustration. In fact, his extreme patience has been interpreted by some as a fault.

Many people, including Robinson himself, anticipated that his biggest problem would be dealing with the media, but nothing could be further from reality, even during the trying early days of the season. On the contrary, Robinson now says the toughest aspect of managing is dealing with the players and their personal problems.

If there is fault to be found, it might be that Robinson is sometimes too outspoken and that he perhaps lacks the ability to motivate certain players. This is not unusual. Many superstars-turned-managers have experienced the same problem, primarily because they never required outside motivation themselves and thus are unaware of the need, or unable to project that kind of leadership.

There have been times of embarrassment, particularly the night the Minnesota Twins batted out of turn undetected by Robinson, in an 11–10 loss. Robinson also had to admit he was wrong at least once: on June 14 when he invoked a curfew on the road after insisting one wouldn't be necessary.

Essentially, however, Frank Robinson has been a sound manager, better perhaps than the Indians' fifth-place standing reflects. How sound will be determined in the second half of the season.

12. "Ellis Can't Play for Me and I Don't Want Him To"

CLEVELAND, OHIO, JULY 17—"It was great. It was like three weeks and the best part was that nobody recognized me," said Frank Robinson after returning from a three-day vacation with his family at Niagara Falls. When the Indians resumed the season with a 6–3 loss to the Oakland A's, Robinson's smile disappeared.

"I don't know what it is, but we always play at our worst against Oakland," he grumbled. "We make mistakes and the A's always capitalize. Our pitchers can't handle their hitters, and our hitters can't handle their pitchers." Robinson set a goal for this six-game home stand. "I'd like to pick up at least two games on Boston, which I don't think is asking for too much."

JULY 18—Jim Kern was informed of his demotion again to Oklahoma City to permit Fritz Peterson to return from the disabled list. Kern's initial inclination was to go home, but he finally consented to go back to the minor leagues. "The thing that bothers me," said Kern, "is that they are afraid to release a couple of old guys, so I've got to be the one to go." Frank Robinson said the decision was reached because "Jim's arm is still questionable." Kern countered, "I told the man yesterday I could pitch if he needed me, and I would have told him the same thing tonight."

During the game—a 7–6 loss to the A's—a heated controversy between Robinson and John Ellis surfaced, partly as the culmination of the bad feelings that have festered between the two men since early in the season. When the Indians batted in the seventh, with a runner on second, one out and Oakland two runs ahead, Robinson sent Bill Sudakis to pinch-hit for Ellis. Before Sudakis flied out, Ellis exploded in anger in the dugout, flinging his mask, which caromed off the wall and almost hit Robinson.

The manager did his best to ignore the outburst, but couldn't look away any longer. Restraining his own anger, Robinson said to Ellis as the rest of the team observed, "John, are you pissed off at me?"

"Yeah, I guess I am," Ellis snapped back.

"Well, are you or aren't you?"

"Yes, dammit, I am."

Thrusting his face closer to Ellis, the manager said loudly, "You're lucky to even be here, the way you're hitting."

Ellis did not back off. "Yeah, and you're lucky to be here, too."

"You can bet your ass I'll be here longer than you," retorted the manager as he ordered Ellis into the clubhouse, instructing him to wait there until the game ended.

When it did, with the Indians falling another step behind the Red Sox, Robinson trudged into the locker room, closed the doors, and addressed the players. Looking directly at Ellis, who sat defiantly in the rear of the room, Robinson said, "If there's anybody here who can't play for me, or doesn't like the way I run this club, or is unhappy about *anything* and wants to get away, stand up and speak your piece." Nobody stood up. "All right, I'll be in my office if anybody wants to come in." Robinson stalked out. Nobody followed.

A few minutes later, Robinson summoned Ellis.

"I told him," related the manager, "I am tired of his selfishness. He didn't say anything. Then I said, 'John, I don't think you can play for me anymore,' and he said, 'That's right, I can't.'"

JULY 19—John Ellis wouldn't talk, but Frank Robinson had plenty to say before the Indians lost a doubleheader to the California Angels, 8–0 and 3–2. Now the Indians are 13 games behind Boston.

"I've thought over what happened and I've decided I'm not going to play Ellis anymore," said Robinson. "I've told Phil Seghi how I feel and he said he'll stand behind me. John will be included in everything we do as a team, but he won't play. What happens next is up to the man upstairs [Seghi].

"I'm not doing this because of what happened last night. That was just the last straw. I thought, with time, John would come around, lose his selfishness. But he hasn't and I can't let this go on. If I do, it will have an effect on the other players. The only way I'll play Ellis again this season is if he comes to me and says he'll do anything necessary to help the club. However, even if that happens, he won't be our regular catcher. He'll only play when it's necessary, or when I think he can help us win a game."

Are racial aspects involved in Ellis' differences with Robinson? "I don't know," replied the manager. "I can't look into his head. I can only speak for myself, and I haven't even thought of the possibility of it."

What will happen to Ellis? "I don't want him on my team anymore, but there's nothing we can do now because the trading deadline is passed. We're not going to give him away, and we're not going to release him. We have to keep him, but he won't play."

JULY 20—"If it means playing again, of course I'll go and see the man," said John Ellis, who refused to discuss his argument with Frank Robinson until today. He insisted his anger was not directed at Robinson. "Mostly I was so frustrated because I'm not hitting or driving in runs, I didn't know what to do. I just exploded. The whole season has been one big frustration. Frank thought, because of what I did, I was being selfish, and I realize now he had a right to feel that way. I'm sorry and I'll tell him so. I don't know what the Indians' plans are, but if there's anything I can do to help my situation, I'll do it. If it means going to Frank, I will."

Then Ellis turned angrily to one writer. "You are part of the trouble. You made it sound like this is a black-white thing, and it isn't. That was a disgusting story you wrote."

Robinson said, "If John comes to talk, fine. We can use him as a pinch hitter, but he will not sit on the bench. He will catch in the bullpen. John can't play for me and I don't want him to play for me."

Phil Seghi supported Robinson. "I am backing Frank 100 percent, and I will continue to do so. I believe any manager has the right to select the lineup he thinks is best and to play anybody he thinks is best. I would have done the same thing with Ellis if I were managing the club. This is a case of a manager having the courage to do what he thinks is best without sweeping the thing under the carpet because he's afraid to take appropriate action," intoned Seghi.

The general manager confirmed the Indians' switchboard was deluged with calls after the Robinson–Ellis hassle was reported. Many fans saw race as the issue and called for Robinson's scalp.

Many also wanted to know why Seghi did not support Ken Aspromonte in his dispute with George Hendrick in 1974. Seghi insisted, "I felt the same last year and in my opinion I supported my manager the same way. [Not, however, in the opinion of many close observers and certainly not in Aspromonte's opinion.] The situations are not the same," continued Seghi. "Last year it was a case of a manager believing a player was not putting out 100 percent, of a manager questioning a player's attitudinal behavior, if you're looking for a fancy phrase. This is a case of a player questioning the manager's authority."

In other developments today, Tom Buskey revealed a back problem that has affected his efficiency. "I went to the doctor and had X rays taken. He told me I have a growth of some kind in my lower back. It gives me constant pain, some days more than others, and also affects the sciatic nerve in my left leg," said Buskey. "I've got to live with it the best I can the rest of the season. I'll decide next winter whether to have an operation."

Robinson switched Rick Manning to center field, making Hendrick the Indians' right fielder. "I think it will be our best way to go," said Robinson. "I think Manning's best position will be center; Hendrick's natural position is right. It does not represent any dissatisfaction on my part with the way Hendrick has played, so don't read anything into it."

The switch means that John Lowenstein, Oscar Gamble, and Charlie Spikes will be platooned in left field because "It's the best thing for our future."

Does that mean the Indians finally are conceding they can't win this year? "Not at all," again insisted Robinson. "I don't give up on anything until there is no chance."

Manning celebrated the move by hitting his first "honest" homer. "The other one was an inside-the-park homer and the guys have been kidding me ever since," said the blushing rookie. "They said it wasn't an honest homer because I didn't hit the ball over the fence."

Buddy Bell also homered in a 10–4 victory over the Angels, but preferred to talk about his teammates' attitude. "The spirit around here has been good from the beginning, and it still is. We were really loose today, probably because everybody was slaphappy from what's been happening. It's a good sign. A lot of things have gone on that could have disrupted the unity of any club, but not this one."

JULY 21—John Ellis and Frank Robinson talked and the Indians went on to beat the Angels again, 2–1, on Oscar Gamble's homer in the eleventh inning. The treaty effected between the two men doesn't change Ellis' status. "I'll use John when I see fit, whenever it's necessary, whenever it's best for the team. As far as I'm concerned, it's a mutual agreement," repeated Robinson.

Robinson also told writers Ellis' name would be put on the waiver list next Friday in hopes of making a deal with the Angels. Robinson would like to acquire catcher Ellie Rodriguez, who has fallen from the favor of Dick Williams.

Ellis, contrite now, has apologized to Robinson and thanked the manager for not suspending him. "I hope I'm not traded because of our argument, that Frank will give me another chance and that things will get better," said Ellis.

John's eyes lit up, however, when informed of the Angels' interest in him. "They said they want me?" asked Ellis, pleased. "That's great to know. It's a helluva feeling when you're not wanted."

DALLAS, TEXAS, JULY 22—The Indians embarked upon what Frank Robinson agreed would be a "make-or-break" trip. They'll play 14 games in 13 days in Texas, Detroit, Baltimore, and New York, and will either be back in the race, or out of it when they return to Cleveland on August 4. Said Robinson, "I'd consider a realistic goal is to gain at least five games on the leader so that we'll be only 6½ out by the time we get home again. If we can do that well, we'll be in contention. If we don't, we'll still be alive, but that's all."

The Indians took the field against Gaylord Perry and lost, 4–0, dropping to 12½ games behind Boston. Gaylord retired the last 22 batters in order and registered 13 strikeouts, pitching as he did in 1974, but not as he did earlier this season for the Indians.

Naturally, Gaylord was pleased; it was only his third victory in eight decisions since joining the Rangers. He insisted beating the Indians did not represent anything special. "I want to beat everybody. Most of all I was anxious to prove to the fans here that I haven't lost anything," he said. "I was never worried, just embarrassed. I could have found myself in Cleveland if I had been given more time. Every pitcher goes through bad streaks, and what happened to me was only a bad streak."

Robinson was unhappy, but more than that he was concerned because Duane Kuiper was injured in a collision at second base. The immediate diagnosis was that Kuiper stretched the ligaments in his left knee.

Robinson said little about Perry and didn't bother to complain about Gaylord's "greaseball" pitches. "He loaded up a few but that's not what beat us. We never adjusted to him, and I don't know why. He beat us with good, natural pitches: slider, fast ball, fork ball. It's the hardest I've seen him throw all year."

✿ ✿ ✿

JULY 23—Frank Robinson returned to the active roster to-night: he replaced Duane Kuiper, disabled for at least 15 days. Kuiper's "deep layer capsule tear of the medial collateral liga-ment" means his left leg will be in a cast from hip to ankle for two weeks. Robinson, disabled since July 4, has decided to have the torn tendon in his left shoulder surgically repaired next fall "so I can lead a normal life. Don't be misled; the oper-ation does not mean I am going to play next season. I still plan to retire as a player. There's no way I'll change my mind."

The Indians lost to the Rangers, 9–8 in 13 innings, a game Robinson called "a bummer, as bad a game as we've played all season. Last night we played in a daze, and tonight we played like we had not seen a field in six months, or like we were finishing a 30-game trip. I'll bet [Texas pitcher] Bill Hands didn't throw 30 legitimate strikes. We were swinging at pitches in the dirt. On the bases we were unbelievably bad. In the field, the same. I honestly don't know what's wrong."

Part of the problem was six errors. There also were mistakes that could not be charged in the boxscore, like Charlie Spikes' miscalculation of a fly ball. It fell for a double and tied the score in the thirteenth, after the Indians went ahead on some aggressive base running by Rick Manning, who went 3 for 6, the only Indian worthy of praise. "Rick forced the Rangers to make the kind of mistakes we were making," said Robinson. "He instinctively knows what to do and does it." Jackie Brown, one pitcher the Indians received from the Rangers in the Gaylord Perry trade, was the loser, providing more embar-rassment for Robinson and Phil Seghi.

There were a couple of questionable calls by the umpiring crew of Lou DiMuro, Bill Kunkel, Dave Phillips, and Jim Evans. "Do me a favor," Robinson asked reporters. "Don't ask me about the umpires. I'll take off on them again, and I don't want to."

Exiled John Ellis made his first appearance in the lineup as a pinch hitter in the eighth inning. He remained in the game, grounding into a rally-killing double play, flying out, and walking. He also committed an error that led to the Rangers' seventh run. Without it the Indians would have won. Ellis' sta-tus, however, is unchanged. "Nothing is different," said Robinson, refusing to yield while Ellis goes silently about his business.

❋ ❋ ❋

JULY 24—John Lowenstein's homer was wasted when a storm hit Arlington Stadium in the first inning, raining out the series finale against the Rangers. Robinson held a team meeting.

"I am looking for answers because I don't understand what's happening. I didn't say anything after we got beat last night because I might have said some things I would have regretted. Now I want to find out if anybody has any ideas," Robinson told the players.

After the meeting, he reported, "We all talked. I didn't raise any hell, though I did bring up the mistakes we've been making. Most of all we're not thinking, not preparing ourselves, and there's not enough enthusiasm, not enough togetherness. I'm not displeased with our attitude, but one of the problems is that we're leaving our good attitude in the clubhouse when the game begins."

One player gave another indication of a change in Robinson's philosophy about umpires. "He asked us if he is creating pressure by arguing with the umpires. Nobody really answered, but I think Frank believes he *is* hurting us. I think it's part of the trouble, but it's not the whole problem. We're just not playing well."

Harvey Haddix had another theory. "What bothers me so much is that too many guys don't get upset when we lose. They're always the same after a game, win or lose. I can't understand that."

DETROIT, MICHIGAN, JULY 25—The Indians slid deeper into the basement tonight, losing to the Detroit Tigers, 4–3. Don Hood was chased in the sixth inning, and Jackie Brown failed again to impress.

"Because Tom Buskey was unable to pitch again, it has reached the stage where we'll have to make a decision," acknowledged Frank Robinson. "Buskey can pitch with pain, so when he says he can't, I know his back is really bothering him. Phil Seghi will be here in the morning and we'll talk about it. Maybe we'll get someone to come in right away."

The sitting and waiting, amidst rumors he'll be traded, disturbs John Ellis very much. Before the game Ellis asked this writer to come to his room. "I want to give you my side of the story of what happened between Robinson and me, but I don't want you to write it until after I'm traded. I want my friends to know I'm not the bad guy Robinson is making me out to be. There were circumstances that brought this thing to a head," he said.

"It goes back to when Gaylord and Jim Perry were still with the club. We'd go over the hitters, with Robinson advising us how to pitch to certain guys. In the game, often they'd go against Robinson. Robinson, instead of talking to Gaylord or Jim, would come to me. All I could tell him was that Gaylord or Jim wanted to do it his way. Robinson would get mad at me. Finally I told him, 'Go to the pitchers and tell them, don't blame me.'

"This led to an incident in Texas [June 14] when Roric Harrison was pitching and the score was tied, 1–1, in the seventh inning. Toby Harrah was batting with a man on second and two out. I signaled for a slider, away from Harrah like Robinson told us, but Harrison shook me off. He threw a fast ball down the pipe and Harrah hit it for a single and the run came home. After the game Robinson challenged me again, not the pitcher. 'What was that pitch to Harrah?' he wanted to know. I told him it was a fast ball, more outside than inside. I was trying to stick up for my pitcher, but Robinson got mad. So did Harvey Haddix. They decided I was a liar. Roric went to Frank and tried to tell him it was his fault, not mine. When I heard Robinson had called me a liar, I went to see him again.

"I said, 'I'm here not because you second-guessed us, but because you called me a liar,' and from that point on Robinson lost all confidence in me. He excluded me from all their policy-making meetings; he went to the pitchers and infielders instead. How do you think that made me feel?

"After that, I missed two take signs in a game against Milwaukee and was fined $300. I was handed a letter when we were on the plane flying to Boston three days later, telling me about the fine. I thought that was lousy. The least the man could do was tell me personally. That's what I went to see him about in Boston and we had that argument.

"The big reason I was upset was that, earlier, he had threatened me with Mickey Mouse fines. When I had the pulled hamstring muscle, he was going to fine me $50 for not showing up for extra hitting one Saturday morning. The reason I didn't was because I was in the trainer's room getting my leg worked on. Another time he was going to fine me $25 for not showing up early, but again I was in the trainer's room. I didn't tell him I was but I knew my relationship with the man was deteriorating.

"In that meeting in Boston I asked his reason for fining me $300. He called me selfish, said I didn't care about the team. I argued with him. I told him his remarks were real weak, but he kept calling me selfish. I said, 'Okay, I'll pay the damned fine, but let's talk about what's going on between us. Let's try to work together.' He said, 'All you want to do is kiss the pitchers' asses and get them on your side.' From then on things really got out of hand.

"Before we ended the meeting, I asked him, 'Have you fined *everybody* who missed a sign?' He said, 'No.' I said, 'Well, then, I've got nothing more to say.' I walked out of the office and that's the way it has been."

Almost simultaneously, Seghi was asking waivers on Ellis, hoping to arrange a trade. "But I'm not going to give John away," the general manager stressed again. "I've already talked to eight clubs about him and they think they have us over a barrel, but they don't. If we can't get what Ellis is worth, we'll keep him until we're able to deal with 23 clubs [after the interleague trading period begins in October]."

JULY 26—Tom Buskey was placed on the 21-day disabled list today, and minor league pitcher Rick Waits was recalled before the Indians beat the Tigers, 6–0, behind Dennis Eckersley.

The Indians now are tied with Detroit for fifth place, but Boston won again and leads the Indians by 14 games.

Eckersley found a "cure" for his virus. "I felt really lousy until we got some runs," chortled the pitcher. "Then I felt a lot better. My weak stomach suddenly improved."

Frank Robinson felt better, too. "It's easy when you get pitching like that, timely hitting, and good defense. It wasn't Eckersley's best game, but it was very good. He challenged the hitters, which is what I've been telling all our pitchers they should do. The kid is amazing. He pitches like a veteran."

Robinson played, walking three times and hitting a single. He came out of the game with sliding lacerations on his left forearm and a bruised right hand—a Detroit infielder stepped on it. While John Ellis languished another day in the bullpen, Alan Ashby hit another homer, his second in two days.

Buskey, though disappointed, didn't quarrel with the decision to place him on the disabled list. "For the past four days the thing that's bothering me most is the sciatic nerve in my left leg. I can't stride normally," he said. Buskey will return to Cleveland and consult with a neurologist. "I don't know how long it'll be until I can pitch again, but I hope it's soon because I think we still have a chance." A chance to win? "I really believe we do. All the guys do. I still believe I can do the best job in the bullpen. Maybe rest will help my back. The way things have been, I felt I was cheating the team."

Rick Waits, whose record at Oklahoma City was only 1-5 with a 4.42 earned run average, was chosen over several other minor league pitchers with better statistics. When it was speculated that the Indians recalled the southpaw because they're anxious to make the Gaylord Perry trade look good (which it hasn't), Phil Seghi bristled. "I see you're doing some more sniping," he snapped.

JULY 27—The Indians and Tigers fought to a stalemate in their doubleheader battle for fifth place, and both lost more ground to the leaders in the Eastern Division. The Indians blew a five-run lead and dropped the opener, 8–7, but Fritz Peterson and Jim Bibby salvaged the nightcap, 7–2.

Frank Robinson complained, "We should have won both games by the same [7–2] score. One bad call turned the opener around, which goes to show how umpires can hurt a team no matter how unimportant it seems at the time." What call? "I don't want to talk about it. I don't want to talk about the umpires anymore, so please don't ask me." Did Phil Seghi order Robinson to stop criticizing the umpires? "No. I just think it's better that I don't say anything about them."

The ruling in question was made by umpire Don Denkinger in the sixth inning when the Indians were leading, 7–3. Willie Horton was called safe at first base and the Tigers went on to score four runs. "We don't get any of the close ones," lamented

Boog Powell. "Horton was out by a full step. I don't know if it's because Robby ripped the umpires, but something is happening. I guess the only solution is for me to raise more hell. I'm not a complainer, but I've seen a few calls that were made just to get the game over. I know it's true because that's what the umpire told me. I've had others tell me, when I said something to them, 'Look at the score . . . what the hell difference does one play make?' Well, today one play cost us a game."

At the start of the second game, Robinson was absent from home plate where he was to meet with Tiger manager Ralph Houk and umpires Denkinger, Marty Springstead, Larry Barnett, and Hank Morgenweck. Finally, Denkinger stalked to the Indians' dugout and called to Robinson. The manager emerged and strolled slowly to the plate.

John Ellis caught the second game and singled in two official at bats. Robinson indicated he was relenting in his exiling of Ellis, suggesting, too, that he has had second thoughts about his statement that Ellis "won't play again." "I knew before the season started everything I said would be written, but some things have been quoted out of context," said the manager. "What I said was that Ellis would not be my *regular* catcher. I didn't say he'd *never* play again."

BALTIMORE, MARYLAND, JULY 28—Rick Waits recorded his first major league victory as the Indians beat the Baltimore Orioles, 7–5 in 10 innings, because Frank Robinson made a mistake. "I just plain goofed," he admitted. In the last of the ninth after the Orioles tied the score, the Indians failed to make a double play, leaving runners at first and third with two out. Robinson inadvertently visited Jackie Brown for the second time in the same inning, which automatically dictates a change of pitchers.

At the time, Rico Carty was arguing with umpire Nestor Chylak that the Baltimore runner had been doubled at first. "I went out to calm Rico and then I saw Brown looking disgusted. I started toward him and realized it was my second trip to the mound. I hoped the umpires wouldn't notice, but they did. [Plate umpire] Terry Cooney called over, 'You want your pitcher?' I didn't answer him, but I was thinking, Oh, no. I looked to the bullpen and Waits was warming up, but just for a workout.

Catcher John Ellis (left) and coach Jeff Torborg.

Thank God he was. He *had* to come in; I had no other choice."

Waits got out of the inning without further damage, the Indians scored twice in the top of the tenth, but the Orioles came back again, getting runners to first and third with one out. This time Robinson changed pitchers voluntarily, calling in Fred Beene, who promptly retired the next two to save the victory.

"It was kind of weak, but I'll take it," said Waits. "I was shocked when Robinson signaled for me, but there's no way I won't take the victory." Ditto for Robinson.

John Ellis caught again, hit a triple and a double in five trips to the plate. In Cleveland, letters to the two newspapers ran heavily in favor of Ellis and almost unanimously critical of Robinson's handling of the situation. "That doesn't bother me," said Robinson. "I know I'm right. What I'm doing is in the best interest of the team."

Robinson might be right, though his action was harsh; his choice of words pertaining to the benching of Ellis was such that it is difficult for the manager to back off the stand he took. On the other hand, Ellis has played better in his limited opportunities since their quarrel and Robinson's public reprimand, and the catcher's attitude seems to be improved, too, though he remains quiet and uncommunicative publicly.

JULY 29—Because of Minnesota Twins' owner Calvin Griffith, John Ellis will not be traded until the end of the season. Griffith, whose Twins have the worst record (44-58-.431) in the American League, claimed Ellis on the waiver list. It blocked the Indians' efforts to deal the catcher to the California Angels for Ellie Rodriguez as Frank Robinson had hoped. "I claimed Ellis because we need a right-handed hitter and a first baseman, and Ellis is both," said Griffith. "I don't know if I can work anything out with Phil Seghi, but I'm going to try." He couldn't.

Griffith offered light-hitting veteran catcher Phil Roof for Ellis. Seghi asked for young catcher Glenn Borgmann and rookie pitcher Jim Hughes. Neither would agree to the other's proposal.

Seghi blamed the media for overpublicizing the squabble between Ellis and Robinson. "It was blown out of proportion just like the Gaylord Perry story was in spring training. If you guys had not written the way you did, we wouldn't have had either problem. You made it sound like Robby and Ellis can't coexist, but they can." Seghi conveniently ignored the fact that it was Robinson—not the writers—who said, "Ellis can't play for me and I don't want him to."

The Indians lost, 7–1, in a dull game. They were held to six hits by Mike Torrez. Don Hood and Fred Beene walked seven to complicate their chores. Now the Indians are 15 games behind the Red Sox and seven behind the second-place Orioles. Robinson reevaluated his goals. "As long as we're still mathematically alive, we've got a chance to win, but for now, I'm realistically shooting for second place. I always thought we had a chance to win, even though you guys [the writers] and the fans didn't. But all I ever said is that I'd be very disappointed if we did not play .500 baseball. I thought we could; I still do. I thought we'd play better, and I still think we will, but the important thing is that, instead of talking and thinking, we start winning."

JULY 30—John Ellis hit a two-run homer to give the Indians and Dennis Eckersley a 3–1 victory over the Orioles. Surrounded by writers, Frank Robinson shrugged and smiled. "Why is everyone so uptight about Ellis? When a story is carried somewhere else, you guys never get the full quote. In this case the full quote was, 'He'll never be my regular catcher and he'll never play for me again *if* he doesn't come and tell me he's willing to play the game the way I want it played—for the good of the team.'" Does that mean Ellis has changed his attitude? "Yes, that's why he's playing," replied Robinson.

Ellis' homer came on a 3-and-0 pitch from Mike Cuellar, when a take sign seemed to be in order. (It is ironic that Ellis' problems with Robinson began six weeks ago with his ignoring two take signs in one game.) "Yeah, this time I looked twice to make sure I got the hitaway sign right," admitted Ellis. "I wasn't trying for a home run. The way I've been hitting, I was sure they figured I wouldn't be swinging." Ellis' homer, his sixth of the season, was his first since June 14. The victory enabled the Indians to regain fifth place, one game ahead of Detroit.

Later, when it was suggested that Ellis might now be out of

the manager's doghouse, Robinson replied curtly, "I don't have a doghouse and I never did."

NEW YORK, NEW YORK, AUG. 1—Eric Raich was kayoed early and the Indians lost to the New York Yankees and Catfish Hunter, 5–4. After the game Bill Virdon was fired by the Yankees and replaced by Billy Martin.

Frank Robinson had no comment on the action and had little to say about the meeting he and Phil Seghi had earlier in the day with Lee MacPhail. They discussed Robinson's accusations that umpires are discriminating against the Indians because he is baseball's first black manager. At that time, Mac-Phail called Robinson's charges "irresponsible" and "totally incorrect," but now the president was more reserved.

"We had a constructive conversation; there was no reprimand and no fine," asserted MacPhail. "I just wanted to discuss the situation with Frank and Phil." Robinson agreed: "We just talked; it was nothing special."

Did MacPhail warn Robinson? "No, but I'm sure he won't do it again," said the president. Did Robinson feel he had been scolded by MacPhail? "No, it was just a discussion, as I said."

Seghi elaborated. "Lee assured Robby the umpires are not prejudiced. I don't know if Frank believed him, but I hope this ends it. I know how Robby feels, but I wish he hadn't been so outspoken. I hate to think he might be right.

"I also wish Frank had not been so outspoken in that hassle with John Ellis. I think he did the right thing in reprimanding Ellis, but he shouldn't have said that John would *never* play again. He got backed into a corner with that statement, and it hurt his image."

Will Robinson's outspokenness jeopardize his chances of being rehired as the Indians' manager for 1976? "Oh, no," replied Seghi. "He'll be back next year, there's no doubt about it, although I don't want to say it now. We'll get together probably the last week of the season."

AUG. 2—Billy Martin's debut as manager of the Yankees was a rousing success today because a season-long problem of the Indians continued. The Yankees won, 5–3, as the Indians blew a 3–0 lead.

"If I had to point to one thing that's held us back all year," lamented Frank Robinson, "I'd have to say it's the lack of clutch hitting. In April we had the same trouble, and it really hasn't improved since then, except for one stretch."

Traveling secretary Mike Seghi, Phil Seghi's son, interrupted Robinson to say the bus would leave a few minutes later than scheduled. Robinson remarked, "Mike, you're just like this team; you haven't improved one bit all season."

AUG. 3—After the Indians lost the opener of a doubleheader, 12–1, to the Yankees, Frank Robinson had little to say. "Bad isn't the word for it," he offered grudgingly. Have the players given up? "I don't think so. They shouldn't, but I don't know." Then, almost to prove there's some fight left in them, the Indians won the nightcap, 3–2.

The split gave the Indians a 5-8 record for the trip, which Robinson admitted at the onset would "make us or break us." He had set as a "realistic" goal enough victories to gain at least five games on the leader so that the Indians would be only 6½ behind when they returned home. Tonight the Indians are in fifth place, 17½ games behind the Boston Red Sox. The second-place Baltimore Orioles are eight games ahead, New York seven, Milwaukee four, and Detroit is 2½ behind Cleveland.

"Yeah, we fell short of our goal," said Robinson, "but if we'd played just a little better, we could have won four of the games we lost. That would have given us a 9-4 record and probably moved us into third place. One problem is that the Red Sox are playing well. I don't know if anyone can catch them now. But this trip didn't break us. What we've got to do now is put it together in the next two weeks, get going again or forget it."

Publicly, Seghi also refused to surrender. "This trip was not the death knell. We've got two months left. The club has not performed as well as it can, but we have not taken a step backward. I would say it's only a halt in progress for the moment."

The Indians' 47-58 record is 11 games under .500. A year ago, after 105 games, the Indians were in second place with a 56-49 mark, seven games over .500.

13. Wait'll Next Year

CLEVELAND, OHIO, AUG. 4—Phil Seghi and Frank Robinson still speak optimistically about the current season. "Who can be sure what's going to happen these last two months?" asked Seghi after a 6–4 victory over the Detroit Tigers.

"I'm still convinced we're good enough to reach second place," said Robinson. "Only Boston is out of our class."

Seghi added, "I am disappointed the way things have gone but there is enough talent here to build a winner. I see no reason why we should not come back next year with good performances from the fellows who have not hit this year."

It is significant that Robinson now speaks of second place and Seghi of next year.

Robinson reflected on his performance as a rookie manager. "I think I've done a decent job, though I'm not happy with our place in the standings or the way we're playing. I've learned a lot about our personnel and personalities, which has been difficult because we've had such a big turnover. I like to believe, and I *do* believe I'm a better manager now than when the season started. I never felt I knew everything. I had to make adjustments. I realize it's give-and-take. I used to believe it was a manager's right, even his responsibility, to ask *why* a guy did this or that, but I've found it's better if I don't. It's interpreted as second-guessing. It's something John Ellis dislikes so much. Sure, in a way I'm sacrificing my principles, but if it helps, I'm willing to do it. That's what I mean by giving-and-taking."

Is there anything Robinson regrets? "Yes, I'm sorry now we didn't leave spring training with the young people we have now—the Rick Mannings, the Duane Kuipers, the Eric Raiches. I'm sorry we went with so many veterans. If we had come north with the kids, I believe we'd be as much as 10 games better now and close to .500. There are other things I wish I had done differently, but it wouldn't serve any useful purpose to talk about them now."

How about his criticism of the umpires, his dealing with Gaylord Perry, and his public reprimand of John Ellis? Does Robinson wish he'd handled those differently? "No. I still believe I handled them right."

Asked what aspect of the Indians' play disappoints him most, Robinson replied, "I thought we'd hit better as a team, and another major disappointment is that we are not better in the execution of fundamentals. I don't know where we went wrong. How much more effort could we have devoted than we did? Again, I think the big turnover of personnel caused some of the problems. As far as motivating my players, I can't evaluate that. I think the players are the only ones who can. I think about motivation, but only because we're not winning. If we were winning regularly, the subject wouldn't be raised. I've tried different things to find what might work and what doesn't. I've been vocal, spirited, quiet—almost everything. I've tried to be a cheerleader, and I've tried not to be a cheerleader, but I haven't really found anything that works yet, so I'll have to keep trying. But I haven't given up on this season, and I don't think the team has quit either."

AUG. 5—Both teams played poorly: the Tigers were simply worse than the Indians. The 8–4 loss was Detroit's ninth straight. Eric Raich struggled but finally got his sixth victory, after failing five consecutive times since July 4. Rico Carty drove in four runs. Rick Manning reached base five times.

"When you're hot, you're hot, and when you're lucky, you're lucky. I am both hot and lucky," chortled Carty. "I keep telling you guys I am not old. When will you start to believe me?" Manning's average climbed to .306 with two singles. "My goal was .300, but now I'm thinking higher, maybe .320."

AUG . 6—Fritz Peterson has been waiting for tonight since April 28. "For a while I was afraid it might not come, but it did and I am very happy," he said after beating the New York Yankees, 5–3, with superlative relief help from Dave LaRoche. "The only thing that disappoints me is that I couldn't finish the game, but I did what I wanted to do. I was up at 4:30 this morning thinking about it."

Peterson was determined to beat the Yankees. He wanted to show up Gabe Paul, who traded him to Cleveland, and he was anxious to retaliate against a couple of his former teammates "for what they did to me and Mel Stottlemyre when we were with that club." Most of all, Fritz wanted revenge for his humiliation three months ago in Shea Stadium when he was kayoed in the first inning and absorbed a 6–1 defeat. After that game, Peterson said, "I stunk up the place, but I'm going to even the score."

Peterson and Harvey Haddix thought then the Yankees were calling his pitches. "I don't think they tried tonight; if they had, someone might have gotten hurt."

In this game Roy White was hit in the ribs with a fast ball from Peterson in the first inning. "Oh, that was an accident," claimed Peterson. But his eyes twinkled mischievously.

Peterson might not have exacted his revenge without La-Roche's contributions. The Indians were clinging to a 4–3 lead and the Yankees loaded the bases with none out in the eighth. LaRoche struck out the next three batters on 14 pitches, earning a standing ovation and his ninth save. Rico Carty, another hero, blasted his eleventh homer. But nobody was happier than Peterson.

AUG. 7—Frank Robinson's mood turned to despair during a 6–3 loss to the Yankees that might have been averted with more

alert baserunning. "Everything that was taught in spring training by Maury Wills has been forgotten," he lamented. "We've
been killing ourselves with mental mistakes all year. As a team
we do not have good instincts. You can't teach instincts, but
you can try to control the situation. By talking, talking, talking,
you hope you can get through to people, but we didn't again tonight. It was not a well-played game. The less said about it, the
better."

AUG. 8—Before tonight's game, a 4–3 victory over the Kansas City Royals, some Indians participated in a parade as part
of "Rally 'Round Cleveland Day." Frank Robinson was unhappy because 11 players didn't take part.

"It wasn't mandatory, but I asked everybody to participate.
I'm disappointed some didn't because these are responsibilities we all have to the club and the city. We've all got to be willing to give as well as take." Holding his right hand out, palm
up, Robinson added, "Too many players never show the other
side of their hand."

Roric Harrison was the Indians' winning pitcher and gave
credit to a parachutist hired by the Indians to deliver the game
ball from an airplane. "When I saw that guy drifting down,"
said Harrison, "I thought to myself, Boy! That really takes
some guts. I went back to warming up and all of a sudden my
fast ball started popping. My adrenalin started flowing and I
was okay."

AUG. 9—Fourth place was there for the taking, but the Indians lost to the Royals, 6–4. During the game an anonymous
caller tipped this writer that five members of the Indians were
fined $200 each for being caught out after the 1:00 A.M. curfew
in New York the previous Saturday night. Frank Robinson did
not deny the reported disciplinary action, his first for curfew
violation this season. "I was disappointed, mainly because we
had just lost a tough game that afternoon and had a doubleheader the next day. I would have thought the guys would be
trying to take better care of themselves. I'm not giving up this
season, and I don't want my players to give up. That's why I
made the room check. I did it personally, door by door. Not
only can we get into fourth place, we still have a good chance

to catch the Yankees for third, and if we can get things together like we did a month ago, we can reach second place. I don't want anybody to forget it."

AUG. 10—The Indians were beaten by the Royals again today, 5–1, and time is running out. Eric Raich was the loser because he hung a curve that John Mayberry turned into a three-run homer.

One of the players caught violating curfew commented on the story that appeared in *The Plain Dealer* this morning. "Did Frank Robinson really say he had checked every room himself?" the player asked. "Then there is a double standard around here. I deserved to be fined because I was out late and got caught, but some other guys were out and weren't caught. At least they weren't fined. I know because one guy who was with me wasn't checked by Robinson. I also know that two young guys were caught but all Robinson did was warn them. Robinson says he wants to be fair, that he treats everyone alike, but he isn't living up to that."

When questioned about the "double standard," Robinson admitted, "Well, I caught five guys out late but I only fined one of them. He couldn't give me a good reason for being out late. Of the other four, one said he was in a different room and I wasn't aware he'd changed. Two were kids who didn't know any better. One was just dumb: he said he got hungry about 12:30 and went out to get something to eat. I let them go this time, but I think they know I'll come down hard next time."

AUG. 11—Today, an open date, was Bill Sudakis' last workout with the Indians. He was released to make room for Duane Kuiper, now recovered from a knee injury. Sudakis complained, "The least they could have done was tell me before the workout." When he signed with the Indians six weeks ago, a catching emergency existed. Sudakis rejected offers from the Los Angeles Dodgers, a team in Japan, and Hawaii. "I picked the Indians because I thought I'd get more opportunity to prove I belong in the major leagues," he said. Sudakis didn't really get that chance. "The fans booed me when I caught because they like Ellis. When I played first, they booed me, too, because they also like Boog Powell. But that's baseball." Had

Sudakis signed with the Dodgers, he might have become a regular because two days later one of their catchers, Joe Ferguson, broke his arm.

CHICAGO, ILLINOIS, AUG. 12—The Indians launched another trip today with a 6–3 victory over the Chicago White Sox. Frank Robinson mused aloud, "Why don't we do these things more often—at least half the time?"

Though Phil Seghi hasn't made it official, there's no doubt Robinson will be rehired. Part of the reason, of course, is that by firing Robinson, Seghi would be admitting he made a mistake last October. "I think Frank is doing a helluva job as manager, especially when you take into consideration the performances we're getting from so many guys who did so much better last year. I expect much better things in the last 49 games, with the fellows playing like I know they can."

AUG. 13—Little things plagued the Indians tonight, preventing them from taking fourth place. In a 4–3, 12-inning loss to the White Sox, the winning run was forced across the plate on a bases-loaded walk by Rick Waits.

In the second inning the White Sox scored two runs that made the difference. Don Hood balked for the third time this season. At least umpire Bill Haller said Hood balked. Frank Robinson disagreed. The manager was studying the rule book when reporters arrived in his office. "It might be one umpire's interpretation of the balk rule," he said. "More than that, I think it was another case of the other team yelling 'Balk!' on Hood's pick-off motion, and the umpire falling for it."

Shortly after the controversial balk, Hood threw a wild pitch. The second Chicago run scored from second base because John Ellis argued with plate umpire Armando Rodriguez instead of immediately retrieving the ball. Ellis contended the pitch hit the shoe of the batter, Brian Downing, which made it a dead ball. "Ellis should have gone after the ball and *then* argued with the umpire," criticized Robinson.

Later, several members of the White Sox admitted the pitch did hit Downing, that Ellis was right and Rodriguez wrong, and the run should not have been allowed. The confession only heightened the catcher's frustration. "I wish you hadn't told me," snapped Ellis. "I knew I was right. I tried to 'prove' it, but I couldn't. When I got the ball, I dropped it intentionally and, in picking it up, I rubbed it against my shoe, hoping some of the red polish would come off on the ball. Then I could have shown it to Rodriguez and said it came from Downing's shoe. But none of the polish came off. It didn't really surprise me, though. It's been that kind of a year for me. Why should it change now?"

AUG. 14—Misfortune hovers over John Ellis and controversy continues to haunt the Indians. They lost 6–4 to the White Sox; lost another argument with an umpire, Ron Luciano; lost a decision at home plate, involving Duane Kuiper and Brian Downing; and even lost a complaint against Chicago grounds keeper Gene Bossard.

Ellis, who homered and singled, reinjured his right hamstring muscle and was placed on the 15-day disabled list. "Just when I started to hit, this had to happen," complained Ellis. Rookie catcher Rick Cerone was called up from Oklahoma City.

The White Sox won on Pat Kelly's disputed, tie-breaking homer in the seventh. Frank Robinson protested that a fan in the right-center-field bleachers leaned far over the railing, preventing George Hendrick from at least keeping the ball in play. "I know I would have got a glove on it and it wouldn't have gone out of the park except for the fan who caught it," Robinson argued. Later he said, "What's the use? Luciano was there and his opinion was different than ours, but I still think we're right."

Kuiper tried to score the tying run in the eighth but was tagged out by Downing, ending the inning. Kuiper, who has been roughed up often by base runners, tried to jar the ball loose from Downing. He slid into Downing's right thigh as the catcher was blocking the plate. Downing leaped to his feet in pain and anger and shouted at Kuiper. "If I wanted to, I could have started something and beat the ---- out of him," said Downing. "I get the same thing at second base," countered Kuiper. "I expect it, and so should he." Players from both dugouts rushed onto the field but order was restored quickly.

Roric Harrison, the losing pitcher, fumed about the mounds

in White Sox park, accusing Bossard of "doctoring" them. "The one in our bullpen is almost flat, which makes the mound on the field especially steep," complained Harrison. "It took me three or four innings to adjust, and by then I was behind 3-0. I know it sounds like an alibi, but it's the truth. What they've done is a travesty; but I don't blame them if it helps their team."

Ellis' injury was especially frustrating to Robinson because the Indians released Bill Sudakis three days ago.

MINNEAPOLIS, MINNESOTA, AUG. 15—In an uninspiring performance against the Minnesota Twins, the Indians lost 8–4.

Frank Robinson and the coaches met for nearly 2½ hours in the manager's suite in the Leamington Hotel. "Mostly these guys just drank beer at my expense," Robinson tried to laugh off the meeting. When the questioning persisted, Robinson added, "We talked about a lot of things, like why are we losing and what can we do to start winning again."

Harvey Haddix volunteered, "I think we're in agreement that our guys are too passive, especially after the other team takes a lead. Hell, that's when you should be more aggressive. Defensively, we're not making the routine plays and we're giving away too many extra bases because we're not executing the fundamentals right. Offensively, the problem is that we're not hitting at the right time, and nobody can come up with an answer to that. We're not moving base runners along, we're too unwilling to accept a walk, and our base running is horrible. Also, our pitchers are not mean enough. You've got to knock somebody down once in a while. I think the situation boils down to a lack of agressiveness by everybody."

Has Frank Robinson been guilty of a lack of agressiveness? Has he been too patient? "I don't know," replied Haddix.

AUG. 12—Frank Robinson did lose patience today after the Indians were beaten, 9–1, by the Twins, who scored six runs in the first two innings. Robinson slammed shut the clubhouse door and lectured for 15 minutes. "It was the maddest I've ever seen him," acknowledged one player. "I was surprised. Usually he waits until the next day, but today he was too upset. I don't blame him."

"I told them," related Robinson, "I don't like the way we're accepting defeat. I won't stand for it. I told them I expect a change in their attitude or there'll be a lot of people who will regret it. If we're not a better team than we've shown, then I don't know talent."

The trouble on the field began almost immediately. The first two Indians reached base, then each eliminated himself with unwise baserunning. After that the Indians lost easily.

"I'm not blowing smoke. I still think we can reach .500 [this would require 29 victories in the remaining 45 games]," said Robinson, "but my talking about it won't do it. The players have got to want to win harder than they've shown so far."

AUG. 17—Maybe Frank Robinson's outburst did some good. "It's possible it did, but it'll take more than one game to convince me," he said after the Indians overwhelmed the Minnesota Twins, 14–5, ending this trip with a 2–4 record.

The Indians scored three runs in the first inning, eight in the second, and two in the third, giving Fritz Peterson a 13–0 lead. "You figure this club out," suggested Robinson. "I sure as hell can't." Peterson, while happy, admitted "it was embarrassing. It was like being my own mop up man, but I'm not too proud to take it." He gave up 16 hits and was kidded unmercifully by his teammates.

When Rick Manning led the third inning, he was hit on the right leg by the first pitch from Mark Wiley. "Sure it was intentional," charged Robinson, "and sure it made me mad. It's like I told our guys yesterday, when you're getting your ass kicked, you've got to do something like that." Why was there no retaliation? "Well," replied Robinson, "Fritz made his first two pitches close to [Jerry] Terrell." Did they serve their purpose? "I don't know. You'll have to ask Peterson." Said Peterson, "I didn't want to wake up any sleeping dogs."

CLEVELAND, OHIO, AUG. 18—The Indians swept a doubleheader from the Texas Rangers tonight, 4–3 and 4–2, taking over fourth place for the first time since May 9. "This is the kind of consistency I like," said Frank Robinson.

Rick Waits' outstanding relief performance and Boog Powell's twentieth homer won the opener. Waits was tickled to beat his former teammates. "It's not like they hate me or I hate them, but I do have bitter feelings toward that organization. I wanted to prove I can pitch up here."

Waits' feelings toward the Rangers are nothing compared to the bitterness Gaylord Perry holds for Phil Seghi and Robinson.

Gaylord wasn't scheduled to pitch against his former teammates but wished he were. "I'd love to face Robinson and show him I didn't lose my fast ball, that I just misplaced it for a spell," said the pitcher. "Most of all, I'd like to pitch to Robinson so I could stick a ball in his ------- ear. Tell him I said so." Perry's record is 7–6 since joining the Rangers 10 weeks ago, winning six of his last seven starts, the only loss a 2–1 game against Kansas City on two unearned runs. Included in his victories are four shutouts.

"Tell Robinson and Seghi I said that shows how much they know about pitching," continued Perry. "I was only in a slump, like I tried to tell them when I was still over there. Tell them pitchers *do* go into slumps like hitters, even though Robinson doesn't think they do."

Gaylord had one more message for Seghi. "Tell him I want the expense money [$900] they've owed me since the trade." The Rangers paid Jim Bibby and Jackie Brown immediately, but Gaylord is still waiting for his money. According to Seghi, Perry is supposed to request it in writing, specifying the standard amount or presenting itemized expenses. "I told Seghi's son Mike three times," responded Gaylord.

Gaylord went a step further. He contacted Marvin Miller, enlisting the aid of the Players Association in collecting. Phil Seghi is very unhappy, but Gaylord will be paid, and soon.

AUG. 19—Three double plays cost the Indians a 2–1 loss to the Rangers, ending a three-game winning streak and causing one player to question Frank Robinson's strategy.

"Hell, you don't squeeze with the bases loaded, especially in the second inning," he complained. "I don't care who's hitting, you don't do it."

Robinson did. Alan Ashby, batting against Jim Umbarger, pop-bunted the ball to the pitcher, who easily doubled Rico Carty off third. It ended the inning and the Indians' chances.

"I was hoping to surprise them," rationalized Robinson. "Anytime you try a suicide squeeze play, you're hoping to surprise the other team. What I wanted was to get the tying run home and get out of a double-play situation, but the pitcher made a pitch that's almost impossible to bunt on the ground. It was high and tight and, well, it was just one of those things."

Later Robinson announced a revamping of the Indians' pitching plans, dropping Eric Raich and Don Hood from the rotation and replacing them with Jim Bibby and Rick Waits. Both Raich and Hood were displeased but were guarded in their comments.

"Sure I'm unhappy," confirmed Raich. "I think I was just getting straightened out. How will *not* pitching help?"

Hood said, "I don't know what is wrong except I'm not the pitcher I should be. I sat around for two years in Baltimore, never getting a chance to pitch, and I lost everything, including my confidence. I thought it would be different here, but it has turned out to be the same thing."

Robinson explained, "Raich is not doing the job, and Hood has not learned to relax and concentrate. The pitchers I've got in the rotation now are the best we have."

KANSAS CITY, MISSOURI, AUG. 21—Jackie Brown beat the Kansas City Royals, 7–3, paying his first dividend since the Gaylord Perry trade. Frank Robinson decided to start Brown when he discovered he had beaten the Royals four times without retaliation while with the Rangers in 1974. "I won four against the Royals and three against the Indians," said Brown. "That's one thing I thought about when I was traded to Cleveland. I mean, the Indians helped keep me in the league." This was Brown's first victory as a member of the Indians.

"Jackie pitched well, but we got him some runs and that makes it easier," said Robinson. "That's what pleases me most, scoring the way we should have been all season. Maybe we're on our way again. I feel a lot better the way things are going."

AUG. 22—After the Indians beat the Royals, 9–5, Frank Robinson contentedly leaned back in his chair. "Ever since we had our meeting in Minnesota we've been playing as a team. I think, at last, the guys are more conscious of the need to play heads-up baseball. I especially liked the way we came back after the Royals got close. Usually, when we score some runs early, we sit back and let it go at that."

The biggest smile in the clubhouse was worn by Rick Cerone, who caught his first major league game and slapped a hit in the fourth inning. The ball was retrieved. When Rick returned to the dugout, somebody tossed him the souvenir and said, "Here, kid, we lettered it for you. Send it home to your folks." When Cerone saw what was printed on the ball, he was shocked. It read, "8-22-75, Kansas City, First ------- major league hit." The smile quickly returned to his blushing face when somebody else gave him the real ball. "Here, letter it yourself," and Rick breathed a sigh of relief.

AUG. 23—It was Phil Seghi's turn to sigh with relief. The general manager has been unhappy with insinuations that he did not make a good trade for Gaylord Perry two months ago, so when Rick Waits beat the Royals, 7–1, in his first major league start, Seghi glowed. All three pitchers the Indians received for Gaylord—Waits, Jackie Brown, and Jim Bibby—have played prominent roles in the last three games, all victories.

"It could be that Waits will be the most important guy in the deal for Perry," agreed Frank Robinson. "Rick pitched a fine game, but I'm also pleased the way we've come alive at the plate. I think everybody realizes we can still make something out of this season."

Then Waits praised Robinson. "As long as someone wants me, I'll bust my butt for him, and Frank has shown more confidence in me in the four weeks I've been here than anyone did the first five years I was in pro ball."

AUG. 24—The three-game winning streak ended for the Indians with a 5–2 loss to Kansas City. They returned to Cleveland in fourth place, 16½ games behind Boston.

"We just didn't make the adjustments you have to make against a pitcher like Al Fitzmorris," commented Frank Robinson. "It would be nice to go home with a winning streak, but this isn't bad. Anytime you take three out of four on the road, you've got to feel good, and I do. I really like the attitude. Nobody has given up; we're playing together again. For a while back there, we'd get behind and you could feel the letdown. It's different now."

The Indians have won six of their last eight games, lengthening their lead over fifth-place Milwaukee to three and raising their record to 58-67. Though Robinson concedes first place is out of reach, his optimism is showing again. "Player for player we're the match of any team in our division. Our pitching is young and inexperienced for the most part, but we're moving in the right direction. It has taken a long time to get things right, but it's not too late to have a good season." Robinson is correct, though a pennant must wait.

14. *Rain, Rain Go Away*

CLEVELAND, OHIO, AUG. 25—While Dennis Eckersley flirted with a no-hitter, Frank Robinson and Charlie Spikes drilled homers and the Indians continued their surge toward respectability, beating the Chicago White Sox, 5–1. Robinson's homer was his ninth of the season, 583rd of his career, and destined to be his last. It was struck off Jim Kaat.

Eckersley permitted only three soft singles, the first coming with one out in the seventh inning. Later, he lamented, "Sure I wanted a no-hitter. Who knows what's going to happen tomorrow, next week, next year? I think about one every time I pitch."

Robinson is more patient. "I don't mean to take anything away from the kid, but I'm not sure I want him to get a no-hitter. A no-hitter creates pressure, and that's not good. I've seen it hurt young pitchers."

AUG. 26—Rain postponed tonight's game with the White Sox, but Phil Seghi was busy. He claimed from the waiver list pitcher Bob Reynolds of the Detroit Tigers and now the Indians are faced with another roster revision.

"We'll decide tomorrow," said Frank Robinson. "My inclination is to put myself on the disabled list, but I don't know if Phil wants to do it." If Seghi overrules Robinson, Eric Raich will probably be demoted until September 1 when the roster limit is raised from 25 to 40. If Rick Cerone is optioned to Oklahoma City, the Indians will be left with one catcher, Alan Ashby, because John Ellis is on the disabled list. If Fred Beene is released, the Indians will be required to pay him through the end of the season.

"Reynolds hasn't been very successful this season," acknowledged Seghi, "but we think he has capabilities." It is significant that, although the Indians are not doing well financially, they are willing to pay $20,000 for Reynolds this late in the season. When the subject of Ted Bonda's approval of the purchase was raised, Seghi replied curtly, "I didn't ask him, I told him."

AUG. 27—The Indians only split a doubleheader with the White Sox tonight despite excellent pitching by Jim Bibby and Fritz Peterson. Bibby hurled a three-hitter but lost, 2–0, before Peterson won, 5–0, on a four-hitter. "We should have won both games, but I'm pleased we came back to get the second game; it would have been easier to give up after what happened," said Frank Robinson.

Robinson reinjured his left shoulder, swinging at and missing a pitch from Claude Osteen in the first game, though he tried to keep it a secret. "It's better that nobody knows I can't swing with it," he confided later.

The Indians almost succeeded in the ninth inning of the opener when John Lowenstein led with a single and Rico Carty did the same with two out. Robinson was on deck as George Hendrick batted against Rich Gossage. The situation called for a pinch runner for Carty, but Robinson remained impassive as Gossage made three pitches to Hendrick. Finally somebody in the dugout got Robinson's attention and Don Hood ran for Carty. Two pitches later Hendrick grounded out to end the game.

Robinson admitted he never thought of a pinch runner "because I was concentrating on hitting next. One of the coaches should have reminded me. The guy who suggested it was Frank Duffy. As cocaptain, that's part of his job, but he should have done it sooner. I think Duff was reluctant to go over the heads of the coaches."

Before the doubleheader Eric Raich both lost and won. First, he was informed of his demotion for four days to Oklahoma City to make room for Bob Reynolds. Obviously, Phil Seghi overruled Robinson's recommendation to put himself on the disabled list.

Raich participated, however, in a bubble-gum contest in the clubhouse. He won with a bubble measuring 18¼ inches in diameter and now will represent the Indians against other team champions. In the circus-like atmosphere of the locker room were two women—Jackie York, promotions director of the Indians, and Marie Vidmar, photographer for station WEWS-TV. Because their presence there was a first (to the consternation of equipment manager Cy Buynak), most of the reporters ignored the bubble-gum contest, preferring to interview York and Vidmar.

Robinson stood on the fringes shaking his head. "This really helps improve the image of major league ball players, doesn't it?" he asked sarcastically, without waiting for an answer.

AUG. 29—Rick Manning hit his first grand slam home run tonight, leading the Indians to a 9–6 victory over the Minnesota Twins, and then was fined $1 for being a "hot dog."

"I guess I still have a lot to learn, including how to run the bases after I hit a homer," chuckled Manning, blushing at the attention he received in the postgame interview. "The guys fined me in the Kangaroo Court because I hot-dogged it around the bases after I hit the homer. They said I ran the bases too fast after the other homer I hit out of the park, so this time I took it easy—and I get fined for that, too."

Also chuckling was Frank Robinson as he said, "This is the kind of consistency I've been looking for." Robinson went to the plate as a pinch hitter in the eighth inning, but the Twins walked him intentionally. "I knew they would. That's the only reason I put myself in. If they hadn't I don't know what I would have done because I can't swing a bat. My shoulder is too sore, but don't write that now, please," the manager asked. "I might want to do the same thing tomorrow."

AUG. 31—Frank Robinson's fortieth birthday was not especially happy.

Two more games were canceled because of a second straight day of rain. Now it'll be impossible for the Indians to break even in the won-lost column because they'll play only 159 games. The Indians were winning, 2–1, when a downpour washed out tonight's opener short of the 4½ innings that constitute a legal game. There were two outs in the fourth and Buddy Bell tried but failed to make a third out.

"That's how good we're going," moaned Bell. "We can't even make an out when we try." Bell allowed himself to be picked off three times, but Minnesota first baseman Johnny Briggs refused to apply a tag, which would have ended the inning. Finally, Bell attempted to steal second base. Shortstop Jerry Terrell caught the ball behind the bag and he, too, made no effort to tag Bell. "Why should we?" asked Briggs. "We knew what they were trying to do." The Indians wanted to get the inning over so that, by retiring the Twins in the fifth, the game—and the victory—would have counted. "But they can't blame us for not cooperating," added Briggs.

Robinson agreed with Briggs, even though he was disappointed. Umpire Marty Springstead shrugged. "It's not my job to criticize. My job is to be fair to both teams," he said. Thus, nothing counted.

Before Springstead stopped the game, George Hendrick was booed for his apparent lack of hustle in the third inning. Twins' second baseman Rod Carew fumbled Hendrick's grounder, but his throw to first was still in time to get Hendrick. Robinson did not think Hendrick loafed. "The fans booed because they think anytime a guy bobbles a ball, the runner should beat it out. The fans were wrong, not George."

BALTIMORE, MARYLAND, SEPT. 1—Frank Robinson sat in the coffee shop of the Lord Baltimore Hotel and spoke softly as the rain pelted the street: another doubleheader postponed. The Indians will play two games against the Baltimore Orioles tomorrow night.

"I wouldn't say we're at a critical point yet, but this has got to hurt us," conceded Robinson. "All these postponements could take the edge off our guys, not only because we're not playing, but because we're not even able to practice."

However, though the Indians haven't played in three days, they've picked up two games on the Yankees, who are now only four ahead in third place, but by only one in the loss column.

Eight players rejoined the Indians today as the roster limit was raised to 40. In addition to John Ellis and Tom Buskey, who returned from the disabled list, six others were recalled from Oklahoma City—pitchers Eric Raich, Jim Kern, Jim Strickland, and Larry Andersen, first baseman Joe Lis, and outfielder Tommy Smith.

SEPT. 2—Brooks Robinson, the magician who plays third base for the Orioles, stole four hits from the Indians with superlative plays in the field tonight, prolonging the opener of a doubleheader until Baltimore won, 3–2, in 10 innings. The Indians prevailed in the nightcap, 2–1, on a homer by Rico Carty, giving Jim Bibby his third victory in a Cleveland uniform.

Frank Robinson praised Bibby's effort but criticized Don Hood's and Dave LaRoche's work in the opener.

"You can't walk guys like Mark Belanger, as LaRoche did in the eighth inning, and Tom Shopay, as Hood in the tenth. Neither one is a good hitter, and when you put guys like that on base, you're asking to get beat. We asked for it and we got it," snapped Robinson.

The split left the Indians in fourth place, safely ahead of Milwaukee by five games, but 3½ behind the New York Yankees, 10 behind the Orioles, and 16 behind the leading Boston Red Sox.

15. *"I'm Embarrassed and Very Upset"*

MILWAUKEE, WISCONSIN, SEPT. 3—Before the Indians blasted 19 hits for an 11–3 victory over the Milwaukee Brewers, Frank Robinson talked to this reporter about his performance as manager and about the probability of his being rehired. He said he has not discussed a contract for 1976 with Ted Bonda or Phil Seghi, but it has long been expected Robinson will return. His remarks led to yet another controversy.

Robinson began by outlining some of the problems encountered by all rookie managers. "It's difficult for a manager to do a good job in his first year, maybe even in his first two, for several reasons. Usually, a manager inherits players he doesn't know and who don't know him, creating problems from personality conflicts, to the players' lack of understanding strategy. Changes must be made, but it takes time and change itself is disruptive. We've made many changes in our personnel this season and only now are we getting to know each other. It's important, and takes time, for players to know the manager and

adapt to his style. Basically, there's not a great deal of difference among managers in matters of strategy, but there is a lot of
difference in the way managers deal with players.

"Like the problem I had with Gaylord Perry. I think the way
I handled that situation strengthened my position with the other players, but it took time. It's part of what I mean when I say
it's difficult for any manager to do a good job his first year. I'm
looking forward to things being better next year."

Has he discussed an extension of his contract? "No," replied
Robinson without hesitation. "But I think I will. I think it'll
come up soon."

SEPT. 4—The phone in Frank Robinson's suite in the Marc
Plaza Hotel rang all morning. First it was Phil Seghi demanding, "What the hell is going on?" The same question was asked
by International Management Inc., the company representing
Robinson. They called because of a story in *The Press* quoting
Robinson as having been invited by Ted Bonda and Seghi to
return as manager of the Indians.

Robinson phoned this writer. "You'd better come down to
my suite, we've got some things to talk about," he said wearily.

"First, I want to say I don't know how the writer [Bob
Sudyk] could quote me as saying what he did because I never
made the statements attributed to me," insisted Robinson. "I
am embarrassed and very upset by it all. A lot of people are. Sudyk asked me, 'Have you decided if you want to return as manager of the Indians?' I said, 'Yeah, I've thought about it and I
want to come back if I'm asked.' But I haven't been asked, not
by anybody connected with the club. I thought I made that
clear. Sure, we—Bonda, Seghi, and I—have talked casually
about the job I've done, but nothing has been said about next
year, formally or informally. If I were to say anything about
coming back next year, I'd say it to both of you [the reporters
who regularly cover the Indians].

"It's the direct quote that said I met with them [Bonda and
Seghi] and they indicated they want me to continue that upsets
me so much, that upsets everybody so much. Especially Phil.
All I ever said was, 'Yes, I'd like to come back next year.' I also
said I would hope I'd get more than a one-year contract, but
that it's up to the ball club.

"This puts me in a very difficult position with the people I'm associated with. Sure, I could demand a retraction, but what good would it do now? The damage is done. I can't even say I was misquoted; all I can say is that I never made any kind of a statement about being invited back, on the record or off record. I have a feeling I will be asked because they have never indicated they don't want me back. But nothing has been said yet. After I told Sudyk I'd like to return, he asked me, 'Can I speculate that you will be back?' I told him, 'You can do anything you want, but don't get me involved; don't quote me.'"

The story placed Robinson in a particularly difficult situation with International Management. Robinson's friend and personal adviser, Ed Keating, who negotiated his first managerial contract with the Indians, left International Management in a huff. Since then there has been speculation that Robinson will terminate his contract with International Management and retain Keating, who is opening his own management firm.

Seghi substantiated Robinson's denial. "We had a very informal meeting about 10 days ago. We just chitchatted; we asked Frank how he likes managing and how he likes Cleveland. He assured us he was happy. We told him we think he has done a satisfactory, no, make that a *capable* job, and we talked about his physical condition and the operation he'll have on his shoulder. But there was nothing definitive in our discussion. We wound up by agreeing we'd meet again soon to talk about the nitty-gritty things, but there's no big hurry."

Asked pointedly if Robinson would be given a new contract, Seghi replied, "I don't see any reason for not wanting him back. But I don't want to make any announcement because there's nothing yet to announce."

The Press was infuriated by Robinson's and Seghi's denial. Sudyk called Robinson's remarks "vicious . . . the most vicious I've ever read," and vowed he'll not talk to Robinson again. The two met in the bar of the Marc Plaza Hotel. "He insisted we had to discuss it," reported Robinson. "I repeated what I'd said earlier, and that I couldn't understand how he could interpret my remarks as he did. He kept insisting I'd said what I know I didn't. Finally I got up and walked out. What he does now is up to him."

It was clearly a case of misinterpretation, but the fact is there has not been any doubt for at least two months that Robinson would return for another term as manager of the Indians. All that remains—and has remained since midseason—is formal agreement concerning salary, length of contract, and whether Robinson will continue to be a player-manager or serve only as manager. Those details have not yet been discussed, let alone negotiated, as Seghi stressed.

At a meeting of the Pen and Mike Club in Milwaukee, Robinson talked about the problems he has experienced, and referred to the erroneous report of his rehiring. He painstakingly continued to deny it, emphasizing throughout, " *if* I return as manager of the Indians."

Robinson also talked about his ability to motivate, apparently lacking until recently. "Now I realize that players today must be motivated more than before. Kids today are given too many things too soon. Players get to the big leagues and make a lot of money quickly. Once they get here, nobody wants to sit. If they don't play, immediately they want to be traded. It's a sign of our times, I guess. It's also something I didn't realize would be a problem until I got into it.

"As for the pressure I anticipated from the media, which I really thought would be the toughest part of my job, well, that ended early. As soon as we fell into fourth place, the reporters weren't interested in me anymore.

"There's something else I've learned, too. It's that I've got two feet and one mouth and it's easy to make use of all of them at the same time, as I have done more than once."

The Indians won tonight, 10–5, over the Brewers. Under other circumstances it would have received more attention; three straight victories and 12 in the last 16 games. But the victory got only scant notice in the Cleveland papers the next day because of this latest controversy.

CLEVELAND, OHIO, SEPT. 5—Lost in what Frank Robinson said and what he meant as well as in Phil Seghi's guarded admission, "I don't see any reason for not wanting Robinson back," is the fact that major league baseball's first black manager has been successful in the judgment of his superiors. Granted, Robinson has not led the Indians to hoped-for glory, but there is no doubt he has done a satisfactory (or as Seghi says, "a *capable* ") job of managing. If nothing else, he has *survived* his first year.

On the field tonight , the Indians' three-game winning streak was snapped convincingly in an 11–2 loss to the Detroit Tigers. Robinson shrugged it off. "We just got beat," he said. "Actually, we weren't too smart. We hit a lot of line drives, most of them right at somebody. They hit a lot of flares, bloopers that our guys couldn't reach."

Despite the defeat, the Indians gained a half game on New York, which dropped a doubleheader. Now the Yankees are only three games ahead but even with Cleveland in losses.

SEPT. 6—Before the Indians beat the Tigers, 4–2, today, Frank Robinson revealed that on two occasions this season, in his despair, he almost resigned as manager of the Indians. Now, of course, he's glad he didn't.

"Both times I came this close to deciding, The hell with it, I've had enough," said Robinson, holding his thumb and forefinger an eighth of an inch apart. "Then, with time to think about it, I said to myself, You've never been a quitter before, why be one now?"

Robinson's first disillusionment, he said, came in mid-June. "We were on that bad trip to Kansas City and Texas. We weren't playing well and I had some doubts about myself and my ability to get the most out of my players." The Indians embarked upon that trip with a three-game losing streak and extended it to seven before they beat the Rangers, 5–1, on June 15. That was the day after Robinson invoked a curfew, admitting he'd been wrong in not having one.

"The other time I came close to quitting was when we were in Oakland and I had that thing with [umpire] Larry Barnett." That was on July 7. After Robinson was ejected, he had accused the umpires of discrimination and publicly low-rated them.

"Those were the worst times for me. I was very depressed, even if I didn't show it. But I got over it both times and there are no doubts now. I think I've done a decent job, everything considered."

* * *

SEPT. 7—Now, certainly, there is no disillusionment on the part of Frank Robinson. He leaned back contentedly and smiled. "We couldn't be playing better." The Indians swept a doubleheader, 7–2 and 9–0, and Tigers' manager Ralph Houk pronounced, "This is the most solid I have seen the Indians play in quite awhile. Their bats are hot and a lot could happen that will cause people to sit up and take notice a year from now."

Houk's mention of "a year from now" is the source of the only frustration Robinson feels, with the Indians now only 1½ games behind the third-place Yankees. "I thought in spring training and early in the season we could play this well, and it's frustrating that we didn't," said Robinson, a frown creasing his face. "If we had, we'd be fighting for a pennant instead of third place or hoping we can reach second."

SEPT. 8—After Don Hood and the Indians beat the Boston Red Sox, 4–1, Frank Robinson made a wish. Unfortunately, it can't be granted. "I wish," he said, "the schedule had two more months to go."

It's no wonder. The Indians slowed Boston's dash toward the division championship as Hood scattered seven hits. They took advantage of several sloppy plays by the Red Sox to defeat 18-game winner Rick Wise. An interference call against Carlton Fisk made it possible for Frank Duffy to hit a bases-loaded single good for three runs.

"We're playing as a team; every game it's somebody else picking us up," chortled Robinson. "It's why I wish we had two more months to play."

SEPT. 9—The Indians beat the Red Sox again, 3–2, on Alan Ashby's tenth inning single as Rick Waits pitched a five-hitter. The trade for Gaylord Perry is beginning to tip in the Indians' favor because of recent pitching by Waits and Jim Bibby.

Frank Robinson also was happy with the attitude of the club as expressed by Waits: "Right now we're the best team in the American League. We can't catch Boston anymore, but we can take any club one on one. We have the pitching, the defense, and that certain something that it takes to be a winner."

Losing pitcher Bill Lee agreed, albeit grudgingly. "We were beaten by a team that is, right now, far superior to us. The Indians keep coming at you. But, hell, everything is so bad here—the city, the ball park, the lights, the field, the clubhouse—the Indians have a psychological advantage over all the visiting teams," he said dourly.

SEPT. 10—The Indians finally reached the coveted .500 level tonight, but only briefly. They won the opener of a double-header against the Baltimore Orioles, 7–1, to balance their won-lost mark at 70-70. It also was their eighteenth victory in 23 games since Frank Robinson angrily locked the clubhouse door and lectured the players about their unaggressive play. "Considering the results of that meeting, I wish I'd done it sooner, like last spring training, or even last winter," admitted the manager between games. It is the first time since May 4 the Indians have won as many games as they lost.

The euphoria of .500 disappeared when the Orioles won the nightcap, 6–5, because of a thirteenth inning "double" over Charlie Spikes's head. "That ball has got to be caught," grumbled Robinson, no longer smiling. "No way it should be a hit. Charlie just misplayed it, and we lost."

SEPT. 11—The Indians lamented that it didn't rain hard enough to postpone what turned out to be a 10–2 loss to Jim Palmer and the Orioles. "It seemed like our guys played from the beginning like they expected the game to be rained out. When they realized it wasn't going to happen, it was too late," complained Frank Robinson. The defeat reduced the Indians' record to 70-72 and raised their third-place deficit to three. "We played a lousy game, maybe the worst since we started playing so well last month." He was right.

While Robinson was unhappy, Earl Weaver was complimentary about the Indians' resurgence and Robinson's work. "This Cleveland club is a terror to play right now," said the Orioles' manager. "Frank has done an excellent job of pulling the Indians together. They're all going good and it's tough to send any pitcher against them."

Since the All-Star Game, the Indians, under Robinson's sometimes too patient leadership, have won 30 and lost 26. Only Baltimore (40-21) and Boston (34-23) have better records in that period.

Unfortunately, time is swiftly running out.

16. "The Man Never Gives Up, Does He?"

NEW YORK, NEW YORK, SEPT. 13—Not only were the Indians mathematically eliminated from pennant contention tonight in splitting a doubleheader with the New York Yankees, their chances of finishing third were also severely damaged. Fritz Peterson pitched a five-hitter to win the opener, 7–1, but the Yankees beat Jim Bibby, 4–3, in the nightcap, leaving the Indians in fourth place, three games behind the Yankees and two below .500.

"We've still got a chance for third," stubbornly insisted Frank Robinson, obsessed daily with the fulfillment of that secondary goal. "I'm not quitting and I don't want anybody else to quit either."

There's no doubt Robinson's fierce determination affects the Indians, who are playing their best, most consistent baseball of the season.

This has impressed many baseball men, like Gabe Paul, who knows Robinson well. "From what I've seen, Frank is doing a helluva job," said Paul. "I'm impressed by the way he keeps the Indians going, even though they're out of it and have been for a while. But I'm not surprised. I was impressed by the Indians even when they weren't playing well."

Peterson has a theory on the improvement. "Maybe it's because Robby was so good when we weren't playing well. He never put any extra pressure on us even when we were so lousy. Maybe that's a reason we were able to turn it all around."

SEPT. 14—Although Frank Robinson has tolerated umpires the last six weeks, today he argued a ruling by George Maloney that was obviously wrong. "I know we won't win, but I'm going to file a protest anyway," said Robinson following a 6–2 loss to the Yankees and Catfish Hunter.

In the Yankees' first inning—with Bobby Bonds on third, Sandy Alomar on first, and one out—Thurman Munson hit the ball back to Rick Waits. Bonds was trapped off third and caught in a rundown. Meanwhile, Alomar came around and reached third when Alan Ashby ran Bonds back to that base. Third base technically belonged to Bonds. Bonds, seeing Alomar on the base, ran past the bag a few feet toward left field. Ashby tagged Alomar as he stood on the base, then pursued Bonds and tagged him, too. Both runners should have been declared out. However, Maloney, who seemed as confused as Bonds and Alomar, called Alomar out but allowed Bonds to remain on third.

Robinson raced from the dugout to argue with Maloney and senior umpire Russel Goetz, but the decision stood. Robinson then announced he was playing the game under protest.

Later Maloney claimed—and was substantiated by Goetz—that time was called after Alomar had been tagged by Ashby. Thus, Bonds was safe. "I did it to avoid confusion," said Maloney. "He can't call time until the ball is dead," insisted Robinson, correctly. "I can call time whenever I want," countered Maloney with Goetz nodding in agreement.

Ashby testified: "I tagged Alomar and then I tagged Bonds, and *then* Maloney called time out."

The next batter was retired, ending the inning without a run. Goetz pointed out, "It [the disputed decision] doesn't matter because it didn't change the course of the game." But it *might*

Paul Tepley, Cleveland *Press*

Frank Robinson and son, Kevin.

Paul Tepley, Cleveland *Press*

Frank Robinson vs. umpire Russell Goetz.

have, which further angered Robinson. "That's their way out, by saying it didn't matter. But it changed the rotation of the batting order for the rest of the game." The Yankees scored three runs in the third inning, as Roy White homered with two out, and three more in the seventh. The Indians should win the protest, but as Robinson speculated, they probably won't.

DETROIT, MICHIGAN, SEPT. 16—Ralph Houk lounged in the Detroit Tigers' dugout and talked about Frank Robinson. "I think he has done a helluva good job; there's no denying he has kept the Indians going when there's not much at stake and that might be one of the toughest parts of managing." Houk should know. He started managing in the big leagues in 1961 and has been at it ever since, except for two years as general manager of the Yankees. "Another reason I think Frank has done a good job," continued Houk, "is that somebody deserves the credit for those kids being in the lineup—Dennis Eckersley, Rick Manning, and Duane Kuiper—and he must be the guy who did it."

Then Eckersley took the mound and beat Houk's Tigers, 9–2, for his fourth straight victory, raising his record to 13–5. The rookie was uncharacteristically indifferent. "Aw, I had trouble concentrating, my arm was a little stiff, my fast ball was just okay, and my breaking balls were only so-so. I was lucky."

SEPT. 17—While Roric Harrison shook his head in disgust, Jackie Brown, occupying an adjacent stool in the Indians' clubhouse, smiled and said, "I wish the season were just beginning instead of ending." Harrison's mood, however, was the opposite. He frowned and said, "I can't believe how lousy I've been throwing the ball the last two weeks." He was ineffective again tonight in a 4–0 loss to the Tigers, before Brown came on in the third inning and pitched well.

SEPT 18—The weather refused to clear, so the Indians and Tigers played in the rain, and Frank Robinson's smile returned. The Indians won, 2–1, on Boog Powell's twenty-fourth homer and a ninth-inning, saving play by Duane Kuiper. Now they're ready for another make-or-break weekend series against the Yankees in Cleveland.

Well aware that the Yankees are 3½ games ahead but up by

only two losses, Robinson said, "We almost have to win all four games against the Yankees, although we'll be all right if we only win three."

"The man never gives up, does he?" one of the Indians asked.

CLEVELAND, OHIO, SEPT. 19—In perhaps their best game all season, the Indians took one step toward third place. "It's all a matter of pride, pride in yourself and your teammates, which is something this club hasn't had in a long time," commented Frank Robinson after the Indians beat the New York Yankees, 3–2. Fritz Peterson was credited with his tenth straight victory and fourteenth of the season, an amazing turnabout since he injured his hand three months ago.

"It's gratifying to see this happening," said Robinson. "For a long time this organization was a loser. It had the image, the reputation, for quitting as soon as things got tough, but not anymore. Everybody is going all out. They're playing like it's April or May instead of September." Robinson declined to take credit for the transformation. "I don't think it's a reflection on me; it's a matter of the guys coming together and doing the things they're capable of doing. I'm only sorry we didn't do it sooner."

Now the Indians are only one game below .500 and trail the Yankees by 2½.

Earlier, Lee MacPhail ruled against the Indians' protest of the 6–2 Yankee victory five days ago. "I'm not surprised," shrugged Robinson, though he still maintains—and rightly so—the umpires were wrong. "One lied and the other backed him up. MacPhail had to go along with them."

SEPT. 20—Frank Robinson said more about umpires tonight, but restrained himself in his argument and postgame remarks. He again had good reason to criticize and this time was substantiated by television replay cameras, though again to no avail. In the sixth inning umpire Larry McCoy called Frank Duffy out at the plate though films proved he was safe. The Indians lost, 4–1, to the Yankees.

"It's all very simple now, thanks to McCoy," said Robinson. "We need to win two tomorrow or forget it."

Robinson batted twice in what was his final appearance as an active player. His bid for a homer in the second inning was caught a few feet in front of the center-field fence, and he was called out on strikes in the fifth. "I didn't swing because it was a bad pitch," he explained without complaint.

"I'd like to play more and it would be nice to get closer to 3000 hits and 600 homers [he has 2928 hits and 583 homers] but I know I can't. You can't play if you can't swing. My shoulder is too bad. It hurts constantly. It has been very bad since that night [August 27] I batted against Claude Osteen."

Is he disappointed about not reaching his goals? "If I were just a player, I would be," replied Robinson, "but I've had 19 good years. I was hopeful of a twentieth, but it just didn't work out. No, I'm not disappointed. I feel I was fortunate to have the kind of playing career I've had."

SEPT. 21—Frank Robinson is more stubborn than realistic. Rick Waits and Dave LaRoche beat the Yankees, 3-2, in the opener of a doubleheader, but Dennis Eckersley and three relievers were shelled in an 11-5 loss to the Yankees in the nightcap.

"Before you ask me, no I haven't given up," said Robinson softly. "I'm not conceding third place until it's no longer possible mathematically."

SEPT. 22—The Indians kept their hopes alive tonight, but Frank Robinson wasn't pleased. "I'm unhappy about some things that happened, but I'm not saying anything because I might regret it," he snapped, following a 7-6 victory over the Milwaukee Brewers.

One of those "things" was that Alan Ashby missed a suicide squeeze bunt signal. Robinson was also angry because several nonregulars and pitchers neglected to report to the field for pregame exercises and running. "Just because we only have six games left is no reason to quit," Robinson chastised them. "The season isn't over until the last game, and until then I want everybody doing what they're supposed to do."

Robinson kept the clubhouse door closed for 10 minutes. He called Ashby into his office but did not levy the standard $100 fine for missing a sign. "I guess I'm getting soft," he admitted.

"Alan and I talked, he said he just screwed up, so I let him off with a warning. He's been doing such a good job for us, I felt I could be lenient."

Rico Carty spent the night in the hospital after being hit in the head by a pitch from the Brewers' Tom Murphy. Carty's injury was not serious, though he'll not play anymore this season.

Even more important than what happened on the field was what transpired in Phil Seghi's office earlier today. He and Ted Bonda met twice with Robinson, opening financial negotiations for rehiring the manager. Robinson named his price; a salary of about $80,000, including fringe benefits, though he'd work for less money in exchange for a two- or three-year contract as a manager only.

"They know what I want, now it's up to them," Robinson confided to a friend after the meeting.

Seghi continued to be evasive, however. "Sure, we talked, but I have nothing to report," the general manager maintained. Does he forsee a problem? "I don't think so, but we have nothing definitive."

Seghi and Bonda also met with Ed Keating. "Keating being in my office was irrelevant. He just came to the park to see Robinson, and then he came up to see me. Don't forget, Keating represents other guys, not just Robinson."

SEPT. 23—At 9:00 A.M. Phil Seghi stood amidst the secretaries and their desks in the outer offices of the Indians' headquarters and read from a one-page, mimeographed release. He addressed three sleepy writers, no more. Even public-relations director Randy Adamack was elsewhere, though he eventually appeared. More reporters, one local television camera crew, and Frank Robinson showed up later.

Absent were Nick Mileti, the general partner of the Indians, Ted Bonda, Bowie Kuhn, Lee MacPhail, Robinson's wife Barbara, representatives of the three television networks, 100 reporters from New York, Chicago, Washington, Boston, and elsewhere, and the 50 or 60 photographers who attended the announcement of Robinson's first hiring. Ed Keating was missing, too, though he will continue to represent Robinson in his new company, Keating Management Agency.

Seghi removed the pipe from his mouth, cleared his throat, and read: "Cleveland Indians General Manager Phil Seghi announced this morning that Frank Robinson will return to manage the Tribe in 1976. Seghi said, 'I'm pleased to announce that Frank will manage the Cleveland Indians again next year. I feel that he has done a good job, and I look forward to working with him and having a successful year in 1976.'"

No klieg lights, not even a camera flash.

"Are there any questions?" asked Seghi. "Yes," replied one writer. "Can we go into your office and sit down?"

About 9:20 Robinson sauntered in, wearing a red leisure suit, a sport shirt open at the neck, and a tired expression. He quipped with reporters and spoke into a tape recorder words that shocked Seghi momentarily.

"Well, if I were sitting there in the general manager's seat and had to rehire Frank Robinson, I would not do it," he said with a straight face. "Anybody could bring a club home in fourth place. That's no big deal. It's like being on a banana peel, going nowhere. It goes to show you, 'those' kind of people can't handle responsibility."

Robinson grinned broadly and retaped the interview.

He took a few phone calls, but there was no congratulatory telegram like the one signed by President Ford 355 days earlier. "Oh," Robinson remembered, "I did get one telegram. It was from a fellow I played ball with in high school."

"There never was any doubt that I wanted Frank back," said Seghi. "We signed him to a one-year contract [strictly as a manager] because that's our policy. I see no reason managers can't do a good job on a year-to-year basis; it's been proven they can. If a manager is doing a good job, he has no fear of not being rehired the following season.

"The low point of this year, in my eyes, was on June 21, when we were 15 games under .500 with a 24-39 record," continued Seghi. "But I never blamed Frank for the ineffectiveness of some of the talent."

Said Robinson, "If I didn't feel all right about a one-year contract, I wouldn't have signed. Sure, I would've liked two or three years, but I understand it's not the club's policy. Right now I have no intention of playing again. It's possible, but not

probable I'll change my mind, and the outcome of the operation will have no bearing on my decision."

If Robinson should decide to play again, will he be paid as
much as he earned this year [$180,000]? "If I decide to play
and manage next year," he answered, "I'll get *more* than I got
this year. You can make book on it." As manager, Robinson's
salary will be about $80,000.

Tonight, almost incidentally, the Indians beat the Brewers,
4–3, boosting their record to .500 (77-77). A Cleveland team has
never finished a season at .500 since 1968 when the Indians
won 86 and lost 75.

John Lowenstein, who has been a member of the current Indians longer than anyone else, chortled, "Finally, after five
years, I'm with a club that's as good as it is bad!"

SEPT. 24—Maybe it was the weather (chill factor, 28 degrees)
that made the Indians think it was last April and the bad old
days. "This is the worst I've ever seen it for a baseball game,"
commented Harold Bossard, Stadium grounds keeper for 40
years.

The Indians lost to the Brewers, 10–3, closing out the home
portion of their season.

"I'm disappointed anytime we lose, no more, no less because
this was our last game at home," said Frank Robinson. "The
only way I look at it is that if we had won, we'd only need to
split the four games in Boston to finish above .500. Now we
have to win three of the last four. I don't think anybody let
down because this was the last game in Cleveland; we just
didn't play well."

BOSTON, MASSACHUSETTS, SEPT. 26—In the rain, fog, and
gloom of Fenway Park tonight the Boston Red Sox virtually
clinched the Eastern Division championship and, consequent-
ly, shattered the dream Frank Robinson and the Indians had
nurtured since this season began.

The Red Sox won two 4–0 shutouts, eliminating the Indians'
third place and .500 hopes.

"It's hard for me to understand what happened to us," mum-
bled Robinson. "The Red Sox came to play; we didn't. We

weren't prepared emotionally, which I find hard to understand. We were all uptight and they were loosey-goosey, but it should have been the other way around. I hope it's different tomorrow. I hope we have enough pride not to smell up the joint again."

SEPT. 27—Though the Red Sox lost to the Indians, 5–2, today, they backed into the Eastern Division title as the New York Yankees eliminated the Baltimore Orioles by taking a doubleheader. The final score of New York's second game didn't come in until 2½ hours after the Red Sox lost to the Indians, and by then all the Boston players had left Fenway Park.

Red Sox manager Darrell Johnson remained with reporters, sweating out the Yankees' sweep. When it was official, he toasted his champions, then praised Robinson. "The first two series we played against Cleveland, Frank was terrible," said Johnson, "but the next time we saw the Indians he was different; he made a big change for the better. Once he did, he was a much better manager. Overall, I think Frank did a fine job with that team."

The Indians' victory was achieved on Rick Waits's six-hitter, raising his record to 6-2 and providing another reason for Phil Seghi to smile about the Gaylord Perry trade. Waits became the only left-hander to pitch a complete game victory against the Red Sox in Fenway Park this season.

SEPT. 28—Frank Robinson's first season as major league baseball's first black manager ended today. The Indians beat the champion Red Sox, 11–4, in a game without meaning for the first time all year.

The victory gave the Indians an 11-7 record against the Red Sox in 1975; they were the only team in the American League to capture a season series against the eventual pennant winners.

The Indians finished fourth with a 79-80 mark, 15½ lengths behind Boston, 11 behind Baltimore, and 2½ behind New York. Far back were Milwaukee, 12½ behind Cleveland, and Detroit, 23 behind.

Statistically, it represented only a slight improvement over 1974, when the Indians also finished fourth, with a 77-85 record, but were only 14 games behind the champion Orioles. When the intangibles are weighed, however, this season looks better.

"I'm glad it's over because there's nothing left to shoot for," sighed Robinson as the players dressed. "I'm a little sad, too. It's always that way at the end of a summer when you don't win. I'd love to be just starting the season with this team because of the way we've come together the last two months. That's another reason I'm sad, that we didn't put it together earlier than we did.

"But I'm already looking forward to next spring, getting off to a good start and picking up where we've left off."

To the players Robinson said simply, "Thank you for all you've done, for having such a good attitude, for working so hard. Stay in shape; I'll see you next spring. We're going to be a team to be reckoned with. We're going to give a lot of teams hell.

"Thanks again for making my first season a success."

Epilogue

CLEVELAND, OHIO, SEPT. 29—Was it only yesterday that Frank Robinson was proclaimed major league baseball's first black manager? It was called a progressive step, which was paradoxical. For a while the man was a novelty, indeed a pioneer, under constant scrutiny.

But somewhere between there and here color ceased to be an issue. Maybe it happened, as Robinson himself suggested, when the continued mediocrity of the Indians manifested itself. Or maybe, as observers among baseball executives and members of the media offered, it happened when Robinson proved capable of maintaining order in the face of frustration. The date cannot be pinpointed, but suddenly Robinson was no longer a novelty.

When the Indians began to win regularly, when they continued to drive forward while other teams were stumbling at season's end, when the only incentive was the sheer satisfaction of doing well, Robinson's ability was no longer doubted.

Then Robinson was rehired, not as a black manager—

because being black proved neither a liability nor an asset—but as a *manager.*

The Indians under Robinson did not win the pennant in 1975. They did not, in fact, substantially improve upon their 1974 record. At the end of 1975, however, after winning 27 of their last 42 games, there was legitimate reason for optimism: the Indians were a good team that finished strong, infused with young talent and filled with a pride long missing. This was not merely a spontaneous reaction to Robinson's presence, but the direct result of the rookie manager's efforts.

From the beginning Robinson was confronted with tests: by pitcher Gaylord Perry, by catcher John Ellis, with umpires, with the media, with his attitude on curfew and fines. These were all headlined, of course, possibly disproportionately.

There was criticism of Robinson's ability to motivate—not uncommon among superstars-turned-managers—and his tendency to be too patient, two aspects of his leadership that improved with experience.

Robinson said early in the season, "I think a lot about motivation, but only because we're not winning. When you're winning, nobody worries about motivation, do they?" When asked if he as a player ever needed motivation, he replied without hesitation, "No, never. I motivated myself."

Coach Tom McCraw commented on Robinson's patience. "If anything, Frank has been too lenient. He's just coming out of the player ranks himself and he's bending over backwards to make it easy for his players. He knows how he was treated as a player and wants to give his players every break. It took awhile before he fined a guy and put his foot down.

"Next year he won't be the same. Next year will be the time to judge the man. He's going to be judged this year anyway, but to get the true picture you have to judge him under the same circumstances as other managers. Next year he'll be just another manager and that's when we'll see more of the real Frank Robinson."

Looking back, Robinson maintained, "I always did what I thought was right, what I thought was best for the team. I have no regrets, and if I had things to do all over again, I'd do everything the same way."

Then Robinson left for his home in Los Angeles, secure in

the fulfillment of his wish six months earlier: "I'm looking forward to the day when people will stop writing, 'Frank Robinson, baseball's first black manager,' and just write, 'Frank Robinson, manager of the Cleveland Indians.' "

The rest of it, indeed, can be saved for his epitaph.

Appendix

FRANK ROBINSON PLAYING RECORD

Year	Club	G	AB	R	H	2B	3B	HR	RBI	BA	PO	A	E	FA
1953	Ogden	72	270	70	94	20	6	17	83	.348	105	28	18	861
1954	Tulsa	8	30	4	8	0	0	0	1	.267	17	15	1	.970
1954	Columbia	132	491	112	165	32	9	25	110	.336	258	63	18	.947
1955	Columbia	80	243	50	64	15	7	12	52	.263	203	3	4	.981
1956	Cincinnati	152	572	122	166	27	6	38	83	.290	323	5	8	.976
1957	Cincinnati	150	611	97	197	29	5	29	75	.322	487	36	6	.989
1958	Cincinnati	148	554	90	149	25	6	31	83	.269	314	24	6	.983
1959	Cincinnati	146	540	106	168	31	4	36	125	.311	1049	78	18	.934
1960	Cincinnati	139	464	86	138	33	6	31	83	.297	775	62	10	.988
1961	Cincinnati	153	545	117	176	32	7	37	124	.323	284	15	3	.990
1962	Cincinnati	162	609	134	208	51	2	39	136	.342	315	10	2	.994
1963	Cincinnati	140	482	79	125	19	3	21	91	.259	238	13	4	.984
1964	Cincinnati	156	568	103	174	38	6	29	96	.306	279	7	4	.986
1965	Cincinnati	156	582	109	172	33	5	33	113	.296	282	5	3	.990
1966	Baltimore	155	576	122	182	34	2	49	122	.316	282	0	5	.983
1967	Baltimore	129	479	83	149	23	7	30	94	.311	207	8	2	.991
1968	Baltimore	130	421	69	113	27	1	15	52	.268	193	5	7	.966
1969	Baltimore	148	539	111	166	19	5	32	100	.308	367	19	5	.987
1970	Baltimore	132	471	88	144	24	1	25	78	.306	262	11	4	.986
1971	Baltimore	133	455	82	128	16	2	28	99	.281	449	20	11	.977
1972	Los Angeles	103	342	41	86	6	1	19	59	.251	168	6	6	.967
1973	California	147	534	85	142	29	0	30	97	.266	38	3	1	.976
1974	Cal.-Cleve.	144	477	81	117	27	3	22	68	.245	23	0	1	.958
1975	Cleveland	49	118	19	28	5	0	9	24	.237	0	0	0	.000
Major League Totals		2772	9939	1824	2928	528	72	583	1802	.295	6335	333	106	.984

CHAMPIONSHIP SERIES RECORD

Year	Club	G	AB	R	H	2B	3B	HR	RBI	BA	PO	A	E	FA
1969	Baltimore	3	12	1	4	2	0	1	2	.333	2	0	1	.667
1970	Baltimore	3	10	3	2	0	0	1	2	.200	2	0	0	1.000
1971	Baltimore	3	12	2	1	1	0	0	1	.083	7	0	1	1.000
Totals		9	34	6	7	3	0	2	5	.206	11	0	1	.917

WORLD SERIES RECORD

Year	Club	G	AB	R	H	2B	3B	HR	RBI	BA	PO	A	E	FA
1961	Cincinnati	5	15	3	3	2	09	12	4	.200	5	0	0	1.000
1966	Baltimore	4	14	4	4	0	1	2	3	.286	6	0	0	1.000
1969	Baltimore	5	16	2	3	0	0	1	1	.188	13	0	0	1.000
1970	Baltimore	5	22	5	6	0	0	2	4	.273	7	0	0	1.000
1971	Baltimore	7	25	5	7	0	0	2	2	.280	12	0	0	1.000
Totals		26	92	19	23	2	1	8	14	.250	43	0	0	1.000

ALL-STAR GAME RECORD

Year	League	AB	R	H	2B	3B	HR	RBI	BA	PO	A	E	FA
1956	National	2	0	0	0	0	0	0	.000	1	0	0	1.000
1957	National	2	0	1	0	0	0	0	.500	5	0	0	1.000
1959	National	3	1	3	0	0	1	1	1.000	3	0	1	.750
1961	National	1	0	1	0	0	0	0	1.000	2	0	0	1.000
1962	National	3	0	0	0	0	0	0	.000	1	0	0	1.000
1965	National	1	0	0	0	0	0	0	.000	0	0	0	.000
1966	American	4	0	0	0	0	0	0	.000	2	0	0	1.000
1969	American	2	0	0	0	0	0	0	.000	0	0	0	.000
1970	American	3	0	0	0	0	0	0	.000	1	0	0	1.000
1971	American	2	1	1	0	0	1	2	.500	2	0	0	1.000
1974	American	1	0	0	0	0	0	0	.000	0	0	0	.000
Totals		24	2	6	0	0	2	3	.250	17	0	1	.944

1975 CLEVELAND INDIANS FINAL STATISTICS

GAMES PLAYED: 159

BATTER	PCT	G	AB	R	H	2B	3B	HR	RBI	BB	SO	SH-SF	HP	SB-CS	E
Ashby	.224	90	254	32	57	10	1	5	32	30	42	16 0	1	3 2	6
Bell	.271	153	553	66	150	20	4	10	59	51	72	10 4	1	6 5	25
*Berry	.200	25	40	6	8	1	0	0	1	1	7	0 0	1	0 1	2
*Brohamer	.244	69	217	15	53	5	0	6	16	14	14	2 1	0	2 2	8
Carty	.308	118	383	57	118	19	1	18	64	45	31	0 6	2	2 2	3
Cerone	.250	7	12	1	3	1	0	0	0	1	0	1 0	0	0 0	0
Crosby	.234	61	128	12	30	3	0	0	7	13	14	4 0	0	0 4	7
Duffy	.243	146	482	44	117	22	2	1	47	27	60	6 4	2	10 10	16
*Ellis	.230	92	296	22	68	11	1	7	32	14	33	0 4	2	0 1	13
*Gamble	.261	121	348	60	91	16	3	15	45	53	39	1 1	2	11 5	2
Hendrick	.258	145	561	82	145	21	2	24	86	40	78	4 8	0	6 7	6
Kuiper	.292	90	346	42	101	11	1	0	25	30	26	4 0	8	19 18	12
*Lee	.130	13	23	3	3	1	0	0	0	2	5	0 0	1	1 0	0
Lis	.308	9	13	4	4	2	0	2	8	3	3	0 1	1	0 0	0
Lowenstein	.242	91	265	37	64	5	1	12	33	28	28	3 1	0	15 10	2
Manning	.285	120	480	69	137	16	5	3	35	44	62	7 2	2	19 11	9
*McCraw	.275	23	51	7	14	1	1	2	5	7	7	1 0	0	4 1	1
Powell	.297	134	435	64	129	18	0	27	86	59	72	1 6	1	1 3	3
Robinson	.237	49	118	19	28	5	0	9	24	29	15	1 1	0	0 0	0
Smith	.125	8	8	0	1	0	0	0	2	0	1	0 1	0	0 0	0
Spikes	.229	111	345	41	79	13	3	11	33	30	51	3 0	0	7 6	5
*Sudakis	.196	20	46	4	9	0	0	1	3	4	7	0 0	0	0 1	0
Sudakis St	.154	50	104	8	16	2	0	2	9	16	22	0 2	1	1 2	1
DH Hitters	.255		591	86	15	23	2	30	91	79	68	3 6	2	8 8	0
PH Hitters	.330		103	12	34	6	0	3	28	14	20	0 0	0	1 1	0
Pitchers	.000	0	0	0	0	0	0	0	0	0	0	0 0	0	0 0	14
Totals	**.261**		**5404**	**688**	**1409**	**201**	**25**	**153**	**643**	**525**	**667**	**64 40**	**24**	**106**	**89 134**

*No longer with team.

PITCHER	ERA	W	L	AP	GS	CG	SV	SHO	IP	H	R	ER	HR	BB	SO	HB	WP
Andersen	4.76	0	0	3	0	0	0	0	5.2	4	3	3	0	2	4	0	2
Beene	6.94	1	0	19	1	0	1	0	46.2	63	42	36	4	25	20	3	6
Bibby	3.20	5	9	24	12	2	1	0	112.2	99	48	40	7	50	62	0	3
*Bosman	4.08	0	2	6	3	0	0	0	28.2	33	17	13	3	8	11	3	0
Brown	4.28	1	2	25	3	1	1	0	69.1	72	40	33	9	29	41	0	2
Buskey	2.57	5	3	50	0	0	7	0	77.0	69	27	22	7	29	29	1	4
Eckersley	2.60	13	7	34	24	6	2	2	186.2	147	61	54	16	90	152	7	4
Harrison	4.79	7	7	19	19	4	0	0	126.0	137	71	67	9	46	52	4	5
Hood	4.39	6	10	29	19	2	0	0	135.1	136	76	66	16	57	51	0	6
Kern	3.77	1	2	13	7	0	0	0	71.2	60	31	30	5	45	55	5	3
LaRoche	2.19	5	3	61	0	0	17	0	82.1	61	26	20	5	57	94	2	4
*Odom	2.61	1	0	3	1	1	0	1	10.1	4	3	3	1	8	10	0	0
*Perry, G	3.55	6	9	15	15	10	0	1	121.2	120	57	48	16	34	85	1	2
*Perry, J	6.69	1	6	8	6	0	0	0	37.2	46	34	28	8	18	11	0	0
Peterson	3.94	14	8	25	25	6	0	2	146.1	154	73	64	15	40	47	6	2
Raich	5.54	7	8	18	17	2	0	0	92.2	118	61	57	12	31	34	1	4
Reynolds	4.46	0	2	5	0	0	2	0	9.2	11	7	5	0	3	5	0	2
Strickland	1.93	0	0	4	0	0	0	0	4.2	4	1	1	0	2	3	1	0
Waits	2.94	6	2	16	7	3	1	0	70.1	57	25	23	3	25	34	1	2
Totals	**3.84**	**79**	**80**	**377**	**159**	**37**	**32**	**6**	**1435.1**	**1395**	**703**	**613**	**136**	**599**	**800**	**35**	**51**

*No longer with team.

1975 CLEVELAND INDIANS FINAL STATISTICS

VS AL WEST	HOME		ROAD		TOTAL	
	W	L	W	L	W	L
California	3	3	6	0	9	3
Chicago	3	3	2	4	5	7
Kansas City	3	3	3	3	6	6
Minnesota	1	2	2	4	3	6
Oakland	1	5	1	5	2	10
Texas	4	3	1	4	5	7
Totals	15	19	15	20	30	39

VS AL EAST	HOME		ROAD		TOTAL	
	W	L	W	L	W	L
Baltimore	4	6	4	4	8	10
Boston	5	4	6	3	11	7
Cleveland	0	0	0	0	0	0
Detroit	7	2	5	4	12	6
Milwaukee	4	5	5	4	9	9
New York	6	3	3	6	9	9
Totals	26	20	23	21	49	41
Grand Total	41	39	38	41	79	80

	WON	LOST
Day	28	26
Night	51	54
Sho-Indv	6	8
Sho-Team	6	11
1-Run Gm	27	23
2-Run Gm	12	12
Extra Inn	7	10
Vs Right	55	56
Vs Left	24	24
Dbl-Hdr	3	2
Split		12
Starters	62	65
Relief	17	15
Streaks	6	7

	CLEV	OPP
Errors	134	146
Double Play	156	168
Comp Games	37	48
Stolen Bases	106	121
Caught Stlg	89	74
Doubles	201	230
Triples	25	30
Homers—Home	79	85
Homers—Road	74	51
Homers—Tot	153	136
Lf on Base	1066	1143

ATTENDANCE

	HOME	ROAD
Total	977,039	1,037,045
Avg	14160	14206
Dates	69	73
Games	80	79